SEARCHING FOR THE FRANKLIN EXPEDITION

Private Journal

of a cruise

in the

Brig Rescue

in search of

Sir John Franklin

R Carter

SEARCHING FOR THE FRANKLIN EXPEDITION

The Arctic Journal of
Robert Randolph Carter

Edited by Harold B. Gill Jr. and Joanne Young

NAVAL INSTITUTE PRESS
Annapolis, Maryland

© 1998 by Harold B. Gill Jr. and Joanne Young
Transcribed and published with the permission of the owners,
Mr. and Mrs. C. Hill Carter Jr.

Frontispiece: Carter's own title page. Its calligraphy showed Carter's
original spacing and type for the canvas-covered book given him
by Samuel Griffin, the *Rescue*'s captain, which he believed would
be a journal only expressing his own feelings—one he thought
no one but his family and close friends would read.
Courtesy of the Colonial Williamsburg Foundation

Library of Congress Cataloging-in-Publication Data
Carter, Robert Randolph, 1826–
    Searching for the Franklin expedition : the Arctic journal of
Robert Randolph Carter / edited by Harold B. Gill, Jr. and Joanne
Young.
        p.   cm.
    Includes bibliographical references.
    ISBN 1-55750-321-4 (alk. paper)
    1. Carter, Robert Randolph, 1826–   —Diaries. 2. Grinnell
Expedition (1st : 1850–1851) 3. Franklin, John, Sir, 1786–1847.
4. Northwest Passage. 5. Arctic regions—Discovery and exploration.
6. Canada, Northern—Discovery and exploration. I. Gill, Harold B.
II. Young, Joanne, 1922–   . III. Title.
G665 1850 .C36   1998
919.804—dc21   98-5219

Printed in the United States of America on acid-free paper ♾
98 99 00 01 02 03 04 05   9 8 7 6 5 4 3 2
First printing

CONTENTS

Introduction   *1*

The Journal of Robert Randolph Carter   *17*

Epilogue   *163*

Notes   *177*

Glossary   *189*

Bibliography   *193*

Index   *197*

SEARCHING
FOR THE
FRANKLIN
EXPEDITION

TWENTY-FOUR-YEAR-OLD Robert Randolph Carter, who wrote his "personal journal" in 1850–51, was first officer of the brig *Rescue* on the U.S. Grinnell Expedition to the Arctic and an 1849 graduate of the Naval Academy at Annapolis, Maryland. The expedition joined British ships in search of British naval captain Sir John Franklin, his two ships, and 129 men of the Royal Navy who had vanished into the frozen region of northern Canada on a quest for the Northwest Passage in 1845.

The mysterious disappearance of the Franklin Expedition had become an international cause célèbre by 1850, and Royal Navy ships had searched desperately to find the missing ships and their men. Now the U.S. Navy had joined the hunt for the explorer with the blessings of Congress and President Zachary Taylor, as well as the financial aid of shipowner Henry Grinnell.

Carter, author of this day-by-day account, was the second oldest son of Hill and Mary Randolph Carter of Shirley Plantation. This estate on the James River in Charles City County, Virginia, was patented in 1613 by Governor Thomas West, Lord Delaware, as West and Sherley Hundred. (His wife was born Cessayly Sherley.) The plantation had been in the Hill-Carter fam-

ily since 1656, when Edward Hill I was noted in official records as being "of
Shirley Hundred," but Hill was granted 450 acres in the county in 1638 "for
personal adventure and transportation of 8 persons."[1] The lives of members
of that family were bound to the sea as strongly as to their rolling acres of
Virginia land. The next two generations of Edwards Hill—II and III—each
served as naval officer and customs collector for the upper James River and
judge of the Admiralty Court, as well as owned a shipyard and their own
oceangoing merchant ships. When heiress Elizabeth Hill married Secretary
of the Colony John Carter, eldest son of Robert "King" Carter, one of the
wealthiest men in America, in 1723, their wharves at Shirley continued to
serve as a vital port for overseas trade. From here their crops were shipped to
England and manufactured goods imported to them. When Elizabeth's
father died in 1726, the estate came into the Carter family, and her husband
built a magnificent complex of Georgian brick buildings. The manor house
and two flanking houses faced the river, while four major buildings surrounded a courtyard to the rear.[2] Their son, Charles, embellished the mansion in the 1770s with superb hand-carved woodwork and furnishings
purchased from both English and American craftsmen. Robert R. Carter's
father, Hill, was a member of the seventh generation to be master of Shirley,
an active participant in Virginia's government, the church, and a recognized
leader in scientific agriculture.

Hill served in the navy during the War of 1812 and was a midshipman
aboard the *Peacock* when it defeated the British vessel *Epervier* off Cape
Canaveral on 29 April 1814. Congress had presented him with an engraved
sword for his participation in that battle.[3]

Following in his father's footsteps, Robert joined the navy at sixteen as a
midshipman and served his first duty in March 1842, on the famous frigate
Constitution, and then until August of the following year on the sloop of war
Falmouth in the Caribbean as part of the Home Squadron. Next he was sent
to the *Savannah* in the Pacific Squadron during the Mexican War. When it
was sent home in mid-1847 to discharge those crewmen whose enlistments
had expired, he was transferred to the storeship *Erie,* which took part in the
occupation of Mazatlan in November. The following June he sailed back to
New York and returned to Shirley on leave, the first time he had seen his family in six years.[4]

A few months later he reported to the U.S. Naval School at Maryland's historic old Fort Severn in Annapolis, established in 1845 by Secretary of the

Navy George Bancroft. His serial number, 00184, testified to how few had preceded him at the academy.[5] He graduated as a "passed midshipman" in 1849, but it was later in the nineteenth century before graduates were given the commission of ensign. Before that, those who passed had to wait for an opening in the allotted number of officers for each rank, and in the interim were given only an acting rank on an expedition.

When Carter graduated, the U.S. Navy for the first time had turned its attention to scientific exploration and surveying. Its first such expedition had been the U.S. Exploring Expedition, commanded by Lt. Charles Wilkes in 1838–42.

At midcentury neither this country nor England—the leading sea power —was at war. It was the era of the clipper ship, with its sharp, long, and narrow hull, the tall spars and cloud of sails, and most of all speed. A clipper wasn't a navy ship; it was the merchant marine of its day. Primarily it sped from the East Coast to China and back again with tea-filled hulls and imports in great demand. But it touched world ports formerly little known, and it opened countries from the Arctic at the north to Cape Horn at the south, and even down to Antarctica, the realm of the Wilkes Expedition. Other reliable but slower sailing ships vied for trade with the clippers. International commerce went hand-in-hand with science. Its scope was endless, with the U.S. Navy as its guard, protecting U.S. ships and shores from more than the pirates of colonial days.

Few governments knew much about continents outside their own boundaries. Now there was both a need to know and the luxury of time to explore. Though some in Congress carped that such explorations were unnecessary and frivolous, others thought differently; and the navy launched a series of expeditions to the world's four corners.

Robert Randolph Carter took part in three of these—the U.S. Grinnell Expedition to the Arctic, in which he sailed aboard the *Rescue* (1850–51); the Exploration and Survey of the China Seas, the Northern Pacific, and Bering Strait, hydrographic counterpart of Commo. Matthew Perry's diplomatic mission to Japan, in which he was acting master (junior lieutenant and navigation officer) of the flagship *Vincennes* (1853–55); and the second La Plata Expedition to South America under Capt. Thomas Jefferson Page aboard the steamer *Argentina* (1858–60). They all had one primary purpose: to survey and discover more scientific and commercial facts about the antebellum nineteenth-century world in which the navy was operating.

The Polar regions were not outside the field of interest. The expedition planned for 1850 was the first official U.S. Navy exploratory one into the Arctic seas. Not the least of the Arctic expedition's appeal to young Robert Randolph Carter in 1850 was joining the long armada of mariners in a three-hundred-year quest for the Northwest Passage, a short water route to the Orient. It began when that admiral of the ocean seas, Christopher Columbus, discovered a continental barrier blocking his path. Henry VII, first English monarch to covet its discovery, had in 1497 sent John Cabot in search of such a passageway. Many explorers followed—equally unsuccessfully. Their names were blood-stirring, seemingly synonymous with courage and adventure: Giovanni da Verrazano, intrepid Italian who sailed under the French flag in 1524; Jacques Cartier, also sailing for France a decade later in search of a new route to China, who found on the Newfoundland coast a gulf and river he named St. Lawrence because he discovered them on the feast day of that saint. There was Sir Humphrey Gilbert of England whose 1566 treatise on finding a Northwest Passage inspired others even after he drowned at sea in 1583 homeward bound from establishing a Newfoundland colony. There was also Sir Martin Frobisher, Elizabethan ship captain, trader, and pirate in the queen's service searching for that passage in the 1570s because, as his fellow seaman George Best wrote, it was "the only thing of the world that was left yet undone."[6]

Henry Hudson who sailed both for England, then Holland, then again for English merchants, died for his efforts in 1611 when he and his son and seven loyal sailors were cast adrift in what is now Hudson Bay by hope-starved mutineers who, with no outlet to the Pacific in sight, accused him of failure and sailed home. Dutch colonization in New York and English claims to Canada were based on his exploits, but a route through the Arctic to the Far East was little closer to discovery.[7]

Other explorers followed in their paths—among them pilot William Baffin in 1616, and Capt. James Cook, who tried vainly from 1776 to 1779, while other British naval officers were trying to subdue the rebellious American colonies, to find an eastward route from the Bering Sea to Hudson Bay. Even so, when Cdr. John Ross, James Clark Ross, Lt. William Edward Parry, and Capt. John Franklin took up the search again almost half a century later, the quest was still at the nadir it had been when Frobisher's party found it the only challenge "yet undone."

Few merchants or their governments still thought such a treacherous northern waterway, with its drifting ice floes and uncertain weather, would be economically feasible for trade. However, all seafaring nations were eager to acquire more scientific knowledge of this vast region at the top of the world.

In the U.S. Navy, Lt. Matthew Fontaine Maury, superintendent of the Depot of Charts and Instruments under the Bureau of Ordnance and Hydrography,[8] was especially anxious to obtain data to prove his theory of the existence there of a vast open polar sea he called Polina. This theory was advanced in England in 1817 by William Scoresby the younger, a noted whaler, after observing ice drifting south along eastern Greenland, leading him to believe there was a sea connecting the Atlantic and Pacific oceans. He had also observed that whales carrying harpoons from Greenland were killed south of Bering Strait, and other whales were brought in near Greenland bearing harpoons from the Bering Sea area. Maury had noted this same phenomenon. His recommendations carried more weight than Scoresby's did in England for the simple reason that Maury was a naval officer and Scoresby a whaler. The fact that the latter could bolster his recommendations with years of first-hand experience and observation did little to influence the stiff disdain of Royal Navy officers, to their later grief.[9]

Maury's study of ocean winds and currents and the fact that Arctic whale species couldn't survive in tropic waters if they were to round South America tended to confirm his belief that a passage across the top of the North American continent was open at least occasionally. Maury believed that a warm undercurrent flowed northward through Davis Strait and that there "must be a place somewhere in the Arctic Seas where this current ceases to flow north, and begins to flow south as a surface current." He theorized that where the warm current surfaces, there is "an open sea in the Arctic Ocean."[10]

On Maury's staff was thirty-four-year-old Lt. Edwin J. DeHaven, who had been acting master of the *Vincennes*, flagship of Commodore Wilkes in the 1838–42 globe-girdling Exploring Expedition, which confirmed the existence of Antarctica and opened an era of naval geographical exploration, charting, and surveying. Lieutenant DeHaven, already an experienced polar explorer, agreed to head the Grinnell Expedition. He was considered an authority on meteorology and oceanography and was thought to be a wise choice to lead the searchers. W. Parker Snow of the British ship *Prince Albert* described DeHaven "as fine a specimen of a seaman, and a rough and ready officer as I had ever seen. . . . With a sharp, quick eye, a countenance bronzed and apparently inured to all weathers, his voice gave unmistakable signs of energy, promptitude, and decision. There was no mistaking the man. He was undoubtedly well-fitted to lead the expedition, and I felt charmed to see it." DeHaven's instructions were "to look, when he should get well up into Wellington Channel, for an open sea to the northward and westward."[11]

Sir John Franklin, aged fifty-nine and one of the Royal Navy's most eminent Arctic explorers, had put out from England on 18 May 1845, with 129 officers and men in two bark-rigged state-of-the-art sailing ships, *Erebus* and *Terror*.[12] Sir John flew his pennant aboard the somewhat larger *Erebus,* and Capt. Francis R. M. Crozier commanded the *Terror*. They were to map what the Admiralty firmly believed would be the final link between the Atlantic and Pacific Oceans north of continental Canada. It was the best equipped expedition that had ever entered the Arctic, both ships fitted with steam-driven screw propellers. They carried the finest instruments and equipment available, and food enough to last three years. They were hailed by a Scottish whaler north of Baffin Island at the entrance to Lancaster Sound on 26 July— and that was the last the world had heard of them.[13]

Waiting anxiously in England were not only members of the Royal Navy's Arctic Council, some of whom had accompanied Franklin on previous explorations, but his beautiful, tireless, and articulate wife, Lady Jane. In 1848–49, a year after the most conservative estimates for Sir John's safe return, seven rescue attempts from Great Britain began. Three ships were sent by way of Greenland westward, three sailed east above the Bering Strait, and one party pushed north overland to Canada's Arctic coast.

One of these expeditions approaching from the Atlantic in the *Enterprise* and *Investigator* was commanded by Sir James Clark Ross, a popular and imposing Scotsman of forty-eight years. He had explored the region from 1829–34 with his uncle, Sir John Ross, and in 1831 had located the north magnetic pole. They had been aboard the *Victory,* a unique but appropriate ship for the far North—a small, steam-assisted paddlewheeler, originally a mere 85 tons and even when modified for Arctic travel only 150 tons. His return to search for Franklin and Crozier, his close friend since midshipman days, in Prince Regent Inlet east of Boothia Peninsula, was partly motivated by their shared experiences. From 1839 to 1843 the younger Ross had led an Antarctic expedition in the same two ships, *Erebus* and *Terror,* on which Franklin set out for the north two years later. In 1841, after discovering both the Ross Sea and Victoria Land, Sir James had wintered in Tasmania (then called Van Diemen's Land), a penal colony off Australia where Franklin was serving as governor for the queen. But even the knowledgeable Ross had no success in finding any trace of his old comrades.

Lady Jane kept up a relentless campaign for more thorough investigations, including her effort to enlist the help of the U.S. Navy by appealing twice in 1849 to President Zachary Taylor. New York shipowners and merchants involved in the prosperous whaling and seal industries, such as Henry Grinnell, added their petitions to Congress to join the search. On 4 January 1850, the president sent Lady Jane's letters to Congress which in turn routed them to its Committee on Naval Affairs. In spite of the keen interest of Lieutenant Maury, the expedition would probably have appeared too costly for the navy to undertake if the project had not been strongly promoted by shipowner Grinnell, of Grinnell, Minturn and Company of New York, who also had corresponded with Lady Jane. He offered to privately furnish and outfit two of his company's ships for the mission, and with the help of Whig senator Henry Clay was able to convince Congress to make it an official operation in spite of the opposition of Senate Democrats. It may have helped their cause, also, that Grinnell's older brother, Joseph, a former member of the firm when it acted solely as shipping agent for New Bedford whale-oil merchants, was an influ-ential Whig member of Congress from Massachusetts.[14]

In 1850 twelve vessels sailed for Baffin Bay and the region above northern Canada. Two were under seventy-three-year-old Sir John Ross, who had promised Franklin to go in search of him if necessary in the ninety-one-ton schooner *Felix,* purchased by subscriptions from the Hudson's Bay Company, with his own sturdy twelve-ton mahogany yacht *Mary* as tender and relief vessel.[15] In addition there was the schooner *Prince Albert,* commanded by the Royal Navy's Capt. Charles C. Forsythe, with a civilian aide, Parker Snow, sent out by Lady Jane Franklin. Capt. Horatio Austin, also of the Royal Navy, commanded a squadron in the bark HBM *Resolute* with a screw steam tender, *Pioneer* (Lt. Sherard Osborn), and Austin's second-in-command, Capt. Erasmus Ommanney, in the bark *Assistance* with its steam tender, *Intrepid,* Lt. J. B. Cator commanding. Others were equally impressive: Capt. William Penny, a veteran whaling captain, with his brigs *Lady Franklin* and *Sophia*; and a converted tea ship, the *North Star,* bringing in supplies for the expeditions. In addition to these British ships was the U.S. Navy's Grinnell Expedition, headed by Lieutenant DeHaven in the *Advance* and Acting Master Samuel P. Griffin in the *Rescue,* with Acting Master Robert R. Carter aboard as first officer.[16]

It was strange that so much worldwide attention centered on the fate of Sir John, a pleasant looking but unremarkable man, endowed with neither brilliance nor a colorful personality. He was only moderately tall with a stocky build, and his hairline retreated completely out of sight above dark eyebrows over wide-set brown eyes. He was extremely proper, if not stiff-necked, and tended to "pull his rank" with subordinates, hardly a loveable quality; and his judgment on early explorations had not been above reproach. Apparently, however, he had hidden virtues. A middle-aged widower with a young daughter, Eleanor, he had attracted the utter devotion of a dynamic, wealthy, well-bred, and well-endowed young woman (nee Jane Griffith) often in the public eye, and they were soon married.

Perhaps it was a case of "opposites attract." Lady Jane was a rare individualist in those Victorian days who, quite different from the usual sippers of tea and embroiderers of fine needlework, pursued her own agenda. She scaled mountains, navigated white-water rapids, and traveled to exotic lands. She knew everyone "worth knowing" and counted royalty and industrial moguls among her intimate circle.

To be fair, Sir John had a remarkable pit bull tenacity, courage, and honesty, traits that had won him followers over a career that began at age fifteen, serving under the great Lord Horatio Nelson at the battle of Copenhagen in 1801 and four years later at Trafalgar. The Battle of New Orleans in 1815, where the British were roundly defeated by Andrew Jackson, added little to his laurels except for having been honorably wounded in action.

In 1818 he was given command of HBM *Trent* in a four-ship squadron to sail on a Polar expedition assigned to find an entrance to the so-called Polar Sea and then steer west, ultimately, to the Pacific. The *Dorothea* was so severely damaged by ice in the Spitsbergen Islands in the Greenland Sea, north of Norway, that the *Trent* had to escort her back to England. John Ross, commanding the other two ships, entered Lancaster Sound from Baffin Bay, but Ross thought he saw a mountain range ahead and turned back. Ross's second-in-command, Lt. William Edward Parry, reported in England, however, that he thought the sound was navigable to the west and the following year was sent out again to pursue that route. Meanwhile, Franklin led an overland expedition from Canada's Great Slave Lake to the coast through unexplored territory. He accomplished some important mapping; but ignoring the warnings of Indian guides, after taking a year to reach the freezing northern sea, Franklin took a hard-headed stand.

"We were ordered to explore eastward!" he told his exhausted men, and in spite of extremely bad weather, he commanded them to launch their canoes. One month and 500 miles later, half-starved, they were forced to abandon the canoes and head back on foot across 150 miles of frozen tundra to their previous year's winter camp. Ten of the fifteen French Canadian voyageurs who had accompanied the five naval officers died before help arrived. They would have all died except for the heroic efforts of Midshipman George Back and three Canadians, who set out on improvised snowshoes to get help from the Indians whose advice Franklin had ignored. Chief Akaitcho at once sent out a party of hunters with food for the survivors, who numbered only four when they were found, two of them tending a small fire over which they were "cooking" pieces of leather gear for their next meal.[17]

When they returned to England, few would have faulted Franklin if he'd asked for a change of venue for his next assignment. On the contrary, in 1825 he was back in Canada, traveling down the Mackenzie River to its mouth on the Beaufort Sea to finish his survey of the coastline.

With him, and proof of the protective loyalty bestowed on Franklin by associates, was John Richardson, a versatile naturalist and surgeon who had been one of the four still alive when George Back had returned with their Indian friends. At Mackenzie Bay, beyond the river's mouth, Richardson and one party traveled east and surveyed 900 miles that summer, while Franklin successfully charted only 350 miles to the west after an attack by hostile Eskimos he stopped to observe despite their hostility, and difficult navigation which piled up several of his boats on unseen rocks. At home, the British hailed their exploits on this venture, cheering Sir John as an Arctic hero, a man who, in picturesque terms, "had eaten his boots."[18]

This much was common knowledge in 1850, when the U.S. Navy's Grinnell Expedition and numerous British search missions were planned. The British Admiralty asked the advice of the Arctic Council—an exclusive fraternity of flag officers who had left their names on various capes and waterways west of Greenland in previous explorations. Among the councilmen were Frederick W. Beechey (Beechey Island), George Back (Back River, sometimes called Great Fish River), Second Secretary of the Admiralty John Barrow (Barrow Strait), John Richardson (Richardson Point), James Clark Ross (James Ross Strait), and William Edward Parry (Parry Islands.)

"If Franklin's ships were 'beset,' [frozen immovably in the Arctic ice pack] what would he have been likely to do?" they were asked.[19] James Clark Ross thought they would have tried to reach Baffin Bay, at the north, or if they were beset farther south, either the Mackenzie or Coppermine River, "whichever was the nearest." Sir George Back (knighted long after that misbegotten attempt in 1819 to reach the Northwest Passage from Great Slave Lake) flatly rejected the possibility of "any attempts on the part of Sir John Franklin to send boats or detachments over the ice to any point of the mainland eastward of the Mackenzie River." He knew from bitter experience how fruitless this would have been. Dr. Richard King urged that a relief party go down the Great Fish River to the western shore of Boothia Peninsula where he thought the expedition was beset (as indeed it was).[20]

Most, however, did not take into account Franklin's demonstrated overriding determination to follow orders at all costs. Only Lady Jane, apparently, took seriously the fact that those orders in 1845, which Sir John helped draft, dictated that he was to sail west through Lancaster Sound, as Ross and Parry had done earlier, then head south to that part of the anticipated passage to the Bering Sea along the Canadian shore which he and Richardson had already charted. If this route were blocked by ice, his secondary option would be to sail north in Wellington Channel. Neither did any member of the council know firsthand what weather conditions there—always the most unpredictable factor determining Arctic routes—had been in the late summer and autumn of 1845. Which sea lanes were open and which ones impassable when the *Erebus* and *Terror* sailed west in Lancaster Sound?

When Carter arrived in New York in May 1850, he quickly met their own dedicated patron, Henry Grinnell. He also met Henry's younger brother, Moses Hicks Grinnell, a member of the firm and former congressman from New York, both sons of ship captain Cornelius Grinnell of New Bedford, Massachusetts.[21] Their headquarters were the luxurious Astor House, whose accommodations were provided by the management; and the Grinnells had already stocked the ships' libraries with books, many written by earlier Arctic explorers.

Lieutenant Maury had also been at work since before congressional approval, providing DeHaven with what scientific instruments he would need and recommending that he buy others, and giving him instructions for scientific observations and specimens to collect. There was little time for all of this to be assembled, as official instructions were dated 15 May, only a week before the ships were to depart in order to be in Lancaster Sound before the end of Arctic summer. They gave explicit directions: "Having passed Barrow's

Straits, you will turn your attention northward to Wellington Channel, and westward to Cape Walker, and be governed by circumstances as to the course you will then take." If ice prevented passage through Barrow's Straits, the search should then turn its attention to Jones Sound and Smith Sound, and if these too were closed, DeHaven should return to New York.

On 1 May 1850, Carter recorded in his personal log that he'd received orders to report to New York City to prepare to sail in the brig *Rescue,* appropriately named for its mission. Griffin had failed to mention that it was a small brig of only 90 tons, 65 feet long, or that the ship's company would number only sixteen. The flagship, *Advance,* was an 88-foot hermaphrodite brig of 144 tons displacement with a twenty-one foot beam, and a complement of fifteen officers and men. (Carter's former ship, the *Savannah,* was 175 feet, had been rated at 1,726 tons, and carried 480 men.[22] It was in stark contrast to what he would call "the U.S. Arctic fleet.")

Carter's "Private Journal" is exactly that—a canvas-covered book the approximate size of today's legal pad, with lined pages, its top line slightly above the others like a ledger. On this he customarily wrote a title describing the mission or a particular activity covered on that date. As he explained in his allegorical "foreword," written like a passage from the Bible, the book was given to him by Sam Griffin, the *Rescue*'s captain, to keep as a personal log. In it he was to write from his own viewpoint, not as keeper of the official log. This he did.

When he was disgusted, he "griped" in true navy fashion. When he was homesick, he said so. When he disagreed with higher-ranking officers (as on observing the Sabbath), he noted his disgust; and when he was happy, he gloried in it. This differed from the published journals of contemporary Royal Navy officers, who seldom recorded any discord in their ranks. However, Carter once said Griffin "would make a good Prince of Unreason for a May Day frolic," and another time called DeHaven's plans for land journeys "a double extract of the essence of humbug!" He had a refreshing air of frankness, and at the same time seems to have been a cool, professional officer, not always in agreement with those who made the ultimate decisions, but still loyal and efficient. It seems, though, that he was "out of the loop" on decision making and planning. It was not until 4 July 1850—after more than a month at sea—that Carter could write, "I see for the first time something of the plan of our cruise if circumstances permit."

Occasionally, he said the cabin (meaning those who shared it) "had a sore head," but his following comments usually proved they had good reason for being disgruntled. His irrepressible sense of humor; his anger when he discovered contractors had failed to provide necessary pipe parts to assemble stoves to heat the *Rescue*; his ingenuity in contriving a tiny burner to make tea; their unique, if useless, attempts to manufacture shot for hunting after their own supply was exhausted; his fascination with Arctic wildlife all made him such a thoroughly "modern" human being that the part he played in history became almost secondary.

Carter's "private journal" has never before been published. His son-in-law, Rear Adm. J. H. Oliver, married to Carter's daughter, Marion, sent at least a partial copy to the Stefansson Collection at Dartmouth College, at the request of Villjalmur Stefansson, head of their Arctic history department, in the 1920s, and another to the U.S. Navy Department. The original remained at Shirley Plantation until the Carters put it on loan to the Colonial Williamsburg Foundation Library in 1991.

No other full day-to-day journal of any member of the U.S. Grinnell Expedition has ever appeared, and its style differs markedly from Elijah Kent Kane's book, *The U.S. Grinnell Expedition in Search of Sir John Franklin, a Personal Narrative*. Kane's romantic account was written "after the fact" and benefited from the time and care "the little doc," as Carter called him, was able to put into it. Kane, however, told far less of the men's daily routine and clearly omitted any irritation among its company, looking forward to a wider readership than did Carter, who felt his journal would interest no one but his family. (For their benefit Carter left blanks for a few words he thought might hurt the ladies' sensibilities. For example, he humorously described Griffin's lazy Newfoundland, a "large bear dog," on 4 August 1851; left a blank; and probably meant to say it was a splendid "stud" dog, since he commented that "nothing was made in vain and [he has] been tried at every thing else without success.")

Carter used wind forces based on the Beaufort scale (defined in the glossary) for his weather notes and abbreviations that appeared on the last page of his journal, as they do here (page 161).

Due to the hurried spelling and punctuation, we have spelled out Carter's abbreviations, such as "A" for "Advance" and "sly" for "southerly." We have kept his uncorrected spelling (except when it was obviously a slip of the pen) and sentences that are longer than they would have been if he had reread them later. For ease of reading, however, we have inserted occasional commas and periods where they seemed appropriate. Carter had studied both French and Latin as a boy, and used each language where appropriate, as he did all his life. He continued to draw the interesting things he saw, without benefit of a camera, wherever he traveled, as did most naval officers of that era. In his writings and in his drawings, Robert Randolph Carter told the story of this country's contribution to the search for Sir John Franklin and his men. His recognition of defeat in that cause was mingled with his regret when DeHaven headed back to New York and they had to abandon their attempt. "So good-bye, Sir John. The Yankees have failed to help you and can only pray for you. God Almighty aid you to escape," he wrote on 15 August 1851. Carter's words said a lot about him and even more about the navy. They had done their very best, and that is all that could have been expected.

Carter opened the pages of his journal with an account, written in the style of a biblical scribe, explaining how he came to join the expedition and keep the journal "in the days of King Zacharia" (President Zachary Taylor). It gives an important background to his "personal log," although it isn't part of the journal of the voyage itself:

> Sitting on the transom was a reefer gay.[23]
> He fixed his book
> His pen he took.
> And these were the words that he did write.

It came to pass in the days of King Zacharia that there was a man of Virginia, Robert Carter by name, who was sojourning in the city of Annapolis in the land called Maryland. And this man was a disciple of the several wise men assembled at that city, according to the laws of the land, for the purpose of instructing Midshipmen in their various branches of knowledge so that when they come to be examined by the old Captains, they may be considered worthy to become Passed Midshipmen.

And whilst there this man did become a *friend* of another disciple in the same School, Samuel [Griffin] by name. For albeit these two men had been much together at sea, and since they had taken upon them to serve their country, yet heretofore they did not discover to each other that they were of congenial tastes and did not love one another much. Howbeit there they did become intimate and did profess *friendship*.

And it came to pass that in the course of time these two men were examined and accepted, and they went their ways and were separated for a season. But they did vow to remember one another and to write one to the other. Then . . . obeying the will of our good King, whilst Robert was dwelling on the border of the James, by City Point as thou goest unto Norfolk, in his father's house, there came one day unto him an epistle, and lo! it was from Samuel and had come from Gotham (that great city) and it did say, "Behold, now I am on my Journey from Gotham to the land of my fathers; Appoint me thy place where we may meet, and I will rest there a day, for I have somewhat to tell thee, which concerneth thee and me, and doth surely open a way whereby we may do much for ourselves and the world."

And Robert said, "Let us meet at Annapolis!" And he arose and went up thither and did there await his friend. So they two met there and were rejoiced to see one another. Then the man Samuel took up his yarn, and thus said: "Art thou but just come into the world that thou dost not know that when Winter is ended that a Man of Gotham, rich and good, will prepare and send out two ships in search of Sir John Franklin, a servant of the great queen across the pond, who is gone, no man knoweth whither, among the Arctic ice?"

And he said, "Yea, I know all this."

And Samuel said, "Grinnell the Gothamite is the man, and lo, he hath bid me go and command one of these his ships, and now I pray thee go with me and thou shalt be my first mate, for I have preferred thee above others, and have mentioned thy name to Grinnell as he whom I would have to go with me."

And the man Robert did consider for some days and did take counsel with his friends of Annapolis who did advise him not to go. Then did the two journey together until they came unto the city of the King [Washington D.C.] and saw how that the service which they proposed to undertake would be acceptable to the King's minister, their Boss [Secretary of the Navy William B. Preston]. Yet did not Robert consent to go with Samuel his friend until as they journeyed together toward the South.

When they came to the place where their roads parted, Samuel saith, "Wilt thou go with me and do as I have told thee when the vessels are ready?" And he said, "I will go." Then said he unto him, "Take heed that thy kinsfolk dissuade thee not." And Robert said, "I have said, and will I not do?" Then they two parted and went unto their own houses.

But the friends of Robert did earnestly persuade him to retract his promise and did urge him vehemently not to go (all except his Mother who said, "Thou art in the hands of the Lord; his will be done.") Nevertheless, he harkened not unto their voices but consented and went.

And it came to pass that at the commencement of May 1850, that Robert did receive orders from the Secretary of the Navy to go to New York and report for duty in the Expedition about to Proceed in search of Sir John, agreeable to his application. Which orders he obeyed and did report at New York for this duty on the 13th of May where he found his friend Samuel waiting for him.

Now it came to pass that after they had been some days on the waters that Samuel saith unto Robert, "Behold, now thou shalt keep a journal of this cruise. But thou shalt put therein thine own thoughts and ideas." Wherefore, oh Captain Sam! behold this book where in whatsoever seemeth unmeet is written especially in accordance with my feelings at the time of the entry thereof.

> *Quisqius huc leget*
> *Quod tibi horrendum videtur*
> *Mihi amoenum est*
> *Si delectat maneas*
> *Si tardet abeas*
> *Utrumque Gratum.*[24]

THE JOURNAL

Private Journal of a Cruise in the Brig Rescue in Search of Sir John Franklin

R. R. Carter

Brooklyn Navy Yard. Getting the Brig Rescue Ready for a Cruise to the Arctic Seas

Monday, May 13th 1850

Staying at the Hotel Astor.[1] Broke out early and went over to the Navy Yard to report and commence work. Astonished to find the brigs so small. Wish I was clear of the scrape. However, put on a good face and went to work stowing the Rescue's hold, regular mates 1st and second, take account of everything, and then see it stowed. Reported to the Commo[dore] (Salter[2]), got a hint about not being in uniform. Work until 6 P.M. and then go over to the Astor to dine. Considerably disgusted or rather disappointed in my anticipations.

Tuesday, May 14th

Same thing; over early, dine at six and a half. Pretty dirty work stowing and filling in with Coal. The Brig is of 91 tons burden strengthened with beams and knees, and forw[ar]d is made very strong with timbers radiating from an upright post some eight feet abaft the cutwater,[3] said to be double decked and double planked, beside the sheathing and quantities of non-conducting material between the planking, the ceiling forward and aft between the car-lings[4] lined with cork ½ inch thick. But she is too small, I think, and certainly an ugly model, much inferior to the Advance. The constant employment does not give me time to think much of the state of affairs, but I am considerably surprised to hear that an older P. Midm [Passed Midshipman] is ordered to this vessel beside myself. However Griffin says that he will be detached, and I am content. Talk about sailing on the coming Saturday. Got a short respite at 12 and ordered an immense quantity of warm clothing at Brook's great establishment,[5] also boots made of canvass uppers, leather & cork soles and lined loosely with flanel.

Wednesday, May 15th 1850

Rained hard all day, could not stow anything so I did not go over but wrote letters all day and dined for the first time at the Astor. Sad day altogether; wrote several farewells and two to A[nnapolis].

Thursday, May 16th 1850

Early to work today and stow quantities of grub &c. Broadhead[6] appears as the P.M. ordered above me. Griffin, B., and Murdaugh[7] receive Act[in]g Master's appointments and I am left in the lurch, however work away in case all comes right, but am resolved to resign sooner than go out under such circumstances. Go along until Tuesday morning only. I commence sleeping aboard on Saturday night and so of course get no grub (breakfast) until the evening when I go over to the Astor, take a grand meal, and write to Annapolis and return at night.

Friday 17th

All of us invited to dine with Grinnell at 6:30. Soon as the work is done, hurry over and dress with speed. Griffin throws a few drops of Jockey Club[8] into my eyes causing most intense pain for some minutes, and we appear at 7 perfectly ravenous. A magnificent dinner, lasts until midnight, ladies couldn't leave until 11. Everyone talks of the Expedition and how much we are to do, all of course certain that we are to find Sir John and the N. W. Passage and return in one season. My reflections are "with those two little boats just land me safely anywhere in a Christian country after two years of intense suffering, hardship, and disgust, and I will be thankful." So I commence talking of anything but the future prospect to old Moses Grinnell who is a smart and fine man. Miss Grinnell doesn't [look] pretty at all though I judge her metalic charms are powerful. 12 mid't: Wish I was home.

Tuesday 19th–21st

Received an Acting Master's appointment in the Expedition and was right glad thereof. Broadhead was detached. This day was passed in a hurry, getting aboard small things, stowing cabin stores without a steward, and running about the Yard. Too much haste entirely. Don't think that I took account of more than half the things that came onboard. Kept up a constant squabble with the officers delivering the things. Got three hours leave and went over to New York. Drew $334 advance and sent home a check for $300 through L. W.[9] on NY Bank. Mailed the miniature and a Gr[10] set with three stones.

Brooklyn Navy Yard. Off She Goes

Wednesday, May 22nd 1850

Another hurrying day. Getting aboard many stores. Broke out the hold after almost finishing it and took out 5 bbls whiskey from nine which had been stored and returned them, so making room for more useful articles. Find that our hold has not the capacity to store all the necessaries for the cruise and in consequence a larger share of the most useful articles, which unfortunately came last, had to be put in the Advance. Pity we didn't know of this sooner, as we might have left out about one half the Beef & other things less useful. Cabin in a royal old state visited by a lady, Miss Grinnell, who rushed down during a shower and found me sans habit stowing grub.

Thursday, May 23rd, 1850

Memorable day! Hail it with a song. Off she goes, and off she must go.

Hurried off. Rushing things aboard. Drove all over the city collecting articles of great need. The Pocket Chronometer of which the rate had been lost by its stopping came from Stewards without a rate. At 1:30 the men were brought on board and in half an hour we were towed out by a steamer, in a wet dirty Northeasterly wind. On the way to the hook[11] trying to get things a little to rights. Fixing logs, lanterns, compasses &c. At 7 cast off and were left on the Ocean with the following souls aboard the Rescue:

S. P. Griffin	Actg Master	in Command
R. R. Carter	" "	1st Officer
Henry Brooks	Boatswain	2nd "
Benj. Vreeland	Asst. Surg.	Surgeon
Robert Bruce (Armorer)	Wm Lincoln (B. Mate)	
John Williams (Qr Master)	David Davis (S. M. M.)	
Geo Willie (Carp. M.)	Alex Daly (Sea.)	James Stewart (Sea.)
Rufus Bagg (OS)	Smith Benjamin (Sea.)	James Johnson (Sea.)
A. Knauss (Cook)[12]	Wm Kurner (Stew'd)	

Outside of Sandy Hook

Thursday Continued

The Advance cast off a few minutes afterward and we made sail together, standing about East by South with a light Northeasterly wind. Not much sea but the brig seems very lively in the water, more so even than the Pilot boat Washington No. 4 which accompanies us for several days having on board Mr Grinnell and two sons. Nearly calm during the night.

Friday, May 24th

Light weather still. In the afternoon a little breeze from Southeastward. Find that the Advance can sail around us, has to spare us much canvass and heave to often to keep in sight. A little sea and this vile boat seems to think it her duty to make every motion except that of going through the water. Oh, what an ass I was for joining this business!
At 12M Lat Obs 40°19' N   Long Chro 73°26'W.

Saturday, May 25, 1850

Light and mod't winds and damp disagreeable Easterly weather. What a beast of a boat this is. I'd give my eternal fortune just to be put ashore anywhere in the U. States. At 2 P.M. the Washington came up and boarded us, took letters (none from me) bade us farewell, sailed round both the vessels and went back toward New York. The motion of the brig makes me sick, and I am heartily disgusted to commence.
Lat Obs 40.25 N   Long 72.52 W. Chro.

Sunday May 26th

Worse than yesterday. Wet Easterly weather and a short steep Sea. Never saw such a wet vessel. Leaks also making 6 inches an hour pop out every watch. A murrian[13] on the persons accountable for the refitting of the brig. I guess Commo DeHaven is disgusted to have to wait for us so constantly.
Lat 39°39'N   Long 71°57'W

Monday, May 27, 1850

A moderate westerly wind and quite a sea during the night. Did ever anyone see such a beast. She is certainly Amphibious. She takes the water in whenever she can, seems to delight in rolling to windward so as to get a whole sea aboard, then by rising forward throws it aft with a rush. Confound this business of hurrying off in any business. The carpenter's work is wretchedly done —decks, deadlights,[14] and hatches leak like sieves. Cabin and Forecastle both wet. Spoke the Advance who says that she is dry below. Again I reflect what a fool I am to expose myself to such discomforts and vexations. Would give all I have to be pitched into the middle of James River opposite Shirley, or launched into the mudhole at the foot of the college green at Annapolis. Watch & watch[15] and navigate, besides keeping the log book & slate,[16] for I have to write Brooks' remarks and whatever he remembers of the R. F. C. Ws.[17] at the end of each of his watches. Am also very seasick.

Wrote three pages of unhappiness mixed with tenderness and faith to L[ouise].[18] With a light fair wind we manage to keep up with the Advance.

Tuesday May 28th

A fresh Northwest breeze, foggy, misty and unpleasant. During the night very fresh and a heavy sea, Advance beating us all to pieces. Wet fore and aft above and below. I wonder what we will do when we get into cold weather at this li[c]k.
Lat. DR[19] 40°29'N   Long DR 67°11'W.

Wednesday, May 29th, 1850

Lat. 40°29' N   Long. 65°2' W
Fresh N. W. and clear. Ran her all day until 5 P.M., washing her decks at every roll. In the afternoon the sea rose pretty high, and we laboured heavily, steered wildly, and water knee deep on deck all the time. I tried to persuade Capt. Griffin to heave to at four, but he was intent on following the Advance who

gains constantly ahead and seems entirely unmindful of her unhappy consort. From 2 to 4 she kept something at her main like a signal for a course, but were jumping about so that it was impossible to keep her in the field of the telescope so as to read it, so we did not answer. At 5 even Griffin could stand it no longer, so he laid her to under reduced sail and were at once comparatively comfortable. The Advance kept on and disappeared in less than an hour bearing NE by E. Happy ridance, Mr. Commo., if that's the way you serve us. Lat. ⊙ 40°29'N   Long 65°24'W Chro

Thur 30th   41.04 N   63.54 W Obs.

Light weather from Northward and Northeastward, damp, tolerably smooth sea. Opened the hold and found that a good deal of water had got in and wet some dry goods. Served out boots, socks, &c., to the men, some of whom needed them much. Find that we are deceived in our crew and that more than half have yet to learn the first principles. Our poor Steward[20] can't speak English or anything but French and would suit a monsieur for a nurse or Valet much better than a Yankee reefer's mess boy.

Fri. 31st 41°39'N   63°27'W DR

Rather fresh Easterly and very wet weather. A horrible high and wallsided sea. Very bad business this, no place to take exercise. I think I will never sail in so small a craft again if I can help it. But still I have a ravenous appetite and do ample justice to the grub which, by the way, the Boatswain has to teach the Cuisinier to cook, and it seems a pity to give the sailors most all the cabin spuds, but of course I am for doing it. The Gulph Stream may do us a little good, but if this is the weather we always have with it, I wish we were out. This is positively the dampest kind of weather. I have some clothes wet since we left N York and in fact have never yet been dry.

Sat. June 1st—Lat 41°37'N Long 63°5'W

Light and calm, thick fog and rain, a nasty sea. The brig wallowing according to her fashion. Oh, Mr. Grinnell, I wish you were here and I in your house during all my watch below, and p'haps this should be written in a livelier strain. Doc[21] says that this is a famous old first of June and is Ex'peck'd.

Sun. June 2nd—Lat. 41°47'N DR Long 62°23'W DR

Another wet day. But a fair wind and toward evening quite fresh. At 5:30 the sun appeared for a few minutes and I caught three glimpses at him which using Lat DR put us 19 miles to Eastward of Long. DR. Those two U. S. chronometers concur in saying that Bliss and Creighton's pretty faced one is like other fair faces, deceitful, and I accordingly use one of them.[22] Had quite a quiet day and am thankful. Wish I could spend every Sabbath chez mon père. Had a gas with the Captain in the last Dog [watch][23] upon the prospects of having cold feet and hands in this wet vessel. He wears a flanel shirt, using himself to cold I suppose. I prefer to be comfortable while I can, for suppose we get lost I will have a more comfortable reminiscense of the first part of the cruise. Laws a massy[24] what a set of sailors. Providential that we have so long a time before getting to where they will be more necessary. Long. by sight mentioned—62°04'.

Mon. June 3rd   42°23'N   59°19'W Obsd.

Pretty fair weather today. Cleared up about noon and staid so. Dried my clothes for the first time. The Barometer rose to 30.15 and stayed there within a few hundredths, so that its indicators of fair weather for once proved true. The porpoises have also made true sign, the wind having come from the direction which they swam four times in succession within the last week. I find that we have no chart of Disco Island or any other harbour in Baffin Bay. Griffin says that we have to trust to luck and a hard bottom to get into a port there. Got an afternoon sight and find that in spite of Gulph Stream and cloudy days our DR and Obs. Long. were only 6 miles different; Lats. difference 17 miles.

Wrote a letter A-ward[25] in hopes of meeting a cod fisherman tomorrow or next day. Thermometer shows low temperatures for the Gulf and I am in hopes that we are done with it. Brooks finished a complete suit of Buffalo skin which a l'air [appears] to be very warm. Elegant Rice Pudding for dinner.

Tues., June 4th 43°04'N   57°43'W Obs.

Lovely soft sweet day. Got up pitch, tar, turpentine &c to try and make the Spar deck[26] tight. Took sights with my watch by myself which came out within nine miles. Poor Doc stuffing a poor little land bird (Common as dirt) which came off to us in distress some days ago. He calls that Taxidermy or some such name. Wrote a letter home but hardly hope to see fisherman tomorrow, wind dying away and hauling ahead, but Barom. still keeps high. The first night watch an Easterly wind and a misty rain. We ought to have a wonderfully good end to this cruise if bad beginnings have anything to do with it.

Wednesday June 5th   43°29'N   57°09'W

Commences a wet misty Easterly light air—monstrous unfav[ora]ble for folks bound Eastward. Barom. higher than ever—30.35. Getting used to this wet cold temperature fast. Prospect for finding Comm. DeHaven at Disco getting slim. Griffin got out in his India rubber skiff and thinks there is a Northerly current of eight miles a day. A poor Merid[ian][27] all on account of misty atmosphere. Porpoises swam to Westward in First watch. Captain Griffin pulled up close to a Booby[28] sleeping on the water, with the doctor's gun loaded with No. 4 [shot] and with the first barrel caused him to awake but did not make him fly; but seeing the boat approach, he rose leisurely and having received the second barrel, flew a short distance. Waited for two similar discharges which he received with perfect indifference but retired a little farther into the thick fog. The dr's gun, says he (the Dr), is the finest ever purchased in ——— shop, New York, and the barrels belonged to his own father &c. Commenced reading Ross's *Expedition*[29] this afternoon, being the first opportunity I have had, and find it interesting.

Thurs., June 6th 43°45'N 56°32'W Obs

A wet foggy morning followed by a beautiful clear mild day. Brooks sick. Find ourselves well to Eastward of dead reckoning. A Westerly wind because of the Porpoises. Shook a water cask from the deck,[30] making a little more room for the watch officer to keep him warm. Got Azimuth and Amplitude, both making variation 11 Westerly, 10 less than Bowditch table.[31] Wonder at seeing no vessel bound to Westward and can it be possible that our chronometers are so much wrong. Overhauling and restowing after locker. Find lots of Masters stores wet.

Fri, June 7th 43°59'N   54°09'W Obs

Fine Westerly wind, clear weather, smooth sea. Quite nice. A Southwesterly current, says Griffin. Bad Traverse,[32] say I, and not my marking for I find a marked difference between the marks I make for my watch and those I make for Brooks.

Sat. June 8th, 1850   45°31'N 52°30'W

A rather fresh W S W wind and passing clouds, Bar. falling, 30.30. At Mer. Saw a schooner anchored on the Banks. Looking out anxiously for some fisherman that we may run near and give letters in a bottle. Toward evening hope of this grows faint. The fastest run we have yet had, and a dense fog precludes all possibility. Can't catch a fish. The only time we have really wanted light or head winds, we have it fresh and straight aft us. But it must be for the best. I put three letters that I would like to have sent in a bottle, but twas no use.

Brig Rescue from New York N'd about New Foundland

Sun June 9th 1850   47°30'N 51°48' W Obs.

They're gone—They're gone, no hope now. I've seen a New Foundland fog and am satisfied. Would I had never seen it, indeed it was not my desire. However, the Fog was under the governance of a kind Providence which showed its omnipotence by raising the fog for 15 minutes at Mer and for the same length of time at 3½, giving me an opportunity to see the sun. At Mer we saw the first iceberg, pretty large, but it didn't create much excitement. A large piece of field ice was also seen in the morning, saw several others during the afternoon, all too distant to alter the temp of either air or water. Am illy satisfied with the manner of passing this Sabbath day. Suffer much from rheumatism in the feet which as they are constantly wet must continue so until I am laid up with them unless a change of weather comes. From 6 to midt. a steady rain. Wind fair all day.

Mon. 10th 49°10'N   50°29'W DR
[No entry.]

Temp from 40 to 37   Tues. 11th 49°48'N   49°42'W DR
[No entry.]

Weds. 12th

The suffering and vexation of the last two days in thick fog quite a fresh wind and heavy sea and almost constant rain more than compensate for anything that we can do this cruise. The wind has been almost entirely around the compass without removing the fog but I think it is most dense and rains more from the Eastward than any other quarter. The Barometer is not much of an indicator of the weather for it rises and falls a whole inch without a material change. Saw a great many icebergs, some immense. Passed within 200 yards of a very large one without altering the temperature of air or water. This morning stood directly for one some twenty feet high and thirty yards square and within fifty yards the water fell from 36° to 34° F. air no change. Saw a great number of small ducks which seem to delight in this climate and stay much about the bergs.

The brig is very wet and more uncomfortable than ever. Monday evening found my poor feet too large for my boots, but by rubbing with linament and missing one dog watch got them into a pair of India rubbers. Though at this moment I am quite comfortable and am not anticipating any immediate hardship, I must say that the loss of comfort, probable loss of health and constant vexation of my position here would more than compensate for the achievement most glorious that the annals of earth could record. I do think that no earthly reward could induce me to come again thus far on this cruise and return with comfort.

Thermometer ranging today from 36 to 40. Passed within fifty yards of another berg about 100 feet high and reduced the temperature of air and water one degree each. Got a DA $\odot$[33] and made Lat. very near the DR. Long twenty miles to the Westward of DR by morning and afternoon sight.

Thursday, June 13th   53°23'N DR 51°34'W DR

Fresh westerly weather until morning or rather until 8 A.M. for day comes now at 1 A.M. During the forenoon a steady fast rain. A heavy cross sea wetting her all over wherever. How I wish I was to home. Confounded be the art of building wet vessels. If all the fresh water that has been put into the sea within the bounds of our horizon since we left New York could have fallen upon Sahara, the desert would flourish as the rose. The Barometer predicted this weather pretty truly according to Purdy's book.[34]

Friday, June 14th   53°55'N   51°49'W Obs.

A rather pleasant day, good deal of calm and not much sun. Thermometer during the day 42°.

Truly the battle will not be to the strong if we accomplish anything this cruise. I have just learned the class of vessels John Bull sends on this duty 3 or 400 tons with propellers and ahead of us a month. In our vessel there is scarcely a man who has seen an iceberg before and no such person as an ice mate aboard. Griffin says that he wanted no such person because his caution would cause us to shun enterprises which our ignorance of the danger might lead us to undertake, so this then is our trust—that we are to accomplish everything by chance. I only hope our ignorance mayn't become apparent by the futility of our actions. I am quite homesick today. There is so little variety in our company. One companion is not enough and if he be out of sorts, que desdicha! Got some rather poor observations of ⊙ [the sun] today which confirms the DA of 12th. Saw one iceberg in the afternoon.

	DR	obs
Sat. June 15, 1850	53°37'N	52°21'W

Moderate Southeasterly weather cloudy foggy and lots of rain with a heavy S. E. swell make the first part of this day anything but comfortable. Oh self, self. Thou *all* and thy interest the main spring and motive of *every* action. I begin to believe what Griffin has said in jest more than once. I came expecting hard work and I find it, even when it might be easier. Watch and watch, navigate and keep the log of course so that very little of my watch below is mine, especially as I am often requested to make out requisitions etc. or attend to any job which requires a responsible officer.[35] All this I have done with pleasure and turned out at 7 A.M. after mid watch whenever the sun was out and now Griffin pretends to, or does wish for another in my place, saying that I was taken as a dernier [last] resort. Rather discouraging for a commencement but I hope he may learn to apreciate me before we part.

	DR	
Sun., June 16th	56°58'N	52°16'W

Horrible day, a strong N.W. gale. Barom was down to 29.29 when it commenced and rose gradually but the wind rose faster, and at meridian it blew heavy and made a sea that I never want to see again. Laid the Brig to but couldn't lay ourselves to too for there was no stillness in her. I was sick as a horse but went it like a trooper. But just let any one say brig of 90 tons to me after this cruise—that's all I want.

The gale put us all in a good humor, however, and we are first rate friends. It lasted 16 hours pretty heavy, hauling to Southward as it went down but neither brought nor left us any clear weather.

	Obs	
Mon., June 17th, 1850	57°45'N	52°26'W

Wind aft—light, cloudy and damp. I wonder if people going from Gotham to the Arctic ever have any dry weather. The brig keeps up a constant rolling in honour of yesterday. The sun fooled me today by keeping me on the taffrail[36] from 7 to 8 bells for nothing, but he forgot and showed his face at 2 and at 6 bells and I caught him with a DA giving us our reckoning very near the DR. We gave the brig rather too much drift in the gale a mile an hour dead to leeward but she did better. Called on the Dr. today for some of his stuff which I am labouring under now.

Tuesday, June 18th   58°48'   53°02'W Obs

A soft sweet day. Wind about S. S. W. and light. More sun than we have had since we sailed and only one shower. I am truly thankful for it. But my evil genius pursues me for I attempted to shoot a sea bird so that it would fall on deck and had the pain to see the poor wounded creature fall into the water where I may be the cause of its suffering a lingering death. This has ruined my pleasure for this day at least, so beautiful that one ought to be at peace with all creation to thank the Author.

A school of Greenland whales[37] passed us going to the NW. Their noses are squared off as nicely as if they had been sawed by rule. They appear very small. Griffin shot at one with a rifle and says he hit him.

Morning and afternoon sights differ 8 seconds, in Longitude about four miles. Must be bad steering for I had fine sights and can generally bring them nearer. But we are uncertain about the variation which on the charts is about 48° and in Bowditch much less.

Obs
Wednesday, June 19th 1850   59°23'N 53°11'W

Commenced a calm drizling midwatch. Cleared up in the morning, and during the day calm and pleasant. Temp. of air at mer. 50°F. At mid't 39°. Water 41 all the time. The Observations have put us to Westward of DR for the last week. Today found no current. Doc killed three birds like gulls.

Got out the boats and tried them. The temperature of the atmosphere makes it oppressive. I wore no coat. There was no hour during the night that we could not read by the twilight although it was cloudy. After laughing at Doc for missing a number of fine shots, took my gun and missed two very easy ones which I can't understand. Seven gulls were killed by us today and are being prepared for dinner tomorrow.

DR
Thurs., June 20th   59°36'N   53°12'W

A foggy night; a mild cloudy day, calm all the time. I killed three gulls in the morning watch and cleaned and stowed away my gun which ain't worth shuck.

The gulls of yesterday were skinned, parboiled overnight, and made into a sea pie[38] disguised with quantities of pork and spuds, but they were too strong for me although the men said that they liked them, comparing them to boiled Porpoise. Sir J. Ross may have been accustomed to a more gamey flavour than I am, but he may have all the gulls for me when there is any salt horse about.

Fitted four of the sweeps[39] furnished us, and put all hands at them with about the same result that we would have had by applying them to Trinity Church, New York. Rain in the afternoon.

DR

Friday, June 21st   60°09'N   53°21'W
Commenced a light Southerly air hauling to N. W. (true Mer) and freshning. Bar. rising slowly. Therm. falling. Very cloudy overhead. A short steep sea making it unpleasant. Afternoon clear and soft. Got Amp[litude] variation 56° W.☉ 9.15. Water discoloured very much. Therm. 38 at night, very cold to the feelings. Bar. stands at 29.80. Wind hauling Southward and moderating.

Obs.   Cro.

Sat. June 22nd   61°28'N   52°33'W
Commenced mod. NW wind, cold rain, cloudy morning, heavy sea running. Saw a company of sea birds at morning drill. Can't get over bad soft tack for a week in succession every morning and pronounce the Steward and cook a couple of humbugs, somewhat to Capt. Griffin's surprise.

Lat Obs 11 miles to Southward of DR allowing 56° Var. Ends rainy, misty, moderate.

DR   cro

Sunday June 23rd   63°14'N   53°03'W
More pleasant. A light Southerly wind and mild overcast. Saw great many pieces of ice and few large ones. Passed quantities of sea weed. All the bergs covered with birds. Got a piece of ice about ½ ton floating by itself and found it beautifully clear and fresh.

Obs   cro

Monday. 24th   64°24'N   53°37'W
Commencing as the sabbath ended. At 11 A.M. it gets foggy and damp. I saw the coast of Greenland first. At 5 A.M. a high rugged point of land bearing S by E and at 11 it appeared again, same sort of land bearing ENE. Passed

quantities of kelp. Saw less ice than yesterday though we are rarely out of sight of some two or three bergs. Therm. from 39° to 36°

DA

Tuesday, June 25th   67°04'N   55°33'W

Commenced and until 10 A.M. a fresh gale, foggy and lots of rain with a tremendous sea. Wind south (true mer.) At 12 calm. Bar. fell 0.2 during the blow being 29.84 at 12. Therm. 37°. At 4 it cleared up beautifully, wind East-ward light. Got DA ☉ & Az☉. A cloud preventing an inferior Mer. ☉, found ourselves 26' to Westward. Saw many icebergs, some too large to float in this water so they must be aground. Sounded in 60 fms water Lat. 67°12' Long. 55°35'. Put hooks to the lead in hopes of catching Halibut but no bites in a dog watch during which the hooks were exposed. Sea log is a humbug. I shall therefore abreviate the remarks in future. Griffin shot a Dovekie.[40]

Make the Coast of Greenland—Whalefish Islands—Disco Bay

Wednesday June 26th, 1850

Lat:	Long.	Wind	Temp Air	Weather
68°00'N	55°48'	S'd m.	34° to 36°	Hazy and foggy.

Saw quantities of ice, some immense bergs and many fragments. Good many birds, principally Loons. Forgot to mention yesterday passing a H[ermaphro-dite] Brig[41] in shore of us standing to Southward in sight from aloft. Many conjectures; some think it is the Advance but she was going the wrong way. At 7:00 P.M. saw the snow capped peaks of Disco and low land to Eastward. The Observation putting us 20 miles to Southward of D. R. put Capt. Griffin in doubt, and he thinks that he has run in too far to Northward and that the land to Southward is Disco, and hauls by the wind trying to fetch a high point to the Southward & Eastward round which he wishes to pass. At midt drawing in with the land see many islands. In running in from yesterday's position crossed a stream of large bergs; 35 were in sight from deck at one time.

Whalefish Isds Thursday June 27th 1850
At 2 A.M.

Lat	Long	Wind	Temp Air	Weather	
68°42'	53°42'	S'd f	48° to 36°+	Thick and rainy	Ends clear

My mid watch beating up for the point to Southward when at 2 I saw the masts of vessels over a low part of the island to leeward and stood for the point round which they must have entered. Call Griffin who is still dubious even about the land to leeward being an island and thinks the vessels seen were in Godhaven; however sails on to see. When at 4.30 in passing a bay saw the Advance at anchor to our mutual delight. Hurrah my reckoning is all right and our solitary cruise up stood in quicker and anchored at 5.45 in 14 fms on the port bow of the Advance a little inside of her, got head and stern fast to the rock on either side of the safe little harbour formed by a cluster of small islands with several outlets. But oh, such a desolate looking shore. The master of the Advance boarded us just at the enterance bringing the Danish Governor a ci devant matelot [that former sailor] who lives at Whalefish islands with an Esquimaux wife and whose service to us consisted in drinking as much of our liquor as he could get and in making much harder bargains for the skins we need than the natives themselves taking in exchange the same currency viz old clothes, handkerchiefs and above all white shirts.

The news is also quite fine. Advance only two days here Commo Austin[42] with two Barques 450 tons and two Steamers left only a few days ago and the Barque[43] which brought over his extra stores going to return in a few days to England. Glorious chance to send letters. A party of the Esquimaux came off in their kayaks (the famous Esquimaux canoe) which surpass what I had read of them in beauty sur-tous [especially] and construction. But the English had got all the skin clothing and we can only scrape up a few poor ones. All the natives of this settlement have evidently seen white folks afore. Most of them have their cheeks and noses frosted.

Reflection from sililoquy, Pretty fair luck this, come in No Chart of Disco bay no idea of situation of the harbour nor appearance of the islands from a distance not even its position accurately. Providence directed me to take a look at the land we were beating away from just as we could see the vessels through the opening or we would have been working to windward, in all this wind and rain. Am very thankful for this mercy as also for that which gave me the sun just at 12 the day before as Capt Griffin says that he ran by my observations although he doubted their accuracy from the unusual difference from DR. The Advance reports a Northerly current all along the coast but she was much nearer the land. Our DR having heretofore agreed so well and running so much across the stream clearly proves a Southerly current for us too. Employed from breakfast until supper making out an abstract of the passage for the Commo to send to the Observatory[44] and was complimented for its neatness.

Whalefish Isd Friday June 28th

Pretty fair weather a haze over the sun. Easterly wind light. Temp air from 48° to 35° water 35°. Ashore at 9 and Mer for sights, got poor ones. Mer Alt also doubtful[.] Gives Lat 69.00'N. Parry gives Lat 68°59'13"N Long 53°12'55"W.

Caulking the deck and getting things out of the hold that we shall need. Got about 40 galls water to fill up, from a stream on the island to Westward of the harbour.

The Advances boat returned from Liefly the residence of the Inspector, as he is called, or Governor general of all the Danish Settlements on the coast,[45] bringing only a few Skins and reporting that no more are to be had. That it is a small settlement of some 250, natives and all. A beautiful harbour entirely land locked. At 9 P.M. the days work being over, but sun not down by some weeks yet, went ashore and saw the settlement; and such a place; they say that there are some 100 inhabitants. Judging from the space and house room they occupy I should suppose that there are about the same number that Commo Jones captured at Monterey (5 and 11 dogs).[46] Our friend the Gov has a small frame house for summer and one of the rooms has a floor. There is also a large house of wood for the reception of seal blubber to be delivered at certain periods to Danish vessels. The natives have houses made of the turf which grows all over the islands in every crevice of the rocks and serves also for fuel being very good for that when dried. The huts are very low, flat roof of turf, only a small door and a little hole for exit of smoke. The common sleeping place is a platform (all of this settlement) made of boards which they must have purchased (as there is not a shrub even on the island) and so small that they must be piled up when all are turned in. The huts contain with difficulty the whole family.

The Govs hut has a stove besides the moss lamp. Most of the men wear clothes of foreign manufacture, however ragged and filthy, in preference to their seal skin clothes and are very vain of them, looking with contempt on one clothed in very pretty skin clothes. The women wear breeches, their boots being of a neater make than the mens coming to the knee. The children were all well clothed in skin clothes, pants fitting well and boots, all of the seal skin which is altogether the hair seal. The whole settlement is a most filthy place. The huts and tents (they use tents in summer) especially so and their food consisting almost entirely of seal and fish prepared in a manner too disgusting to our tastes to be worth mentioning. They get a coarse brown flour from Denmark. There were two large kayaks made of the same material as the small ones viz a wooden frame covered with seal skin but made like an open boat, in which they told us the women use always going several in company, as they can't manage the small ones that the men use which is covered entirely having a small circular hole in the center into which the man squeezes with difficulty and wearing a shirt of oiled skin, draws it tightly over a rim around the hole. They are about 20 feet long and about one foot beam but appear very stable, except when they wish to get out which they do by joining two or more of them with the paddles across each other. The paddles are very neatly made of wood pointed or rather bladed with bone, a blade at each end of the paddle, using one for each boat.

When equipped for a hunt they have a harpoon of wood pointed with bone with an iron barb which has a line fast to a skin blown up carried on the after part of the boat so that when the harpoon is thrown the shaft comes off leaving the barb bouyed by the skin which the hunter can pursue. A lance and a circular platform just in front of the man containing his lines hooks bait &c. The natives say that none of them can swim and when they go into rough water always go in company so as to assist each other in trouble.

They have a great many dogs, a half starved wolfish looking set but perfectly inoffensive. They travel much in winter as the whole bay is then a fine road. I was sufficiently amused in an hour and returned to the ship. Took the skiff and set out on a cruise around the bay landing on several of the islands shot a dovekie and a snow bunting.[47] The large island to Southward & Eastward is very rugged and steep. I walked nearly across it finding the moss and turf saturated from the melting of snow. There are large fresh lakes on top of it, one about ¼ mile long appeared to be pretty deep. About 11 it commenced to rain so I returned to the ship by 12½ and enjoyed my first sleep in since leaving New York.

Whalefish Islands Saturday June 29th 1850

Light Westerly wind and cloudy rainy weather finished our trade with the Esquimaux. Some of the men having quite fitted themselves out in skin clothes most of which were purchased from the backs of the natives. The best are the shirt of deer skin with the hair turned in, having a hood to haul over the head. Griffin got a few skins of the Eider duck. Our Commo and the English Lieut. in charge of 0 [?] alias Admiralty agent who came out to see the contract with the store ship fulfilled (A prince of a fellow) dined with us. The Advance sailed as we went to dinner and after I got mine we started, going out through the N. E. passage; found the Advance hove to outside. Gave our friend Lieut Power the letters, another drink, and bade farewell to Whalefish at 9 P.M.

Sunday June 30, 1850

Lat N	Long W	Wind	Weather	Temp Air	Water	Var 72°
69°26	55°48'	Sd. 4	c. m.	39 to 33	35 to 31	

Intend to use the notations directed for the ships log see explanation on last page of this book.[48] Got clear of Disco bay sailing along the land which is high very rugged and looking perfectly desolate, all the valleys filled with snow. Pass quantities of ice and many large bergs which no one notices now. Spent this day most unprofitably.

Monday July 1st 1850

Lat N	Long W	Wind	Weather	Temp Air	Water	Var 6½ pts
70°38'	56°08'	W'd 3 to 0	cbm & bf	35 to 33	35 to 30	

My mid watch went aloft and discovered a pack of ice extending from a point on Port bow as far toward the land as the eye could reach.[49] Sailed up toward it following the Advance. On nearing it hauled to Eastward and stood in shore along the edge of the pack in a dense fog (which came up at 6 A.M.) hearing the roar and shocks like thunder all day. At 8.30 P.M. followed the Advance through a stream of sailing ice and on reaching the clear water to Northward the fog rose and showed the land Cape Cranstown bearing N by E ½ E. North end of Ubekfent Island E. S. E. Very funny business bumping and scraping through a stream of ice quite exciting and from the novelty rather pleasant. Although while to leeward of and sailing through the ice the therm stood at 32 and every thing was frosted from the mist it was not cold to the feelings even on the topsail yard where I spent the hour which we sailed through the stream. Dressed on deck as usual washing in water at 30° with more comfort than sometimes with air and water 10° higher if there were a fresh wind.

At midt Doc made a rum egg flip for night cap not good eggs being of the ducks of Whalefish and quantities of which might be picked up on the uninhabited islands as also other sea birds Eggs.

Tuesday July 2nd 1850

Lat N.	Long W.	Wind	Force	Weather	Air	Water	Var
71°28'	55°52'	S'd	1.3	b.bcm. & o.	38°–33°	35°–33°	74

Sailing along the land near the Advance. In the afternoon calm, went aboard, having swept the brig up to her. The land is awfully dreary looking, much snow on it. It is very high abrupt and anything but green. Saw large flocks of ducks in Shore. Heard the shocks of icebergs breaking one very loud and long thought was an avalanche on shore. Saw one berg of moderate size fall into two with a loud roar. This is only a faint beginning of what we expect, hey?

Wednesday July 3rd 1850

Lat	Long	Wind	Force	Weather	Air	Water	Var
72°02N	55°31'W	North	2–6	b.c.m. f*	38°to 29°	35 to 32	76°W

Rather beat the Advance sailing close hauled in a light breeze. At Meridn there came a fog which concealed everything. 4.50 P.M. came to the edge of the pack, got into perfectly smooth water. Tacked and stood in shore till 8 passing through several streams of ice which is not so pleasant in a dense fog. At 8 stood off again, sailing through a stream of immense bergs which, as we could not see them until very near, made it rather exciting. Near some of the larger ones it was very squally and others making a beautiful bay very inviting to weather out the fog.

Baffins Bay. Meet Sailing Ice

Thursday July 4th 1850   74th⁵⁰

Lat DA	Long	Wind	Force	Weather	Air	Water	Var
72°16'N	57°07W	N.o.W.	4 to o	f* ends b	27–35	31–35	76°

Sailing through much Pancake ice. By 8 Calm and fog getting lighter. At 3 P.M. cleared of[f] beautifully with a light Westerly air showing the Advance ahead of us. Several streams of ice and the land & small island just to Southward of Store I[sland]. Got a D.A. in afternoon. The Commo seems to have been uneasy during our temporal separation as he sent a boat with orders in case of separation by which I see for the first time something of the plan of our cruise if circumstances permit. He fired guns for us last night which we didn't hear.

Had a blow out on Egg nog, made a quantity and served it out to all hands. This lovely evening makes me mons[tr]ous homesick. Oh, I wish I was home, indeed I do.

Friday July 5th 1850

Lat	Long	Wind	Force	Weather	Air	Water	Var
72°27'N	57°20'S	N & E	2–0	beautiful	33°–45°	33°–36	76°

One of those beautiful soft days so welcome to Arctic cruisers because so seldom seen. The land and islands near Uppernavic in sight and to the N & W'd the Pack of ice apparently impenetrable except close in with the land. Beating up against a light air.

During the first watch witnessed the striking phenomenon of objects some distance below the horizon brought into view by refraction or reflection.

Seeing a number of icebergs apparently inverted in the air, some distance from the horizon. I went to the T[op] G[allan]t masthead to see if I could see the real ones. Some were entirely out of sight, of others nearer I could just see the summit touching the corresponding peak of the inverted reflection. Others, still nearer, reminded me of the modern wasp waisted belles with bust and tournure [bustle] reversely distorted, while those of a cubic form appeared twice their natural height. The pack which from aloft looked like a field of ice from deck appeared like an immense wall of snow studded with bergs of every fantastic shape.

Sailing with a 4 knot breeze up to a stream of pancake ice about 30 feet wide and a mile long, found it almost calm to leeward of it, while there was the same fine breeze up to the very edge to windward which we caught as soon as we passed the point. This is not new as former navigators all mention it but I had no idea that so small a quantity of ice would cause the great change. Saw a good many seals. Griffin landed on an immense berg and found it decaying as most of them seem to be keeping a continual roar like distant ordnance.

Saturday July 6th 1850

Lat	Long	Wind	Force	Weather	Air	Water	Var
72°54'N	56°31'W	N.W.	1–0	b	44°–34°	36°–33°	76°W

Working up the Land between the Pack and the shore studded with little islands. In the afternoon about twenty miles from the Land two kayaks came off to us from Uppernavik having only some eggs to trade, but we got them on board and gave them dinner. They confirm the accounts of the enormous appetite of their countrymen but belie the oil yarns as they would not drink either sweet or lamp oil but rum, brandy, and molasses with great gusto so that one was quite a la bete [beastly] when he departed. Sent a few letters by the sober one to care of the Governor at Uppernavik.

At 10 another party came alongside being on their way to Uppernavik from the Northward. They were in an English whaleboat, having three women along.[51] They had several seal and Eider ducks, of both of which the Advance got some but we didn't, much to the annoyance of our Doc who complains of it tomorrow.

They report a clear passage in shore for a long way to the Northward and that the whalers are only some three days of their sailing to the Northward and Austins vessels they have also seen. The men of this party were also very drunk having visited the Advance first. Strange how many of these people can read and many of them write, but it shows the good of the Danish missionaries who have more than civilized these singular beings as far North as 74°N Latitude on this coast. Showing one of them an Esquimaux vocabulary in English characters he pointed out several words spelt wrong for his dialect as the Esquimaux language varies or even changes entirely in different situations. They also have very clear ideas of Religion, Moravian.

Baffin's Bay   Enter the Middle Ice

Sunday July 7th 1850

Lat	Long c	Wind	force	Weather	Air	Water	Var
73°53'N	57°2'7W	S to W	4–0	b m f	58–32	38–30	80

Stood to Northward with a fine Southerly wind, hoping soon to see the Whalers or Austins squadron. Passing rapidly by the numerous islands, when at 1 P.M. the commo stuck her West and in an hour entered the pack where after veering and hauling about, taking the most promising leads, at 8 we were fast, there being little wind. We furled sails and took a tow line from the Advance. From 8 to 12 by cutting, warping, and sailing between the shifting floes, we made about a mile to Northward, the hardest work the men have yet had. At 10 the ice was all around us but a lead about twice our length ahead of us and a crack only to haul through which we succeeded in doing, the ice closing after us too soon for the Advance to follow. So at 12 we made fast for the night. We are sorry that the commo attempts to cross the pack so low down as all the whalemen and former Navigators advise to get more to Northward for doing which we had an open passage and fine wind. Pity, pity! Prospect of spending a long time in the ice however it gives us lots of room to walk and plenty of exercise for us all, as in the excitement of hauling through a tight place it is so natural to jump out and push or pull to point her straight and to heave at the windlass, which I did last night with all my heart. Carried out and planted an ice anchor with no aid. The ice, however, is very rotten and the pieces breaking up so that it is unsafe to wander any distance from the ship or we might get some seal of which many are seen.

Monday July 8th 1850

Lat DR	Long DR	Wind	force	Weather	Air	Water
74°12'N	59°14'W	S'd & W'd	3.	f	34–32	30

Beset in the ice most of the time. Slow progress. Employed all the forenoon cutting a canal for the Advance to pass into our lead which she did at 1 and again took us in tow. The work being novel and keeping me warm in this raw day I offd coat and went at it with a will as did the Commo and his officers. Cutting the ice on which we stand was (in most places) not sufficient for several thickness's had to be removed, the under ones being the most difficult to cut being under water and harder. The average thickness of the ice being about 28 inches, in many places by being thus lapped was six feet thick. We cut about twenty yards in the four hours, using only the ice choppers, the saws not suiting such ice.

I shot a Kittewake[52] for the Doc. Unshipped our rudder and kept it hung up astern all night.

Baffins Bay Working into the Pack

Tuesday July 9th 1850

Lat 2	Long	Wind	force	Weather	Air	Water
74°08'N		NNW	1–0	f. cm. s	35° 32°	31° 29°

Beset nearly all day warping and sailing. The Advance towing us and using our crew. The lines for warp[ing] are manilla whale line about 2¼ inch which carry both vessels along bumping and scraping against the floes and ploughing through broken ice with ease. In the last dog saw the land. The Devils thumb being very conspicuous from its remarkable shape. Long. by the bearings 58°30'. Got good meridian alt with Art[ificial] Hor[izon]. The ice appears very wilful and to delight in shewing us our weakness for in a minute it opens a way which we are all day trying to open without much effect and again it closes in a minute what we have worked at all day. At 9 last night after having been three hours trying to heave and cut into a lead twenty yards a head of us without success, we sent the men below and in five minutes after, all was clear with room for two ships to sail through and so it remained until all hands this morning when as if intentionally before the men were fairly on deck it closed again in five minutes. We observe that a Southwesterly or Westerly wind has the effect of packing the ice very close while an Easterly wind opens many leads and loosens the floes. Saw several seal on the ice but they always keep near the hole through which they rise and disappear very suddenly upon any attempt being made to approach them. A more dreary prospect can hardly be conceived than this pack of ice presents to Southern eyes, but it is a relief to be able to stretch oneself after so long a confinement although it is at the expense of wet feet as the ice is covered with snow which in many places is melted into ponds just crusted over.

Baffin's Bay Beset in the Ice

Wednesday July 10th 1850

Lat.	Long chro	Wind	force	Weather	Air	Water
58°55'		S'd & W'd	4–0	b c m.f	32°	30°

A dull day for folks in a hurry to cross the Bay. Made fast to the same piece of ice, but quite sociable among ourselves cruising from one to tother, played foot ball, whist, and got a specimen of the Ivory Gull.[53]

Thursday July 11th 1850

2☉

Lat ☉	Long chro	Wind	force	Weather	Air	Water	Var by az
74°14'N	58°59'W	N.N.W	1–4	mc. b	36 to 29	29	84.30 Wly

A most beautiful day. Got good sights with the Art Hor on the snow for every thing. The reports of old cruisers in these diggings lead us to think that thirty days will be passed in this way. Passing the Pack find by the obs that in the last two days we have drifted a little to Northward but during that time there has been a Southerly wind. Have not stirred this day either.

Friday July 12th 1850

The Barometer fell with the Northerly wind to 29.01 and commences rising with wind of to-day from South showing that there is little ice to Northward of us.

Lat	Long	Wind	force	Weather	Air	Water	Barom
No observations		S by E	0–8	d.r.c.& b	36°–33°	29	29.01 to 29.45

Saw the first bear to-day just after the rain and a party started in pursuit but he walked away too fast. A most enormous beast he was and striding majestically off as if not conscious of our presence.[54] After dinner we made a start and got some distance from our last resting place with a gentle breeze, the ice being very loose, and as the breeze freshened we pushed through some tight places but when it grew strong the ice became packed and we had to tie up again closely beset having gained some two miles to Westward. The cavil[55] to which our tow-line was fast aboard the Advance having carried away, we were left and made sail. In coming up to her after she was fast we managed to give her a rub which injured the eagle on the N. Pole which I thought might mean that (The Rescue prevents the Eagle from spreading his wings over that point.[)][56]

Saturday July 13th 1850

Lat 2☉	Long cro	Wind	force	Weather	Air	Water
74°22'N	59°14'W	Sly	10–0	b c m. B	38–30	29

The gale abated by 4 A.M. and quite calm pleasant and beautiful weather follows. Saw the Devils Thumb appearing much nearer. In the afternoon discovered a ship about 10 miles to Eastward of us beset like ourselves. Great numbers of seal sunning themselves but too wide awake for us, always disappearing suddenly. At 7 in the evening saw two other vessels more to Northward beset. The atmosphere in the evening is much clearer and objects b[e]low the horizon are seen oftener.

Sunday July 14th 1850

Lat 2☉	Long	Wind	force	Weather	Air	Water
74°22'N		SE Nd	1.0.1	B c m.	38° 32°	31° 29°

Getting dull. Set the men to cutting a canal toward a Westerly lead more for occupation than with any hope of success I suppose. Saw the three vessels all this day, the one to Eastward appeared to get more to Northward but also seems to be in heavy ice as he was much listed at times. Unsatisfactory sabbath to me. I pine for the quiet ones of the last eighteen months.

Monday July 15th 1850

Lat 2☉	Long cr	Wind	force	Weather	Air	Water	Var az
74°20'30"N	59°07'W	N by W	1	o. be. b	37°33°	31° 30°	85°W

Our friend to Eastward was under sail today and got out of sight to Northward. The others also disappeared. We drift apparently with every breeze. Speculate on the prospect of being so long in getting to the mouth of Lancaster Sound as to make it advisable to return home this winter. Took a Lunar which came out rather poorly had to compute $\mathcal{D}$[57] but as it was low the refraction might have affected the distance. I felt unwell and had an attack of vertigo after working out all my sights, about four hours steady figuring.

Endeavouring to Cross the Pack

Tuesday July 16th 1850

Lat $\odot$2	Long c	Wind	force	Weather	Air	Water
74°19'N	59°15'W	NW	0.2	b	36° 30	31° 29°

Saw four barques and a ship standing to the Southward in shore of us, apparently meeting no obstruction from the ice. They are the same mentioned on the 14th.

The ice seems to grow stronger daily, being now very thick and close in every direction.

Wednesday July 17th 1850

Lat $\odot$	Long c	Wind	force	Weather	Air	Water	Var
74°13N	59°15'W	NW	3 to 0	bc. m	36 30	30	85°30'W

Grand Race. Arctic course. Rosinante Benjamin against Benson both Rescue's. One heat 1 mile. Sweepstake Purse two Pursers shirts, Forfeit one sleeve. Times R[osinante] 7m 44s, [Benson] 8m 30s. Source of amusement for Mr Brooks made a skysail yard = 1 Squilgee[58] handle—the shavings for shape. Rigged it and crossed it standing yard made a sail = 1½ captains sheets bent and set it. Lifts and halyards—6 thread stuff Braces = codline.

Thursday July 18th 1850

Lat	Long	Wind	force	Weather	Air	Water
No obs		WNW	1	om. s.	36° 31°	30°

Both crews employed cutting and breaking the ice ahead of the Advance (as their appears to be a prospect of making a little way). Working hard for nine hours and gained one ships length into thinner ice. The next two hours warped about two hundred yards West through the ice. Prospect for wind rather dull, the snow a little annoying as it melts during the day as it falls.

Friday July 19th 1850

Lat ⊙	Long	Wind	force	Weather	Air		Water
74°10'N		Vble	o	o. f. dm.	36°	33°	30°

Employed as yesterday. The Advance reached a pool ½ mile wide. We were just shut out by a floe.

Endeavouring to Get through the Pack

Saturday July 20, 1850

Lat	Long	Wind	force	Weather	Air		Water
No obs.		SE	3.0	bm.	35	32	30

Crossed the pool and entered the rotten ice on tother side making perhaps ½ mile. Worked alone to-day and kept it up until 8 when we secured to the ice alongside the Advance.

Turned out (having the mid watch) at 10 and with a half clad & half armed party rushed half a mile over the ice after a half grown bear which was within half gunshot of the ship but was suffered to walk away in hopes that he was looking for a firmer path to the vessels but seeing him continue on his course we sallied forth to be distanced in half a mile the bear loping off as soon as he saw us at a rate which defied all pursuit. The bear wanted spunk or we would have had a nice fight.

Sunday July 21st 1850

Lat	Long	Wind	force	Weather	Air		Water
No obs		SSE	4 to 0	sr. o.	35	30	30

Commenced at 6 in the afternoon and warped two miles to SW by ten P.M. Shifting for ourselves, the commo having been disgusted at having us a stern of him, however, as soon as we got clear of him, we went ahead and had eventually to send him a tow line. This brig is a poor place to spend Sunday well.

Monday July 22nd 1850

Lat	Long	Wind	force	Weather	Air		Water	
No obs		NW	4 to 1	f*	b	34 30	31	29

Did a quantity of cutting and warping and made very little progress. Officers working as hard as the men, feet wet all the time. Advance about a mile SSW of us.

Tuesday July 23rd 1850

Lat ☉	Long c.	Wind	force	Weather	Air		Water
74°09'N	59°32'W	NW	1	bc	44°	30°	30°

Cut a canal about 80 yds into a pool which led us to the Advance. They tell us of another bear chase, very large but no braver. The beasts are not urged by hunger to fight as they do in winter. Seals are never mentioned now although they are thick as fiddlers in Hades, but too wide awake for us.

This ice business is getting very dull. Work all day like chaineys and make ½ mile. I should have mentioned that every night there is a formation of young ice sometimes ½ inch thick on all the pools, but it is the fresh water which melts from the snow during the day and remains on top of the salt as the temp is rarely low enough to freeze salt water (proof) the ice is almost perfectly fresh.

Wednesday July 24th 1850

Lat ☉	Long c	Wind	force	Weather	Air		Water
74°05'N	59°32'W	NW	2 to 1	b	40°	29°	30°

Mighty small headway to-day. Worked a good deal didn't go twenty yards. Called all hands from peaceful slumber at 11 P.M. and made a few yards before Midt. No variety. Got hold of Crantzs history of Greenland, fine book.[59] Think it much more agreeable to be so near the other vessel on idle days.

Thursday July 25th 1850

Lat ☉	Long c	Wind	force	Weather	Air		Water
74°05'N	59°03'W	N'd & W'd	1	b	34°	29°	30°

By constant heaving at the Advance's capstan warped about 4 miles to Northward & Westward. The young ice being ½ inch thick making the work for the boats very hard in carrying out warps. Every officer but one, Doc, has fallen through the ice and most of the men, I twice. Tisn't very cold after one gets out.

I was in a boat from 8 P.M. until 2 A.M. (tomorrow) carrying out warps steering and paying out while two men worked the paddles (oars being too long to pass the floes). The young ice very bad, cuts the boats bows. The water running from the lines forming sleet in the boats thwarts. This I guess is the hardest work as the two men I first had (Advances) sung out "spell oh," at 12 although I planted most of the anchors myself. The last two worked much better (being Rescues). We made slow progress. Toward the last the floes coming home and closing the passages constantly.

Friday July 26th 1850

Lat ☉	Long c	Wind	Force	Weather	Air	Water
74°03'N	59°45'30"W	NW	4 to 2	b	35° 32°	30°

The same employment as yesterday. Discov'd a case of scurvy in the Forecastle.

Prospect of getting through the pack in time to do anything getting dull. Mr Commodore, I think, that if you dont wish to go to York this winter you had better take this Westerly wind and go in shore and try farther North.

Saturday July 27th 1850

Lat ☉	Long c	Wind	Weather	Air	Water
73°57'N	59°48'W	NW 3 to 1	b	39 28	30

Much work, little go ahead.

Saw a greater refraction than I have seen yet, the reflected bergs appearing among the clouds near the horizon. The Devil playing "Simon says down," with his thumb. The field ice goes South much faster than the bergs in sight which is apparent from our continually approaching those to Southward of us even when we are making some progress through the ice in the opposite direction.[60] Saw clear water to NE about 10 miles off.

Go North in the Pack

Sunday July 28th 1850

Lat ☉	Long c	Wind	force	Weather	Air	Water	Bar
73°54'N	59°58'W	NW SE	4	b. bc	40° 30°	30°	29.15

Cutting and warping until 10 P.M. when we cast off from the commo and both brigs made sail shearing and bumping along toward the open water which appears to Northeastward. The Barometer has been gradually falling for two days so that at 4 P.M. it is 29.15 giving us reason to expect a Southerly fresh wind which accordingly commenced about 10 P.M. and at 12 the Bar is 29.17.

Monday July 29th 1850

Lat ☉	Long c	Wind	force	Weather	Air	Water	Bar
74°54'N	59°57'	SE	7 to 5	cm. o. f.	39°34°	35° 30°	29.50

Hurrah, once more under sail and going it with a rush. Made a degree North by getting into that clear streak. Kept up the go until 1 P.M. when it was so foggy that if there were any clear leads we couldn't find them, so the commo ran us about 100 yds into the edge of a field and we make fast to thick ice, experienceing any amount of bumps, scrapes, and squeezes. By four P.M. all the loose pieces had floated by and left us in a pool but by 8 we are entirely surrounded by an extensive field and a big berg to windward of us. I am for standing by for a rush on the ice if we are squashed. Squeezed a little but were protected although we were as near as I care to be to being crushed by the berg which passed only a few feet from us. Saw a Bear and as he appeared to approach, we prepared to give him a welcome but he changed his course when about 300 yds and went off rapidly making some tremendous leaps astonishing us with his agility. We are now nearly in Melville bay and may expect to be nipped. The field we are moored to is certainly fast to the land which appears about 20 miles dist[ant] so that One degree of Northing has taken us out of the pack but on the same edge which we entered.

Making Northing at the Expense of Westing

Thursday July 30th 1850

Lat	Long	Wind	force	Weather	Air	Water
No obs		SE	5 to o	Of* bcm.	41 34	30

At midday made a move but couldn't get into a lead in sight to NE with much work. The vessels lay alongside of a small berg which like many others in sight has many stones and some sand and earth upon them. Boarded this fellow and find a pool of clear fresh water on his summit, looks like a beautiful basin of marble of a bluish cast, the streaks perfectly immitated by cracks in the ice. This berg hung near us all day and at night commencing to move to North-ward squeezed us very impolitely.

Wednesday July 31st 1850

Lat ☉	Long c	Wind	force	Weather	Air	Water
75°05'N	59°42'W	NW	4.1	o. b. f.	42° 30°	30

Worked hard all the mid watch warping ¼ mile along the edge of our field. This berg giving us a tight race and constantly threatning us with a squeeze, as there was not room for both to pass abreast. I was for making the berg tow us into clear water ahead and at 4 they made fast to him but wishing to put in a second anchor, a large piece split off* while a man was drilling the hole and let him slip into the crack, and thence into the drink to the imminent peril of his life and much to his alarm.[61] By seven we reached the water and commenced beating to NW until 10 when we made fast to a floe finding no lead open and got another heavy squeeze.

There is a large berg near us on the summit of which, more than 100 ft high, there are stones too heavy for a man to lift.

*The place where this anchor was put was over twenty feet from the edge of the berg on which the Advance had rested all day and the man in driving the anchor with all his force made the whole piece fall off and was, of course, precipitated with the anchor into the fissure. Two others were standing on the fragment but caught ropes as they fell.

Melville Bay—A Large Iceberg

Thursday August 1st 1850

Lat ☉	Long c	Wind	force	Weather	Air	Water
75°03'N	59°44'W	NW	1 . 0	f m	40° 25°	30°

Warped and tracked a few miles to Eastward through the ice. Passed some immense bergs. Ice getting very close and no appearance of a Western passage.

Friday August 2nd 1850

Lat ☉	Long c	Wind	force	Weather	Air	Water
75°05'N	59°42'W	NW	1 to 0	b bf	40° 25°	30°

Commenced a most beautiful clear morning, temperature of the air colder than we have had it. Saw the new land distinctly all day. Most of the main Land seems to be covered with snow, all the vallies filled up even with the hills, only a few peaks appearing and it seems as though all the indentations in the coast are filled, so as to make an even and smooth hill or ridge of ice. The ice near us being somewhat loose we made sail and stood in toward the land until at 5 P.M. we could get no farther and now all appears tight as wax no egress except to Southward and the ice too thick to hope for it to melt this summer. After a cold night we generally have a warm day which melts a quantity of snow which running off and floating on the pools and leads of salt water freezes the following night forming ice perfectly fresh and transparent. Four of us went to the largest of a number of bergs in sight and climbed its steep sides to the summit which we found (by timing the fall of a number of bullets) to be 314 feet high. Killed a little auk with a boathook. One can hardly imagine the grandeur of one of these immense bergs. The view from the summit being like that from some lofty peak of land, every thing appears small. The vessels about a mile off appeared too insignificant to notice.

Every outlet to our present place seems closed, no water in sight from the berg. Found stones near the summit.

Endeavouring to Cross Baffin Bay Pack

Saturday August 3rd 1850

Lat	Long	Wind	force	Weather	Air	Water
No obs	Sd	2 & 0	b f		40° 29°	30°

Under sail nearly all day and night made a little Northing. Getting rather dull, all work & no go. In the first watch saw two bears. One was quite near and the party that chased him got shots at him but without having the effect even of heaving him to. Greater part of this day foggy and unpleasant, but we have so much beautiful weather now that a little bad can't cause a complaint.

Sunday August 4th 1850

Lat ☉	Long c	Wind	force	Weather	Air	Water
75°09'N	59°57'S	W'd	1	b	41° 31°	31°

Hove a great deal at the Advances windlass but made no progress to speak of. The young ice has cut the boats badly and also the vessels at the waters edge just abaft the iron on the bows so all this afternoon (Sabath) was spent in listing the brigs with purchases on the masts and nailing on sheathing iron. The Thermometer placed in the sun goes up to 70°. Were heaving at a crack between two floes for an hour of the first watch and had scarcely turned the men in when it opened without any assistance, very wide, showing how entirely futile our efforts are against the unfavourable state of the ice.

Monday August 5th 1850

Lat ☉	Long c	Wind	force	Weather	Air	Water
75°09'N	59°52'W	NW	1	b	29°41°	29° 31°

Warping as persons desperate, made trifling progress compared with the distance yet to go to save our credit for to return without having entered Lancaster Sound will be horrible.

The vessels were fitted out trusting too much to Yankee luck that we would come up and find open sea all the way to Melville Island in which case we should have done marvelously but we are weaker and as illy provided for forcing through the pack than the Whalemen which never attempt it. But what will our people know of that? and how can they see the disparity of our means with those of the English Squadron if they do much and we nothing. I would hardly know which to choose. Remaining in the pack this winter if we can't get into Lancaster Sound or returning to New York; though doubtless duty would demand the latter in order to render the vessels more efficient for a second attempt. This life is not unpleasant in spite of the constant labour and an occasional souse in the drink for it is pleasant to enjoy so much sunshine and being relieved from the annoyances of a heavy sea, although this last cannot be compared with the constant labour to the men, one half of whom are constantly at the capstan or windlass from Sunday morning till Sunday morning again, only relieved occasionally by a few hours of sailing when we are bracing, making and shortning sail the whole time. But there is a fine climate, lots of fresh water, and plenty of snow to walk on. I wonder what James riverians[62] would think to see me go to a fresh pool and break ice an inch thick sit down and wash my feet and do more trimming than Cinderilla's sisters in the open air as comfortably as they do it by a fire. Yet this I do so I trust I shall be able to weather the winter. Measured a moderate sized berg and found it 107 feet high.

Find standing on the Advances knightheads[63] for four hours at night directing the warping with an hourly visit to the topsail yard a poor anodyne inasmuch as I turn in with iced toes and aching nether joints which prevent sleep for at least an hour.

Ice Opening a Little

Tuesday August 6th 1850

Lat ☉	Long c	Wind	force	Weather		Air	Water
75°11'N	59°51'W	WE	3 to 1	b.	bc	42°29°	30°

Working hard as usual during the 24 hours which I am tired repeating, the leads being very intricate and young ice troublesome.

In the first watch saw the exact appearance of a city on the land, steeples, large buildings, and scattered suburbs distinctly represented by the ice. A glacier, or as we call it a berg factory, is also visible at this time. Found a stone of about two hundred weight on a floe. The wind seems to be ahead for us which ever way we point her which some of us think is ominous of our stay near this position for many months as there is little more than one in which we may work. The bottom of Melville bay visible from aloft. Variation Az 89°W.

Wednesday August 7th 1850

Lat ☉	Long c	Wind	force	Weather	Air	Water
75°13'W	59°51'W	NE	1	bc, b & c	42°38°	32°

Leads pretty wide. Wind all day coming from the direction we seek to go. Warping all the time except two hours of the first watch, when the pool being too wide to carry lines across made sail and ran off the desired course to reach a point whence we might again warp. A party visited a large berg 200 feet high.

It is astonishing at what distance a common conversation may be heard in this still weather and it requires no exertion to make a person hear at a miles distance. A great deal of water in sight leading Northward but wind ahead and too light to beat past strong enough to prevent towing and the pools so wide that not being able to send lines across we have to warp some very tedious semicircumferences.

First Bear

Thursday August 8th 1850

Lat ☉	Long c	Wind	force	Weather	Air	Water
75°19'N		E,N	1	bc. & o	42–30	31

A bear swam near the vessel and Griffin went after him in a boat with a small party. By approaching him slowly and quietly he permitted them to come so near that a lucky shot entering the spine paralysed the hinder part of his body so that with difficulty he dragged himself on the nearest floe where they soon dispatched him with cold steel. His dimensions are greater than the average given in History. He was excessively fat but hungry, evident from his permitting them to approach so near and apparent from the emptiness of his stomach. As soon as he was wounded he made for the floe which was fortunate as he would have sank had he been killed in the water. Saw many flocks of little auk going Southward which looks ominous of an early winter. Two vessels were reported from the Masthead to Westward but I guess it was an optical delusion as I could not see them with a glass from the Advances masthead. Passing some immense bergs. I went to one which was really grand and beautiful.

Friday August 9th 1850

Lat ☉	Long c	Wind	force	Weather	Air	Water
78°22'N	59°53'W	N to SE	1	o.b. f*	41°–28°	31° 34°

Under sail all this day and only heaving through cracks four hours of the 12. The 12 hours of night were of course labouring or jammed in ice. Some of the day heaving I would have avoided had not my design been cou[n]termanded by Griffin as I intended to have gone through at the same time as the Advance by keeping very close and Brooks who relieved me to dinner just as I was executing this said that he was about to do so when Capt Griffin forbade it and taking the deck hove through the closed crack in one hour. The Advance escaped the other two hours heave by taking a little different lead and was waiting for us.

Melville Bay Getting Northward a Nip

Saturday August 10th 1850

Lat ☉	Long c	Wind	force	Weather	Air	Water
75°27'N	60°22'W	SW	1	f. bc. o.	39° 25°	36° 30°

Under sail from 8 A.M. till midnight. Wind very light and superficial current making it impossible to steer so that we kept he[r] pointed fair with a boat ahead. Saw immense numbers of little auk. A party from the Advance got 140 of them gave us 2 dozen. They are most delicious, requiring no skining and taste much like our spring Teel. We have tried the bear in every way and all his eatable parts but I cant go it. Too much of the boiled porpoise about it. Got a fine view of Melville monument, but find the bearings altogether different from the chart probably Baffin was in a hurry when he passed here or made some mistake in his Latitude as we had perfect sights with good instruments and different observers making the same Latitude.

Sunday August 11th 1850

Lat	Long	Wind	force	Weather	Air	Water
No obsr		SE	3	f. om.	35° 32°	32 30

The South wind closing up every thing; by 6 A.M. we were fast enough past heaving or anything else. Saw six bear by the mid watch at the same time three of them were watching near seal holes crouched so as to resemble hummocks. A party of four approaching them they escaped with speed. The Advances report having seen seven at one time. Three of them being in the water they got one and regretted not having known that they would float after death as by securing the dead one they let the others escape. These fellows dont fight as the former Navigators represent them to us. In the afternoon two floes closing on us, we were nipped and hove down six streaks.[64] A large piece being forced under her bottom lifted her bows three feet, shored her up, and took a good nap until the end of this sabbath. Read the articles and mustered.

Melville Bay Getting Along Finely

Monday August 12th 1850

Lat ☉	Long c	Wind	Weather	force	Air	Water
75°36'N	60°48'W	NW. SE	f. bm. b	3,0	38° 28°	33

In my mid watch the commo made a start and I attempted to follow being piled up on the ice found it no easy matter to heave off and only succeeded by securing the ship to one floe and the ice under her to another and as the floes seperated we were dragged off. Find strong superficial currents which make it almost impossible to steer, having to use a boat frequently to point her fair. During the day the NW wind opens the leads and gives us beautiful weather but in the evening the studding sail breeze closes the ice and brings thick weather.

Tuesday August 13th 1850

Lat ☉	Long c	Wind	force	Weather	Air	Water
75°42'	64°19'W	E. N.	4 3	cm. b	44°28°	36 32

Lots of water, under sail all the 24 hours. Cant steer a straight course but can work about among the floes and bergs so much faster and easier than we can warp, that it is quite refreshing and we again hope to get into Lancaster sound this fall. The young ice was bad today but the Advance walks through it like a knife. We caught up after the sun made clear water for us. Got some forty little auk; chased a narwhale[65] but he was too cute for us. Brooks says we passed the berg which let Costa into the Drink on the 21st ult[66] but he sees many wonders. Had a fine breeze toward midnight. Griffin says the cabin has a sore head. I enquired how his own was. And he was right for when we are so dependent on each other for comfort off duty we must regard each others situation and station on duty and Griffin had been a little remiss on this point on several late occasions for which he seems sorry and we are friends again. Drew a Scotch cap. Too warm to be comfortable.

Little Auk Cape York Red Snow

Wednesday August 14th 1850

Lat ☉	Long c	Wind	force	Weather	Air	Water
76°01'N	63°22'W	Nd	3,1	b	37° 30°	34 32

Sailing all day. Fairly into Melville Bay now and passing near the land. The number of Little Auk that cover these waters at this season is incredible. They feed on a marine insect of a crimson colour about the size of a house fly which we find in the craw. Griffin and Doctor [Vreeland] killed 160 of the birds this evening and were so busy picking up the game that they were three miles astern before they commenced their return and had to pull with all their force for an hour to catch up.

Thursday August 15th 1850

Lat ☉	Long c	Wind	force	Weather	Air	Water
75°59'	66°47'	Nd.Ed. WSW	3,6	b	40° 34°	35° 31°

Sailing along the coast. At 5 A.M., off Cape York, I heard the whoop of a man and looking ashore saw two men making signs which being reported to Griffin. We in studsails and commenced beating up for them (having signalized to the commo the reason) in hopes of relieving some poor cast away sailors. As we approached we made them out to be Esquimaux and stood back to the Advance who however continued beating up and sent a boat in to them. They were Esquimaux having a sledge with no dogs and nothing to trade, said that five of them lived near the spot, pointing toward their hut which they said was a short distance back. With this important information we filled away[67] doubled Cape York and saw the crimson cliffs and the ravines filled with purple snow. In the afternoon the Commo, Griffin, and both docs went ashore and brought off marvelous accounts of lofty hills, luxuriant valleys, immense Glaciers, and abounding game. Being in the want of water we stood in and in the first watch anchored within stones cast of the shore in a valley surrounded by rocky cliffs.

Friday August 16th 1850

Lat ☉	Long c	Wind	Force	Weather	Air	Water

[No weather entries.]

Poor Mate couldnt take a cruise. Capt went again however. He saw the specimens of about twenty varieties of plants, heard the birds hollow, and saw the others shooting at them and say that the cliffs were full of them and their young. A specimen of young Little Auk was brought off. After filling every empty vessel from a torrent from the snow capped hills, I went on the beach and got a little of the red snow which when melted contains a red substance like chalk but which the docs call a plant (sort of fungus). Examined some of the crimson rock and found it covered with a kind of lichen, colour of brick dust. The hills here are at least 1000 feet high and very steep. The Commo saw a fox. Docr Kane saw a beast like a weasel and got into a bog trying to get a shot at it.[68] I killed three dovekies which came to look at the strangers on a piece of floating ice. And so we left standing up the coast again. Brooks shot a Great Auk.[69] This afternoon being becalmed near the land a little to Eastward of Dudley Digges Point, the Capt and myself took the dingy and pulled in to the beach, passing a glacier where we could see how the Bergs are manufactured. This seems to have been a factory of small bergs as the pieces broken from its edge could scarcely exceed 100 feet in thickness. The Glacier was a whole valley and bay filled with ice extending two miles along the coast and perhaps one from the original shore and ascending gradually till it nearly reaches the summit of the range of hills back of it some 400 feet high. This constantly increases by the washing down of snow from the mountains in the spring, and after growing immense the pieces which are broken off the edge make small bergs filled with dirt and stones. We landed at the foot of a cliff almost perpendicular and clambered up some distance to get specimens of the rock covered with lichen. Saw a Dovekie feeding its young in a cleft of the rock. It brought a small fish and having watched us until she thought we were not looking ran in and disposed of the prey and was off in an instant. Saw great numbers of the Black throated divers.[70] Most of them as they passed up the coast had some sort of fish in their mouth. Saw a Walrus which gave us a minute inspection but kept at a respectful distance. Every little shelf on the side of the point that we landed on was covered with a little sod of grass or tuft of flowers. We shot three of the divers for specimens and tried very hard to get a Giant Petrel[71] but he flew off with the shot we gave him. This was not a satisfactory landing because as the glacier entirely filled the valley we could not walk but only cling to the foot of a cliff and scramble up by the shelves and crevices, however it was a great relief to the monotonous passage of time in a 90 ton brig. The whole Southern sky was of a beautiful violet tinge this evening such as is peculiar to Arctic regions.

Saturday August 17th 1850

Lat ⊙	Long c	Wind	force	Weather	Air	Water
76°09'N	68°08'W	Nd	2,3	b	42°34°	33°

Working to Northward came up with D[udley] Digges Pt and getting a little breeze. Stood to the Westward. I shot a Puffin[72] in my morning watch—a common arctic bird but the first specimen we have seen. After refusing it to the Doc for saying he was common I gave him to him. The Advance beat us terribly to-day. Saw Walstenhome Island and the immense glacier near it.

Sunday August 18th 1850

Lat ⊙	Long c	Wind	force	Weather	Air	Water	Var
76°06'N	71°11'W	SE	2 to 4	bm, f	39°30°	34° 31°	101°W

Sailing finely accross the bay through quantities of sailing ice, a most delightful temperature and fair prospect for Lancaster. Advance spares us all stdsails. Lost sight of Greenland at 6 P.M. Spent a very unprofitable Sabbath. Working up after the FN[73] watch took till dinner watch again at 4 occupied all attention.

Pennys Brigs

Monday August 19th 1850

Lat DR	Long DR	Wind	force	Weather	Air	Water	Var
75°11'N	77°50'W	ESE	4 to 10	f. cm. dom.	38°35°	34	106W

Who'd ha thunk it? Saw two sail astern heading two pts more to Southward than we were, but soon they stood for us and overhauled us rapidly, fast as we were going for Lancaster. A Murian on all slow vessels. The Advance sparing us all stdsails and royal. Well the Brigs came up and the flag brig spoke us. They were Penny's two Brigs, the Lady Franklin and the Sophia, having found the entrance to Jones Sound closed impenetrably coming to hunt in Lancaster for the lost. They report Commo Austin's squadron off Carey Islands on the 6th inst with old Sir John Ross (in the Prince Albert) in tow, also that the North Star having wintered at Wolstenholme Island had gone up the Lancaster sound. Penny himself was the spokesman and didn't speak plain so we lost much that he said. A very genteel man standing by him we took for Goodsir.[74] They took us for Commo because Griffin was the only name mentioned when they left England so when he learned his mistake Penny said goodbye Captain, gave us three cheers and stood on for the Advance but by some strange management as the Englishman passed under her stern she luffed up into the wind which Penny could not do for his studsails and they didn't converse two minutes. Poor Rescue, the smallest, dirtiest, unhappiest little boat, you are the last to enter the sound. Sir John would never see his lady if he waits for you to find him.

My eyes, what splendid craft the Englishmen had, large, high, roomy, full rigged Brigs; every thing looked so clean and comfortable with plenty of room to walk about and a spar deck defying all water. They'll have a nice time. They had bears meat and more birds than we even. They headed about one point more to the Southward than we after leaving us and we wonder where our commo can be going way to the Northward. Made the land at 6 on the West coast of Baffin Bay and are very glad thereof, but are surprized that the Commo still heads so much to the Northward. Weather getting thick and fresh. At 10 P.M. We followed the Advance's example of heaving to but she gets away from us fast and just before the curtain falls on this funny day and Capt Griffin was going to make more sail at a great risk, The Advance vanishes in a fog. A piece of washing ice drifts foul of us right under the bows smashing the dolphin striker[75] at the first pitch, warning the bowsprit at the second, and carrying it way at the third. The fog to leeward lifting reveals a high rocky lee shore and tomorrow finds me turning out for the mid watch to say Poor little Rescue aint you in a fix.

Tuesday August 20th 1850

Lat DR	Long DR	Wind	force	Weather	Air	Water
74°21'N	80°23'W	Eastd	11 to 9	dm. fr	36°	33°

Horrible, wet, uncomfortable, seasick day. May nobody ever see such another unless it be to cure some poor ass of a taste for the sea. Oh wont I be stupid if I ever come to sea again? Strong gales and heavy sea, water everywhere. Secured the bowsprit as well as possible and sent down light yards & Light-mast, laid to all day.

Wednesday August 21st 1850

Lat ☉	Long c	Wind	force	Weather	Air	Water
74°06'	85°26'	ESE	8 to 3	d m. f. o	36° 33°	30°

Out of our reckoning. At 4 A.M. saw the Southern coast and by the trending of the land suppose the point to Westward of us to be Cape Crauford which the observations of the forenoon although imperfect from the fog confirm giving us a strong Southwesterly set. Made all the sail we could and stood toward the Northern coast until we made it and then trying to steer by the land whenever it could be seen; the compasses being very deceitful.

Leopold I[sland] Cape Hurd

Thursday August 22nd 1850

Lat DA	Long c	Wind	force	Weather	Air	Water	Var
74°19'N	89°41'W	ESE	1	o. c. m. f*	36° 33°	34° 30°	113°W

Went on deck for the mid watch and found the vessel heading directly for Port Leopold at the entrance of Prince Regents Inlet NbyW (pc) so I persuaded the Captain to come up and take a look which as soon as he did of course we stuck her for one of the capes on the opposite shore. But we were passing Leopold island which could not be mistaken. Part of this great error might have been the result of thick weather and bad compasses. At 8 saw a barque and a Steamer ahead of us steering toward Wellington Channel, doubtless part of Austins squadron having been to Cape Walker and returning toward Wellington Channel.[76] Fog came on again and staid all day. At 7 in the evening made Cape Hurd right ahead and saw some distance into Radstock Bay. It has a great deal of ice in it. Hauled her up for Cape Riley having to keep away for ice occasionally. About 8 the wind came out dead ahead (WNW) and too light to make anything by beating in this dull craft. It seems that a Southerly wind makes a thick mist and a NW clears up into a dense fog so thick that the capt apprehends danger from running the brig against a bank of it; so until midnight. Saw several whale appearing very unconcerned at our proximity and heard them blowing in every direction during the 1st Watch. I am more than ever convinced that the one thing needful on this cruise is speed for which much ought to be sacrificed. This is plain as the season for operation is so short that no time can be spared and if with open water and light winds we spend half the month in traversing a weeks run we cant expect to do anything. The Advance has already been detained by us at least one week, but she is clear of us now and will probably have searched the sound before we reach the first point in our sailing directions (about fifteen miles to the windward). Tried the Black throated Diver and Dovekies and found them delicious.

Come Up with Capt Ommanney, Austin's Second

Friday August 23rd 1850

Lat ☉	Long con	Wind	force	Wea	Air		Water	Var
74°28'N	90°22'W	NW	1 to 4	f. bc.	36°	32°	35°	115°W

Beating to windward. This little craft doing tolerably working within 8 pts. The Bowsprit being tied up and the light sails set again. Came up with the pack of ice extending apparently accross to the southern shore and leaving a passage on the Northern shore filled with sailing ice. In the 1st dog saw a boat capsized among the ice and picked her up finding oars, sails &c lashed in her and marked Assistance (the name of Austins second barque) beat up within three miles of the barque which was hove to off Cape Riley while the steamer was cruising about it and Beechy Island. Exchanged colors with the Barque. We wonder where the Advance is.

Saturday August 24th 1850

Lat	Long	Wind	Weatr	force	Air		Water	
Cape Riley		WNW, NNW	c, o, f	3, 5	34, 32		31, 30	

At 2 A.M. came up with the English vessels, the Barque being the Assistance and the steamer the Intrepid both of them sent boats. The captain of the Intrepid came himself, was a capital fellow, said the boat was his and had been washed from his davits in the gale on the 20th. The Steamer had worked her way up to Cape Riley and Beechy Island and found on the former some articles which no one but Franklin could have left. Says that the ice is packed in Wellington Channel but passing out and advises to keep near Cape Riley for a day or two when we may find a passage across the strait. Took another pipe and drink and went aboard to keep the rest of his mid watch having only one mate he keeps W and W⁷⁷ (a Lieut. R. N.) Capt Ommanney's compliments offers of assistance &c and would be 'appy to see Capt Griffin aboard in the morning.

We stood down off Gascoigne Inlet and about nine in the morning Griffin goes aboard the Englishman.

Cape Riley Beechey Island Having Beat Penny & the Commo Traces of Franklin

Commenced beating dead to windward, for Cape Riley in a dense fog and through thick streams of heavy sailing ice. By 2 P.M. the fog rising a little the capt went ashore on Cape Riley a mile to windward of us left a bottle for the Advance, picked up some scraps of cloth, leather &c and an empty meat can with Golden (the name of Franklin's victualer) stamped on it. Saw marks of four tents but by the moss upon the stones they must have been there two or three years ago. The English however say that they are convinced that Franklin is not to the Westward but that these marks were left on his return to Eastward in boats, and they dont see the use of hampering the ships in the sound this winter—the Loafers. Griffin says that their ship is the picture of comfort the cabin like a city parlour and warmed by a stove while here we are sleeping with our noses in the open air. Standing too far off found ourselves caught in the ice and had to run her off to leeward of the cape again driving her through a piece of ice twice her beam and four feet thick to get clear. By midt came up with Beechey Island saw two brigs to leeward beating up; suppose them Pennys.

Sunday August 25th 1850

Lat ☉	Long bearings	Wind	force	Weather	Air	Water
74°47'N	92°12'W	NNW	4 & 3	f.o. c	32° 30°	29°

Again I say bad luck to the builders of slow vessels, every thing beats us. The English barque a perfect beast herself beat 8 miles dead to windward of us in the morning watch. Penny came up with us. A schooner which Penny tells us is the Prince Albert, Capt Forsyth, raises her hull astern of us and lastly the Advance shows her fore yard. Griffin boarded Penny and breakfasted with him. He was a month in Melville Bay and wants to know how we ever got through without 'aving any experience in ice management. Griffin says he is not so comfortable as Capt Ommanney but is a nice fellow. By eleven A.M. the barque was out of sight toward Cape Hothany. The Advance instead of coming up now disappears and at 2 having seen Penny tied up to ice in the Pack which appears to extend to Cape Hothany we stood back under all stdsls for Cape Riley and on rounding Beechey I saw her high and dry on the beech at Cape Riley. Stood down and then off and on until this day ends. It seems that she had stood too far inside of the cape, been becalmed, and drifted ashore with the current near high tide (the current runs here two knots) and are under some apprehension lest they will be unable to get off on the next tide and lose the rest of the season in getting her afloat. They say that after the gale of the 20th they were looking for us fell in with Sir John Ross also Forsyth, and looked into Port Leopold thence with light airs to these diggings and so little dreamed of our being ahead of them that they wouldnt open the bottle left for them at the cape (not observing the eagle stamp and Yankee ice pole left to mark it). Ross told them that the North Star is going home after landing her stores at Port Bowen so they write by her and give the letters to Forsyth who having got the news from Cape Riley returned to Prince Regents inlet and will see the North Star. Austin with his steam tender went to Ponds Bay and has not yet entered the sound. Forsyths and Ross' vessels are neither of them larger than ours and they are going to winter up here most probably. Every thing that we have yet seen has the legs of us so we can only creep on and see what others have done so again I wish I was home or had a fast vessel. We saw land some distance farther up Wellington Channel than Parry has recorded and being farther North than the English are probably the discoverers, though I fear that their crows nests are ahead of us.

Traces of Sir John

Monday August 26th 1850

Lat ☉	Long (bearings)	Wind	force	Weather	Air	Water
74.43N	91°55'W	Wd SE	3	OM. S	34° 28°	29°

Beat up against a light air until 3 P.M. (But by the way the Advance hauled off with the next tide a little after Midt) when getting a fair wind we made sail and came up to Pennys vessels which were hove to off Cape Spencer. Penny visited both the vessels saying that after passing us yesterday he had gone up as far toward Cape Hothany as the ice would permit and had been on board the Assistance which could not go much farther, that he had sailed along the pack, accross Wellington Channel and affirms that it has been closed for at least two years; thence he came back and landing on Cape Spencer found articles (which he produced) such as a piece of newspaper, more meat cans (one with the paper label perfect) some small shot, spikes, a clay pipe and lastly a piece of writing paper with the name of McDonald[78] (one of Franklins Doctors.) These things being in such preservation and the stations of their deposit being so near each other I think gives us good cause to conjecture that Franklins party passed lately and going Eastward on sledges (the marks of a sledge were seen) the encampments being about a days journey apart which it is improbable they would have been had he made them while in possession of his vessels. Penny says he is going to examine Cape Hurd, Radstock Bay, and then return hitherward to examine farther up the channel and I think from his remarks that he would be glad to work together with us, that is he examine to the Eastward of Cape Riley while we do here, and then inform each other of the discoveries, as he said he would tell us if he found anything there (But just now he cant pass Beechy Island as the ice has set against it with this wind). Were we to work thus we might all pass next winter more pleasantly than I anticipate doing. I visited the Advance in the calm of the afternoon and thanked Buck[79] for having written to my father by the North Star and our little Fleet Surgeon also who says that he told his friends to write to their friends who know my friends &c. Just to think that we were near the very spot where Penny found all those things for some hours yesterday and might so easily have gone and found them. Penny seems to be a capital old fellow, sayst that we have done better than all put together to come through the pack without experience and without even a crows nest. Goodsir was with him and seems a fine fellow, little like an author. I hope we may winter near them if at all up here. Saw a great many of the white Whale[80] which swing up to and pass under the bottom sometimes touching and uttering a cry resembling a suppressed scream or between a low whistle and a scream.

Tuesday August 27th 1850

Lat	Long	Wind	force	Weather	Air	Water
		Wd	4 to 0	cm. O.	38° 30°	29°

Sailed back to Beechey Island with the Advance. Penny following us and made fast to the land ice Just as old Sir John Ross with the Felix and Mary made fast. Sent a party to search the Southern Shore of Cape Spencer (says the log) say I, Rob Carter took his gun and two men and after crossing a mile and a half of ice, wading through lots of fresh ponds, took a cruise over the hills finding the marks of a sleigh in the loose pebbles about ½ mile long leading from the beach to a hole dug in the ground, found also a soup canister some twine and a clay pipe. The tracks were as distinct as if a carriage wheel had just passed.

After searching this point crossed over to the island where the English were searching and had found the graves of three of Franklins party—Braine, Hartnell, and Torington.[81] The boards at their heads dated Jany and Apl 1846 also on the same spot the marks of his winter quarters for that year, too evident to be mistaken leaving us in little doubt that Franklin had passed his first winter here with his ships and that the traces which we had discovered on Cape Riley and this side of Wellington Channel were those of spring excursions. But how strange that they left no notice of having visited these places and nothing under the cairn on the summit of the Island which the Captain of the Intrepid told us and Capt Ommanney told Griffin that they had examined and rebuilt without finding any writing.

Davis (S[ai]l Maker) of the Rescue tells me that on the morning which Griffin called on Capt Ommanney while in the boat alongside the Assistance the men told him of their having found these graves the day before when examining Beechey Island where the capts say they found no traces but the useless cairn. Then their advising us to search to Eastward and not saying what they intended to do but that with the evidence found they were satisfied that Franklin had returned Eastward and they di[d]nt wish to hamper their ships this winter and immediately after under all sail and steam hastening toward Cape Hothany not waiting for Penny and Forsyth both of whom were in sight astern (see Aug 25th) caused me to suspect that Capts Ommanney & Kator[82] had found notices certainly under the cairn on Beechey Island (which such thoughtful men as Franklin built for some use) perhaps at Cape Riley telling the future course of the sought party and that they had concealed them from us, tried first to avoid Penny and not succeeding deceived him also. This suspicion I communicated to Griffin who, with what all of Griffin's boats crew affirm to have been told them on board the Advance the 24th inst, communicated to our Commo and in five minutes the officers of the five vessels here were in an uproarious state suspecting themselves of being humpbugged by Ommanney and it is amusing to see how hardly some of them take it. Penny swears to shoot him. DeHaven says he'll up helm and go home if it is so; None of us but would eat a small piece of him.[83]

In the afternoon we were ordered to go as far up the channel as the ice permits and thence send a land party up to Cape Bowdin or farther as &c. So we left all this company and going up off Cape Innes Griffin fits out a party (himself, Lovell and four men) and starts with five days provisions leaving me to take care of the brig. He attempts to cross the ice but soon sings out for a boat and pulls in for the land at edge of the pack which having landed them brings me an order to take the brig in near where he landed and send a party to search from Cape Innes toward Cape Spencer and if he is not back in four days to send a party to Cape Bowdin with provisions for him.[84] The ice here is much thicker than the pack in Baffins Bay and as we are fast to the immove-able land ice, a Southerly blow would serve us shabbily I fear.

Wednesday August 28th 1850

Lat ☉	Long c	Wind	force	Weather	Air		Water
74°49'N	91°54W	Wd	0 to 3	bcm, f.	33°	26°	29°

Rather dull for me. After breakfast I brought the ship near the land and started the party to search the coast and near it around Cape Innes and thence toward Cape Spencer. The party consisted of Doc, Brooks, and two petty officers. They asked for muskets and I reluctantly consented telling them to search for any thing dropped by a travelling party or marks of one, and cautioning Mr. Brooks not to let game or anything take him off the coast into the interior. Got a good ☉, poor azin, tolerable time sight, and within a few degrees an amplitude; and took bearings but the compass wont work. I found that by moving it about on the ice it gave different bearings for distant points then bringing it back and placing the legs of the tripod in the same holes it gave still other bearings so my azimuth cant value much. Doc said that he would return to dinner so I waited. Well here is 10 P.M. and no Doc and I am in a quandary got no one whom I can trust to send for the doctor and much less to stay by the ship. Brooks with one man returned at 8 having come about as near as usual to the directions given him and struck off into the valleys after hares two of which he brought along with him, says he left the doctor about 12 and of course found no traces of a party surveying the coast. I blow horns and fire guns as it is foggy but no answering sound as yet.

Thursday August 29th 1850

Lat	Long	Wind	force	Weather	Air		Water		Variation
		Sd	2 to 4	S	27°	32°	29°	28°	139°W

Had a famous old time this morning. Was just about to start a party at 4 o'clock to search for the doctor when several large pieces of thick ice came down upon us and I was an hour getting her clear with all hands, after which it came on thick with snow so that a searching party could do nothing. At 8 Griffin returned having visited undiskivered land and found camping out where there is no fuel and nothing but Irish feathers for beds rather tough. They took no tents but slept during the warmer part of the day and travelled at night.[85] At 12 The Advance came up bringing our Doctor who in the coolest manner had slept there all night instead of returning to us after completing his search. The Advance brings news of Austins arrival at Beechey Island with his barque and steamer so that now there are nine vessels between Capes Riley and Hothany. Griffin thinks that this is a bay only, instead of a channell as he saw land extending apparently accross it. Docs man found a bottle on the top of Point Innes with the head of a newspaper (the London Mail) dated April 24, 1845, but no writing on it.

Worked two hours to get her underway from a deep bight in the ice with the wind directly in and in two hours more beat her down to the beach just North of Cape Spencer where the Advance had a boat ashore and was hove to. Finding the passage between the cape and the pack too narrow to beat through we had to make fast to the pack for the night or rather until this wind changes. Snowing all the time we were at work. Griffin sleeping off the effects of his journey. Murdaugh landed in the Advance's boat and found near the beach some old thrown down huts in which by raking among the stones he got some bits of paper, some lucifer matches &c. The huts were apparently of Esquimaux as they found many bones of whale, seal, about them. Saw Austins, Pennys, and Ross' vessels anchored to the ice cosily under Beechey Island and wish we were also.

Friday August 30th 1850

Lat	Long	Wind	force	Weather	Air	Water
		SSE	3 to 4	c. b. s.	32° 26°	29° 28°

Cold snowy and dull. Cabin got a sore head and some reason for mine as neither Griffin nor the Doc would turn out to mark time for me although after 8 o'clock. Still Griffin expects the result of observations and thinks I ought to teach Brooks (the other watch officer) to assist in taking azimuth while I take the alt and time in order that he and the doctor may have no disturbance. Griffin hinted that I had not done my duty because the azimuth which I took alone when there was no other officer aboard gives a result which even I doubt, and says he can teach me how to do it. (This I had to do on the ice, Therm at 26°, with art hoz, pocket chro, and az comp mounted.) I think Griffin would make a good Prince of Unreason for a May day frolic. Some pieces of heavy ice Surrounding us, had to shift our berth 300 yds to leeward and nearer the Advance. Penny sent a boat aboard the Assistance who is jammed in the pack some distance from Cape Hothany, pretty tightly squeezed and standing by for a campaign on the ice. Her tender the Intrepid has lost her rudder. This boat reports eleven bear in sight at one time. Found one of Brooks hares very fine eating. The fur is also very fine and snow white but comes out too easily.

I think that this party ought to endeavour to return home this season as nothing more can be done now all having been examined up to the impassable barrier and the field for spring excursions too limited for the number of Englishmen to amuse themselves with. There is about enough for Austin to do on this side and Ommanney on the Southern so that until the next open season Penny, Ross, and ourselves can only play fifth wheel while by starting early next spring we may certainly get this far before Austin will be free from his winter quarters. I wish DeHaven would think so, for the prospect of nine months in this little boat while all those John Bulls are in their comfortable cabins is dull. If we cant go home lets do something desperate and winter in the pack where if we are not squashed in the spring we'll be the first out of winter quarters. Austin was at Ponds Bay. Says that not a whaler got through the pack this season, which is good for us.

This snow is very penetrating and cooling with this wind besides making the decks mons[tr]ous slippery. Griffin and myself cured our sore heads with a bottle of champagne and a big dough for dinner with a little London Charivari after it but the Doc took no such medicine.

The Assistance has sent a party to Cape Hothany without finding any traces of Sir John.

Went aboard the Advance this evening and roused the sleeping beauties out for a gas. Murdaugh was aboard the Resolute a few days ago and described their appartments as very fine for winter, each state room connects with a big fire below by flues so that by turning a cock a current of hot air rushes in sufficient to warm and dry a relevée [watch officer] from a four hours rain. I daresay that those fellows came here to spend a pleasant winter as they could scarcely be so comfortable in a house. Quite a contrast with our little "rain come wet me, Sun come dry me" cabin with no stove even, which by the way the English have besides the flues. The commo said something about going home this winter and I asked him if we came next spring to get us a pilot boat even though not strengthened in preference to this dull craft. Returning about 8 took accurate bearings lest I should have to bear up to avoid a bear on my way to the Rescue.

Three Bears before Breakfast

Saturday August 31st 1850

Lat ⊙	Long c	Wind	force	Weather	Air	Water
76.46'N	—	SE	3 to 10	cm. o.	35° 30°	29°

Quite a gale making the moderate temperature very unpleasant to the feelings; much colder to the feeling than any weather we have yet had. The tide was very high and the field to which we are fast drifting Northward and closing in with the land so that both the vessels had to shift their berths, we several times. The ice is so hard that digging for an anchor is a labour of 10 or 15 minutes.

I see now what the arctic writers mean by hummocky ice and how disagreeable travelling over it must be, tenfold worse than new ploughed ground and quite as bad as loose lava.

Three bears swam near the ship at breakfast time and Griffin & myself manned a boat and pulled to the attack. About half way bearward we found that our weapons consisted of my shot gun (one barrel with buck and one with bird shot) and his musket with a doubtful charge however as no time could be spared we went on. His musket snapped the first time but upon being recapped brought one and reloaded by an accidental charge in Brooks pocket brought another and my load of buckshot by coming within ten yards laid out the third. Pretty fair—three bears with three loads.[86] The one I shot is the first male we have got but is small being young all were shot in the head, mine least dammaged, those muskets make such awful holes. The chance of getting out of this pool to the Southward are getting slim, the ice being jammed up against Cape Spencer for a mile and that too with a high tide leaving the chance of finding a harbour horribly small.

Commo made my heart jump for joy by saying that if we get out and find no opening to Southwestward that he will endeavour to return home this winter.

Hope of & Reason for Returning Home

Sunday September 1st 1850

Lat ⊙	Long	Wind	force	Weather	Air	Water
74°48'N		SE	10 to 6	om.	36° 34°	29°

Gale continues till night and the drifting snow renders the open air unpleasant. Passage Southward still closing. Drifted two miles Nd. All in all rather bad. But all for the best as everything yet has turned out. Suppose the commo hadnt got ashore and stayed so long at Cape Riley that we ran back, we would most probably have been jammed with Ommanneys vessels. By the way all our suspicions of him and Capt Kater [Cator] were as unjust and unfounded as galley yarns generally are.

More say [talk] about home. Commo dined here, says that he expects to winter either 300 miles west of this or at home, but is very disheartened at the present prospect—the first time I have heard him at all despond[ent].

The only thing that we can gain by wintering in the Sound is the advantage of Spring foot parties, for which while we're entirely unprepared (not having even a tent, and so few men) the English are fully equipped, have a strong force and less ground than will occupy half their time. And by referring to former winters up here, no vessel has ever been freed from her winter quarters as early as we got here in this season, so backward that not a Whaler got through Baffins Bay.

Monday September 2nd 1850

Lat	Long	Wind	force	Weather	Air	Water
Off Pt Innes		SE. North	3. 1	om, f	38° 32°	29°

Capt Griffin & Brooks went hare hunting without seeing any near enough to shoot. Griffin dined with Penny whom he likes still more. Dr. Kane returned from the English ships (where he has been for three days during the gale) giving glowing accounts of their comforts, he actually had sheets to sleep in every night. He staid on board Austins Ship says that they have regular Man o war discipline, had prayers morning and evening at quarters, and are inspected regularly and make as much ado, reporting &c. about a small piece of drift ice as we do about being nipped and thrown on our beam ends. All the officers and men receive double pay and the officers certain of promotion after this cruise. Aint dat hi? Commo Austin came back with the doc and dined aboard the commo is the jolliest old Englishman ever seen. Talks to our commo about the expeditions to be sent in cohoot in the spring saying that he will fit us out. They are trying to get old Ross home to carry news of the squadron.

One of the baloons for distributing news over the Arctic world was sent up from Beechey Island during the gale. About a thousand bits of paper marked with (Date, Ship, position, future intentions, and naming depots of provisions) put up in packages of ten or more are fast to the baloon and so arranged that by the burning of a slow match a bundle is bursted and scattered at regular intervals during its flight. Three of the papers were found by a party from the Advance about five miles from Beechey Island which were probably some of the first bundle showing that it had worked well thus far. Saw numbers of Narwhal and some were shot but not struck in the right place. It being almost impossible to harpoon this fish—it is oftener caught by shooting it in the spine. The tusks which are several feet long are the finest ivory. During the disagreeable weather of the last few days we have had our hatch doors closed and now we find everything damp with condensed vapour. The Advances say that even in their lockers the clothes are all damp. Sheets wouldnt suit that.

The English officers on hearing our Commo say that his force was 33 men asked in surprize "thirty three all in your vessel"? and perhaps their surprize increased a little when told that the thirty three included officers, men, cooks, and stewards of both vessels. Still we have beaten them with their steam, experience, faster vessels, and strong force.

Leave the East Side of Wellington Strait

Tuesday September 3rd 1850

Lat	Long	Wind	Weather	force	Air	Water
		Nd, NW	f. om.	1. 2	34° 30°	29°

The floe to which we have been fast during the gale commenced drifting South with the ebb tide so at 10.30 we cast of[f] and commenced beating against the tide loosing a little every tack until about 6 P.M. when at slack water we found ourselves very little to Southward of the mornings position we stood to the Westward in a long lead towards Cape Hothany about six miles. At midnight the lead closing with the continuance of the flood we had to tie up. The tides here run about 12 hours each way so that this lead ought to be open tomorrow afternoon with the ebb unless a southerly wind comes when we shall probably be jammed. Dr. Kane shot a seal and got him falsifying the assertions of all the knowing ones that they will sink when killed in the water. He says that the Englishmen have shot several and got them. Going this way dont look homeward and our cakes look doughy.

Wednesday September 4th 1850

Lat ☉	Long c	Wind	force	Weather	Air	Water	Var az
74°47'N	92°29'W	NW	2	bc. b	39° 20°	29° 28°	111°

This is a beautiful morning but rather cool. Dressing on deck Ther 27° the water in the tumbler would freeze after each pouring on the toothbrush but the sun was so welcome that I didn't want to shame him by going below, especially as we have not come to that yet, and a beautiful mess we would have if we did dress below. At 3 the ice opened so that we had a lead as far as we could see to Westward of which taking advantage we make about six miles toward Cape Hothany and by Midnight are fast again. The pack to Southward of us drifting by to Westward at a lick o two knots carrying with it loose pieces several feet higher than our rail making our position any thing but comfortable and letting us see that the marvelous accounts of Ross and Back may have a little truth mixed with the poetry.

A most enormous bear was shot from the Advance just before we made fast here measuring 8 ft 8 in—two inches larger than any on record; a male very old and swam near the ship without fear. We were in hopes that they did not see him as the lead was narrow and the vessels going three knots when suddenly they stood right for him, the port bow bristling with fire arms, however, only two were fired, the first killing and the second missing but they were fired so nearly at the same instant that Lovell and Dr Kane dont know which of them did it. Poor Lovell—he put one ball in the head of the first one they killed but one of the men did the same and he is most ambitious to kill a polar bruin. Saw the Assistance and Intrepid off Cape Hothany under sail but our chance seems rather slim to get there or any where else just now. Therm at 20° and bay ice forming fast. Saw lots of stars to-night the first of the season. Compasses are humplugs. Az gives only 111° var today.

Thursday September 5th 1850

Lat ☉	Long	Wind	force	Weather	Air	Water
74°45'N		NE to West	3. 1	bc. b.	35° 26°	28° 29°

The Advance's bear is immense and can only be compared with small elephants being too large for 'orses and hoxen. Made a start at one P.M. and at quarter fore six made fast to the land ice about 300 yds from the North Cape of Barlows inlet in eleven feet water the Advance being beached just ahead of us but she did it so softly that they had to measure to discover it, and at low water too. The tide commenced to flow and by eight we have lots of ice around us. I took a cruise around the inlet which is a beautiful land locked

harbour extending three miles from the mouth and spacious, as a horse shoe
but I dont know the depths as it was frozen or rather filled with ice of years
standing.[87] We are not near the middle of the enterance which accounts for
our shoal water. We found a dead seal with a fine silk handkerchief tied round
it, and opened a cairn erected only yesterday with a paper in the same bom-
bastic style of Capt Ommanney's other document not mention[in]g which
way he is going nor where provisions are left &c. but that no traces have been
found on Cornwallis Island of which perhaps he has examined one one hun-
dredth and that 1/100 poorly if no better than Beechey Island which they
thoroughly examined without finding Franklins winter quarters with a conspicuous cairn pointing them out. Perhaps this isnt the place to express such
uncharitable sentiments but it does look so ridiculous for that party to be
rushing ahead so as to be first at every place then leaving it unexamined to
say that no traces are found there (Cornwallis Island is a young continent).
Commo Austins barque and steamer crossed the sound to-day and the
steamer is towing her in among the loose ice toward us. One of their boats
has just returned having come in to see whether all that flashing and firing
was for warning to them. And having learned that it was Dr. Kane trying
to get his rifle off took another drink and returned. Thats the rifle as shot
the bear after snapping only once thinks Dr. Kane but Lovell thinks his Polly
longlips done it. We saw three bear this afternoon as we sailed rapidly along
the edge of the field and some of the men fired at one but only alarmed him;
one was feeding on the carcass of a bear left skinned by the Englishmen so I
daresay bruin can eat his fellow bruins without compunctions. This looks
less like home than ever and as Capt Ommanney doubled Cape Hothany this
afternoon I suppose we may tomorrow. Hoping which, I'll take the mete-
orogicals and call my relief.

Barlows Inlet Rescue Escapes a Nip

Friday September 6th 1850

Lat	Long	Wind	force	Weather	Air	Water
Barlow Inlet		W SE	2 to 0	o. f. m*	32° 26°	29° 27°

No possibility of advancing or returning all day being closely surrounded by
ice which drifts South and North with the tides at a great rate. The English
commo also sticks pretty fast and I daresay regrets not squeezing in here last
night as he is in a fine position for drifting out of the Sound a la James Ross.

Murdaugh sounded across the enterance of this inlet and found six and seven fathoms in the channell which runs nearer the Southern cape agreeing with the rule "In entering bays, harbours, &c in Limestone regions avoid the side which terminates in a cliff." Cleaned my bear skin as much as possible which wasnt much though requiring some labour. The bay ice formed so thick during the night that parties have been skating all day. But today it is mild again. The Englishmen came ashore near us but dont come aborde.

Saturday September 7th 1850

Wind	force	Weather	Air	Water
SE Nd	1 to 6	f. o	34° 23°	29°

Ice still closer until 6 P.M. when a North wind getting a little fresh we perceive the whole pack to drift slowly Southward taking commo Austin with it. We being inside of a point on which are a number of grounded bergs maintain our position having the power to force our way further in the harbour if desirable. About this time a large fragment of the floe to which we were fast broke off and both vessels drift rapidly accross the mouth of the harbour toward a berg grounded to leeward of us. The Advance goes clear but the poor little Rescue was caught again. Providentially in the vortex of an angle and was popped out like a melon seed with no dammage the ice very considerately unshipping the rudder just as we most desired it to be done[,] however as the ice could not stop to run it up to the davits that had to be done, and seeing some men humbugging at it to sling it and keep dry feet, I jumped into the water and slung it myself somewhat to their amusement perhaps but at all events better than losing the rudder. Hauled the vessels a short distance farther in and made fast to the lee bergs being protected from this wind by those grounded on the point (above mentioned) but still not in a secure place as quite large pieces drift against us with the tide. Austin is drifting yet and closely beset. Begin to talk about having to winter in this desolate spot where even the bears wont come. I had almost rather winter at home. Read in Parry[88] to-day that he put all his compasses below except the Azimuth which was also a poor dependence and am quite satisfied to learn that I am not the first master to make funny variations by azimuths taken near the same position. The variation I got on the 29th ulto agrees within 2° of Parrys nearest to that position.

Sunday September 8th 1850

Long c	Wind	force	Weather	Air	Water	max Bar
	N to W	5–2	0, bcm	25°23°	28° 26°	30.66 in

Another day of confinement by the ice one of the few remaining and precious days of open season. Expecting a gale all day the Barometer having risen higher than it has ever done before. Austin still beset has drifted about six miles South of us. Old Penny seems to be as cautious as a fox he keeps astern of us all and profits by our experience. He appeared last evening five miles to Northward of this port in a stream of open water next the land ice and holding on to it so as not to share what seems to be Austins misfortune. The bay ice formed thick enough for all the men who can raise skates to be breaking the sabbath all day, and firmly cementing the loose fragments that drifted around us with the last flood tide so that two hours of the afternoon were employed in breaking it around them so that the ebb cleared us again. I spent a very quiet sabbath reading, but this is no place to pass a satisfactory one and more particularly in this weather where one is suffering from cold except while in bed or during active exercise. I sent a bundle of tracts which I selected from our supply into the forecastle but I am affraid that they will hardly be noticed. Every one in the expedition appears so utterly indifferent to the one thing needful in spite of the constant evidence that Providence alone can protect us and in this cruise by special interposition.

Monday September 9th 1850

Wind	force	Weather	Air	Water
West	2–5	om	28° 23°	32° 30°

Got underway at 4 A.M. and stood for Cape Hothany doubling it and commenced beating to the Westward. Austin towed by his steam tender got out of the ice and went to windward fast. Penny caught and passed us, so that by night we are again last because of our dull vessels. Penny boarded us as he passed and got some 300 pounds of bears meat for his dogs of which he has thirty eight. We gave him of an old bear as we think the young one fine eating. Saw Griffith Island twenty miles ahead. The young ice is so troublesome now that we apprehend having to hunt for winter quarters soon, lest our dull vessels should be caught in it and drifted S. E. Home stock so high a few days ago is not worth shucks now and Melville Island stock is up and as such seems the design of Providence. I shall e'en content myself with the prospect of a winter in one of these brigs which the remembrance of last winter renders doubly gloomy. Penny says he sailed some distance up Wellington Channel and thinks Griffin mistaken about its being a bay.

Farthest West. Up with Austin, Ommanney & Penny

Tuesday September 10, 1850

Lat	Long	Wind	force	Weather	Air	Water
		West. Nd	4, 3	o. s*. m.	30° 26°	31° 29°

Until 4 P.M. beating to the Westward when we got a fair wind stopping the snow and cheering us up. At 6.30 we doubled the Southern extremity of Griffith Island and saw Austins four vessels and Pennys brigs fast to a field of ice three miles West of the Island and extending North and South as far as we can see. Came to among them (man o war style). Capt Ommanney had been here only 24 hours having examined a good deal more of Cornwallis Island without finding traces of Sir John. Austin & Penny had been here only twelve hours and all say that there is no going farther. The Intrepid has examined in shore and between Griffith Island & Cornwallis finding a harbour on the latter which they have named Assistance Harbour and where Commo Austin thinks of wintering as the season is shutting up so early and on dit [it is said] that Ommanney is to survey Wellington Channel. So what do now Messrs Yankees but go home if ye can as your instructions direct ye, saying to the effect that if you cant get far enough West to go to [blank] in the spring you will return and examine Jones & Smith Sounds and finding them closed not let the young ice catch you but return to New York. A great deal of the snow that fell into the water was formed into round balls about the size to throw so that the mermaids have millions of them all ready for their sport. One of the English middies spent the evening with us and entertained us much being quite funny. But he tells us that in addition to the double pay and certain promotion, that Govt furnishes them with clothes, and better ones than they could have purchased themselves. The list he gave us of one years allowance being about equal to my whole supply plus two pairs of boots such as we never even saw before. Old Penny is right in saying that those fellows dont deserve any credit, steamboats and all taken into consideration.

Cant Go West Austins Plan

Wednesday September 11th 1850

Lat	Long	Wind	force	Weather	Air	Water
		E. SW.	8 to 2	S	30° 20°	31°

A very dirty day. One incessant snow storm to half of which I have been exposed and find it like everything else nothing when you are used to it. Worked three hours of the morning to wind the ship and warp her a cables length to a good lee. The Assistance's tender cruised about all the forenoon to find an opening to the Westward without success. Penny made sail and stood to S. Westward into some loose ice and the tender reports him fast in it a few miles south of us. Too thick to see half a mile.

I met a most interesting gentleman on board the Advance of the uncommon name of Brown,[89] an English Lieut who was with Sir Jas Ross last cruise in these regions and he gave us among other interesting information an exact account of the equipment and conduction of the Spring parties, of which however I can tell better after we have tried one. Commo Austin sent a letter to our Commo advising him of his plans. The Assistance is to winter near here and survey Wellington Chan and examine as far as possible the Northern shore of Barrow Strait while he endeavours to get farther West in his vessels. Home stock is again in the Market and I think that if there is no going West in a few days we will try still harder to get East and home. Doc wishes for a fair wind to go home and hear Jenny Lind; of course in much finer poetry than the above.[90] The Aurora Borealis wants to know what bug abounds these regions which accompanied Noah on his cruise. I suppose it must be the Ark-tick.

A Rough Day for the Rescue

Thursday September 12th 1850

Lat	Long	Wind	force	Weather	Air	Water
		Nd	8	om. s*	20° 10°	

I have seen days of suffering, hard winds, and some cold work but, this was one in which those unpleasant things, combined with danger, made quite an event in the life of every one of us.

At midnight last night I turned in leaving all calm and secure but in half an hour I felt her bump against the ice, heard the wind roar, and the captain turn out so of course I lay expecting to be called every minute. However not till 1.30 did they make my tally, when I was up quickly and found that our nice lee by a change of wind had become a lee shore against which she was thumping heavily. Captain on the ice planting anchors & wanted me to drop the brig round the point, but changing his mind he came aboard and commenced veering. When just at the point all four anchors broke adrift and we were blown off leaving two men and one of our boats on the ice (near the Advance). Making sail we commenced beating up, under considerable anxiety lest not being able to make any weather we should drift on the ice two miles to leeward of us where human efforts wouldn't have been worth shucks to save the brig and little more to save our lives. But after two or three tacks we found that we gained a little and thought that we would stand off and on until the gale abated when we could make fast to the ice again. So at 4 I turned in having been two & a half hours at the helm, but under such excitement that I scarcely felt the cold, although the Capt had the helm relieved every half hour afterwards, the therm being 18° and snowing fast. At 6 I was again called to relieve the capt who had not slept all night either, having been aboard the Commo until Midt so I worked her up among washing ice until 12 when finding that we had gained enough to run under the lee of Griffith Island and anchor I called him and made the proposition which he determined to attempt seeing the exhausted state of the men (who were now reduced to six, three being sick and two absent[)]. So we ran her to within stones cast of the ice grounded on the beach and let go an anchor in 9 fms water but it wouldn't hold, and we dragged off in a giffey; drifting into a piece of washing ice and smashed the rudder so as to render it almost useless. However made sail and beat up again to within biscuit throw of the shore and let go in 4 fms water which held for a while so that she swung round alongside the land ice and a man jumped ashore to plant an ice anchor but before he could do it the arm of our best bower[91] broke short off and we began to drift off so rapidly that with difficulty the man was dragged aboard leaving the ice anchor. The men were now nearly exhausted but we made sail again hove up the broken anchor and worked up a third time, shortening sail and running alongside of a grounded berg we put ropes over some of its projecting points and were thankful to see them hold until we could get out ice anchors and secure her for the night. By this time all hands were completely worn out so that few were capable of any exertion even to save their lives.

It must be remembered that we had all been doing heavy and annoying work all day, The weather very cold and snowy, while underway constantly looking out for ice which the blinding snow and spray made it difficult to avoid. Our clothes were saturated with the spray in half an hour after starting, but they froze immediately and so were perhaps warmer. But the annoyance was the stiffness of the ropes which were iced and twice their usual size. The head guys, shrouds, and bobstays made a kind of net work which, being dipped as the vessel pitched, soon formed a solid mass of ice out to the bowsprit cap and the sea breaking over the bow rail soon had a solid mass from the knight heads to the windlass and being coated with ice outside she looked like an iceberg under sail. The small boat which we got from the Advance having been smashed against the ice and filling with water made us steer wild, so I cut her adrift with one blow of a hatchet and said good bye as she dove and rose bottom up astern. Only two men had their fingers frost bitten and both might have escaped it by more care, for although cautioned about taking off their mits they wouldn't believe that a minutes exposure could do the business. One was the old Boatswains mate whom I had ordered to put on his mits about six times during the day. Giving the Doctor and Brooks the first & mid watches (they having been in bed all day,) the captain and mate with all hands got some needful repose.

Friday September 13th 1850

Lat	Long	Wind	force	Weather	Air	Water
		N. NW	8–5	15. 5	15° 5°	27°

Were very glad to see the Advance and Commo Austins squadron standing down for the Island at 11 o'clock. But not so glad as they said they were because they didnt expect to see us again supposing of course that we had been caught in the ice to leeward and the Commo having determined to try and go home they feared that having to hunt for us would knock that in the head. They made signal to us to get underway and follow and upon hearing of our crippled condition took us in tow and we are going to Eastward finely. At 8 we were off Cape Hothany and stood accross the channel until 10 A.M. when we fetched up in the young ice. The Advances saw Penny and a schooner anchored close under the land about half way between Capes Martyr & Hothany. We left Commo Austin going into the harbour which the Assistance found for winter quarters. Home stock was up high but the young ice has caused a great fall.

Stopped by Young Ice

Saturday September 14th 1850

Lat	Long	Wind	force	Weather	Air		Water
		SSE	3	om. s	21°	17°	27°

We are afraid that we're caught for the winter. There was open water for several hours as far as we could see to the Eastward but we couldnt get into it until so shortly before it was closed that we sailed only two miles and are again fast in the new ice with a six knot SW wind and the temperature so low that there is little hope of a break up. Commo Austin didnt write by us but asked our Commo to write to the Admiralty which is strange none of his officers seem to have known of our homeward intentions and we suppose that their commander didnt wish them to.

Sunday September 15th 1850

Lat	Long	Wind	force	Weather	Air		Water
		SE. E	4	bo m s	17°	20°	27°

It is sometimes hard to say "Thy will be done." And this my 25th birth day is one of those times. Yes one day of open water would have put us whence we have every reason to suppose returning home certain or at all events in some harbour. But here we are fast, tight as wax in the middle of the mouth of Wellington Strait with a six knot fair wind. There has been no opening to-day and the field has drifted a little to NE so as to bring us within the capes of the strait and near the middle of it. The ice is so thick (4 inc[hes]) that while there was hope of getting on all hands were cutting sawing and breaking upon it, but it is so soft and tenacious that it doesnt crack; a stick makes a hole through it like mud, and closing after the sun, in five minutes it becomes hard as before. The ways of Providence are inscrutable and it is doubtless all for the best, but one can scarcely help thinking it hard to be kept up here away from all that is dear to us away from even the companionship of the English vessels for nine or ten long months at least and away from a safe harbour.

"What! winter in the pack" said old Penny, "Perfect madness!" and then enumerated the many disadvantages and dangers which we now unavoidably must suffer and experience. The danger to be apprehended most is the breaking up of the ice in Spring which being so far off I leave for a future Jeremiatic reflection. But the present inconvenience is that we cant prepare our vessels for winter until six weeks after John Bull in his harbour has been comfortably housed for we dare not put our stores on the ice out here until the lateness of the season makes it improbable that a gale would give them to the mermaids, and in fact Parry says that he saw the ice outside the harbour agitated in the gales during all winter. So here we must remain without fire until winter is well begun. Our appartments are now so cold and damp that the Docs call them unwholesome and those of the men are worse. Could ships and men have a more gloomy prospect? But it may all be for good even in a worldly sense an early break up in the spring might liberate us early enough to be the farthest West next season or if we have an awful time Government may give us extra pay eclat &c. Again! May it not be a just punishment? Ours were the only vessels of the nine up here, in which there was no public worship of God, no mention made of his name nor his goodness in having enabled us to do as much as the English with all their advantages. So perhaps we are brought out from among them lest they be consumed with us. But since with God, miracles are small things I yet hope that he may convince some of us that he has done all for us heretofore by liberating us after all hope has vanished. For it seems that even the worst of us could be better employed almost any where else.

Drifting up Wellington Channel

Monday September 16th 1850

Lat	Long	Wind	force	Weather	Air		Water
		SE	6–5	os. cm.	24°	18°	27°

Another day of fast in this horrid young ice. There was a small opening at 6 o'clock P.M. and we were carried into it about half a mile North in which direction we are daily being carried at a rate very annoying to those who still hope for a liberation this season, very gratifying to those who wish to remain and survey the channel and very perceptible to those who like myself are indifferent which way we go since it is so plainly the hand of Providence guiding us. The young ice has got so strong now that it plays with our vessels like toys swinging and thumping us about constantly so as to keep us constantly at work repairing its dammages. To day after almost finishing our rudder it [the ice] swung the Advance into us nearly crushing our white whale boat and then commenced squeezing us so as to make every timber creak and the poor little brig quake and quiver constantly; leaving it at this rascally sport which having lasted an hour seems still to afford it amusement, I will bid it good night.

Tuesday September 17th 1850

Lat	Long	Wind	force	Weather	Air	Water
		SE	6–3	om. s	24° 20°	31° 28°

Drifting Northward with the pack about five miles NE of Cape Bowden to-day at noon. The ice kept up the squeezing and grinding all night and is much broken. The heavy pack ice coming North seems to have done this and if there is any hope left of getting out this season the loosening of the ice will cherish it until another freeze blasts it entirely. This South wind contrary to anything ever known in these regions seems to have no end. The South wind is rare at this season and generally of short duration.

Give Up the Attempt to Go Home

Wednesday September 18th 1850

Lat	Long	Wind	force	Weather	Air	Water
		SE	2–1	os. om.	23° 20°	

Drifting Northward still, came to a floe of heavy ice and being hard up for water got some fresh ice from it. All hands have given up hopes and the commo doesnt want to go home. Talking of going on land journeys this fall which I call a double extract of the essence of humbug and want to see it tried by some of those who propose sending the party.

Thursday September 19th 1850

Lat	Long	Wind	force	Weather	Air	Water
		North	3–7	om. s	20° 18°	

The wind has been kind enough to change so that the Northerly drift seems checked. It is quite a gale from North but too thick and snowy to see far. The home is done for and the object now is to get in near the land and find a har-bour which a few pools stretching toward the West coast seem to render prac-ticable. So all hands were set to work to see how the cutting into the nearest pool (a large one to Westward of us) would go but I judge that it was thought rather difficult as we were ordered to knock off after two hours work, having made no impression, for although the ice is only a few inches thick it is so piled up and overlapped that all around us six feet of thickness is common. I am in hopes that we may be drifted entirely out of Lancaster Sound before we are liberated as I cant perceive the good of wintering any where near here, it being certain that if the lost party have gone no farther West than our spring parties could reach they would have returned years ago in the same manner that we would go, and besides we know that from the low temperature, and South wind driving the ice on the North shore of Barrow strait that Austin, Penny, & Ross cant be far off and that they intend examining this channel. However our carpenter is making a sledge and a tent is under construction aboard the Advance for the proposed party to go to Assistance Harbour as soon as we are considered fast for the winter.

Friday September 20th 1850

Lat	Long	Wind	force	Weather	Air	Water
		Nd SE	5. 3 to 8	om,s. s*	30°	23°

So be it! No home this winter and that given up I am content, although wintering in the pack to initiated ones has connected with it ideas of suffering, danger, the almost impossibility of return next fall, and the improbability of taking the vessels back at all and lastly the almost certainty that some of our number will find a long home here. Who can say, "it wont be me"?

A fresh South wind commencing at noon and increasing to a gale by midnight send us at a great rate up the channel, and my hopes of being drifted out of the sound with those of the commo of getting into a harbour are driven before it at too rapid a pace to return any more. Some few leads and pools were seen near us but we are still fixed as stone and our cement seems to harden dayly. Better as tis perhaps because having been piled around us in a soft state it did us no injury and now serves to guard us from the shocks and squeezes of the heavy masses drifting about us. I was quite anxious and unhappy while there was a hope of going home but now that has vanished I am as indifferent and trusting that it is for some good end and thankful to say earnestly "Thy will be done."

Rescue a la Ice Anchor

Saturday September 21st 1850

Lat ☉	Long	Wind	force	Weather	Temp Air	
75°20'N		Southd	8 to 3	cm. bc. s.	22°	19°

The fresh Southerly wind made a rupture in the ice about the Advance leaving her adrift in a pool so she makes an ice anchor of the Rescue and moors by us head and stern. Drifted much to the Northward. Got an imperfect (2 ☉ mer) for lat. The sun on the mer being so low as to be scarcely seen in the art hor and entirely useless for longitude. Commo wants us to get alts of stars but thanks to be none have been seen yet through the mist, to give Jack Frost a bite at my fingers holding a sextant for the amusement of commodores and captains of the American Arctic fleet.

Transferred Wm Benson to the Advance, he having been sick with the scurvy for a long time and am in hopes that the little fleet surgeon understands its cure as I see he has gone very actively to work on this patient making him scrub and exercise. The Crows Nest (Lovell & Griffin editors) came out to-night.[92] I haven't read the first number but understand that it is a dirty pill which didnt go down.

Sunday September 22nd 1850

Lat ☉	Long	Wind	force	Weather	Air
75°24'30"		SE NE	2	0m. cm.	25° 19°

Strange indeed does it seem to me that Enlightened Americans should openly profane the Sabbath. All hands have been employed to-day cutting the ice between us and the pool in which the Advance is. By 4 P.M. a canal was cut to within twenty feet of our stern when they discovered that we are entirely imbedded in the crushed and lapped cakes of bay ice which for twenty or thirty feet around us is from 8 to 15 feet thick and of course impossible to get out unless there was room to float off layer after layer of it so the sabbath has been a lost day in every respect. As I have the forenoon watch I had the afternoon below and so o[n]ly lost four hours of the Sabbath in that scrape. Read the Sabbath Manual by J. Edwards[93] and am afraid it behooves me to leave a service where such work may be required. Indeed my conscience spites me, for not having considered this matter before, though I had never any idea that I would ever be places where the Sabbath was purposely made the day of work as it is with us. Last Sunday the Commo mentioned here that to employ his men he has set them to breaking out the hold. Most of the preceding week tho had been idle. The S. Manual, together with several other religious books furnished by some Society[94] in New York I got out of a waste paper locker on board the Advance where are many others being torn up perfectly new. A large bundle of tracts having been exhausted in the same cause. This is perhaps speaking against my superiors & brother officers, but as this is a private journal and only intended for the perusal of my friends at home with whom these officers will probably never come in contact, I deem it no harm and if on our return this should be demanded by the commander of the expedition, I am willing that this days record be the first to meet his eye. This cutting ice with a cold wind and half the time wet to the knees is unpleasant and if the cold feet I have had all day is an earnest of our future winter work I am afraid that some of us will suffer from the effects of this cruise. The Northerly drift has been less to-day and at Midt we have a fine NE Wind. The ice is again piling up around us and our canal is a mound several feet high. I walked to the Advance on ice of to-days formation. The channel seems to widen up here the Western coast taking a Northwesterly direction. Got a good 2 ⊙ for lat.

Ice Exhibiting Its Infant Strength

Monday September 23, 1850

Wind	force	Weather	Air
NE, SE	5–3	om, s*	26° 18°

The ice has been in a state of great excitement all day overlaying and piling itself around the vessels in a manner to give us apprehension for their safety and showing us that with perfect ease it could overwhelm us. I am afraid that it is only waiting for the season to become more inclement to leave those of us who can rush out, sans every thing on the ice. This business of wintering in the pact commences with difficulties, I only hope we may be able to tell how it ends. About a foot of snow has fallen to-day and looks just like home snow falling fast, silently, and in large flakes, so different from the fine driving snow coming into every crevice that we have hitherto had that I went up and enjoyed the scene often being delighted with one reminding me of home as it did. Griffin accuses all hands of desponding at the prospect which gloomy as it is can be rendered more so by constantly expecting the worst. Dr. Kane says "all this extra annoyance just to be called fools for our pains while the Englishmen amply provided, meet only the common evils of the undertaking to be honoured and promoted." Verily we would be fools to repeat the visit under like circumstances.

Tuesday September 24th 1850

Lat ⊙	Long	Wind	force	Weather	Air
73°23'N		NE	3–1	cm. o. s	15° 9°

More squeezing and piling. The little Rescue was forced twelve feet ahead through her bed of hummocks and mounds of this ice are raised in every direction some of them ten feet high. Quite cool to-day but pleasant below with doors shut except for the constant dripping which has no cure and keeps numerous vessels employed at its regular depots and little puddles where its deposits are not known till thus discovered.

First Snow Hut

Wednesday September 25th 1850

Wind	force	Weather	Air	
NE, Sd	1. 4–1	om. bc. m.	19° 12°	

Quite a pleasant day out. Taking active exercise after breakfast was oppressed with heat. This seems so strange, but with no wind and a low temperature, we are comfortable sitting in the open air whereas with a rise of 20° and a moderate breeze it is difficult to keep warm at all and with a fresh one impossible even with violent exercise. Our tent (of felt cloth) was finished and pitched to-day and being found to be too large is to be turned into a depot tent. The floe in which we are so firmly imbedded broke adrift and is a very small one appearing to-day in the middle of a large pool and showing its ability to drift wherever open water will permit it carrying us along captives. I wish it would go down to the banks of Newfoundland on a fishing excursion and get stuck there.

Thursday September 26th 1850

Lat ☉	Long	Wind	force	Weather	Temp Air
75°24'30"N		NW. SW	3 to 1	o. bcm.	15° 10°

Very pleasant day. Commenced a snow or rather an ice house for exercise cutting and carrying the blocks of ice being hard work. Murdaugh & Lovell soon joined me and I daresay we shall have a tower of Babel after a few mornings work using ice for brick and water for cement.

Dr. Kane shot another seal and was as much pleased with himself as after his first one.

Broke out our stove to prepare the pipes (which to save room were ordered to be put up in sheets all punched and cut) and find that we have none at all, the box containing only the parts of the stove and any quantity of shavings. Wouldn't we have been comfortable this winter by ourselves? The Advance has been making her pipes for several days and has nearly enough when lo! the rivets have given out. Verily some of our countrymen are knaves. Knowing how we were hurried off and that none of us would suspect rascality where all seemed to wish to aid, our stove man had a fine opportunity to display his kind. Saw a black fox quite near the vessels but under too much way to give hope of a chase. Our floe has drifted to the Northern side of the water mentioned yesterday and is also leaving the land.

Finding every thing in my bunk damp and some articles touching the beams saturated, I kept a solar lamp burning inside the bunk all day and determined not to draw the curtains at night any more.[95]

Friday September 27th 1850

Wind	force	Weather	Air		Water
NE	2–0	om. s	10°	6°	29°

Rather sombre day and being pretty cool withall not so pleasant. Exercise at the snow hut. Lovell made a swing from Advance's fore yard. Some skating but the ice was too rough and one man looking for smoother got into the drink and being some distance from the strong ice came near joining the mermaids. All hands rushed toward the spot but no one thought to carry a line or board until at the place, giving the man ample time to drown if he had lost his strength or presence of mind as some do when floundering about in this cold water.

Saturday September 28th 1850

Wind	force	Weather	Temp Air	
North	2–0	om. s. bcm	8°	3°

Quite cool to-day but being calm not disagreeable. Crews employed banking ice around the vessels and filling the crevices with snow and water so as to make a casing four feet thick resembling rough masonry. Broke out the sails and some bread from forward and making a tent of part of the sails put them on the ice and removed the after Forecastle bulkhead giving the men more room. The carpenter constructed another sledge of cask staves, the other having proved a failure. My morning exercise was building an arched doorway to our ice hut. I found it very comfortable dressing on deck (temp 4°) although the water froze on my face while washing the hands and indeed it is worth remarking that after being out an hour or two the beard becomes frosted and the mouchetach an icicle but they are still a great protection to the face.

Three of our men have scorbutic symptoms,[96] but as we are beginning to work at winter preparations I hope the constant occupation and increase of room will cure them.

Sunday September 29th 1850

Wind	force	Weather	Air
SE. S	1	bc. os.	13° 3°

Doubtless all is for the best, but my short sightedness cant see it. I pine for one more sabbath among those with whom I can spend it as I would and not feel so conscience smitten at the close of the day. Tis much easier [to] enjoy a sabbath in the way God intended it to be, when one is among those who are devoutly disposed and where one can hear the preached word. Oh I would that I could thank God for each of these seasons instead of having to mourn them as time misspent.

Apart from these things the season is so far advanced that one day resembles another. Every thing is white, the black spots on the hills (vertical or shelving sides of rocks) are gone and all wears the winter coat now so dreary to look upon. Griffin walked to within a few miles of the land and found most of the pools too weak to bear a sledge showing that the water is still quite warm. The two officers from the Advance joined with us in keeping watch putting us in four watches, one looking out for both vessels.

Ice Humbugging Us

Monday Septr 30th 1850

Lat	Wind	force	Weather	Air
	NW. W	2	os. bcm.	8° 1°

The Advance commenced breaking out her cargo and putting it on the ice and after the whole days work with part of our crew assisting no visible impression in her hold. Although the pile of coal and provisions on the ice looks like a cargo for her. Griffin is busy making preparations for camping out having just finished his fourth attempt at a sledge. I have been tinkering all the afternoon using a copper bolt for soldering iron, sealing wax for rosin, pursers scissors for shears, and old meat cans for tin and have made a spirit lamp with three tubes to fit in a perforated case on which to place cooking utensils; it boils 1 quart of water at 32° in 20 minutes. Witnessed the phenomenon of a parhelion—or rather two parhelia—this evening,[97] a mock sun was seen about 12° on each side of the true one and an arch of light (not perfect) extending from one image to the other. That's the first time I ever saw three suns at once. Pity that they cant make a little more heat.

Tuesday October 1st 1850

Wind	force	Weather	Air
SW	4–3	oms	13° 7°

Griffin started on an experimental trip with ten days provisions but the ice began to crack before he was out of signal distance. So his recall brought him back after having gone to within a mile of the shore.

The ice breaking around the Advance caused some apprehension for the stores on the ice and every man and officer was set to work to bundle them in again which was done in one hour, but the coal took several more, only losing about a ton of it, which was in a small pile just where the ice chose to crack. This again disappoints our hopes of getting into winter quarters without much suffering.

Foxes Stove

Wednesday October 2nd 1850

Wind	force	Weather	Air
SW NE	4 1	oms. bcm.	14° 3°

No excitement to-day except a very hungry grey fox which four of us have shot at, each one at different times, without hurting him and supposing it to be a fairy, have set a trap to catch him alive if possible. The Advance working dilligently at her housing. The ice closing and squeezing with a roar like an approaching tornado. It is galling to see the season advancing so rapidly while we lie idle, afraid to commence winter preparations, or to start the party which the commo seems to think it necessary to send to communicate with the English vessels. Our cabins are nice and wet nowadays from the condensation which cant be remedied.

Thursday October 3rd 1850

Wind	force	Weather	Air
North	1–0	bcm. os. f	+8° -8°

Griffin killed two foxes from the vessels deck this morning; one was snow white and very beautiful, the other a light grey very soft fur but ugly colour.

All sorts of traps snares & spring guns were set out for their benefit if any of them visit us to-night. They are very tame both of Griffins victims having been within twenty feet of the muzzle. We borrowed a few pieces of stove pipe from the Advance and put up our stove to dry the cabin which it does pretty well, but makes an intolerable heat. It felt so strange to have dry feet and a dry deck to stand upon when undressing. I am afraid I shall be spoiled with such luxury.

The floe in which we are imbedded has been in motion all day and wont give the young ice time to freeze hard enough to confine it.

Comforts

Friday October 4th 1850

Wind	force	Weather	Air
North	1	bcm	-11° +6°

This day is just an hour and a half old, it being my midwatch, but I must commence the remarks because I have already experienced the most delightful sensation that I anticipate during its progress, that of finding my boots dry upon turning out, moreover I have been sitting at the table since midnight without getting a single drop of water on my head or book. Truly we cant appreciate comfort until it is contrasted with its reverse. Still it did not occur to me last night that this was a comfortless place although every thing was damp from the constant dripping and after sitting an hour it was necessary to take some exercise to thaw out the joints.

Not a fox was caught, the bait was taken from the muzzle of a spring gun by one of the Reynard family showing that even in these regions they are cautious about entering traps. A gun is added to the other traps for to-night. Dined aboard the Advance and found the fox excellent eating, thought it was seal until after dinner several of us confessed that we would not have tasted it knowingly, some thought it preserved meat. The thermometer was quite low this morning and -3° at meridian but the change was hardly sensible. I dressed on deck as comfortably as usual with the Therm at -10°. Several seal were seen in the water near us and Dr Kane says that he killed two of them but they sank. It is strange and annoying to us to see so much open water around us which was scarcely crusted over this calm morning, as it tells of lots of warm water somewhere which by keeping our floe in motion and constant apprehension of a rupture may prevent us from preparing for winter at all. Just to think that all those Englishmen who without any fire or a harbour would be more comfortable than we could be under any circumstances are all safe in winter quarters within a hundred miles.

Drift Southward

Saturday October 5th 1850

Wind	force	Weather	Air
North	4 to 8	om. bm.	+4° 0°

First thing in the morning four geese flew by us bound Southward and gave me a violent attack of home sickness because perhaps in six weeks they will be sitting on some knoll in Mr. Carters wheat field watching for persons whom I'd give worlds to see. Two parhelia were visible during the forenoon. We perceive by the land that we are drifting Southward.

Sunday Oct. 6th 1850

Wind	force	Weather	Air
North	6 to 10	om	7° 2°

Quite a gale all day and the fine snow drift penetrating the most minute crevice, blinding the eye, and darkning every prospect make this a rather unpleasant day to be out. So I reduced my exercise to running a mile. Lovell caught a fox in his dead fall. Our floe is all adrift and will carry us southward at a big lick.

Monday Oct. 7th 1850

Wind	force	Weather	Air
North	6	bm. b.	9° 5°

We find ourselves close in with the Land just North of Barlows inlet surrounded with heavy hummock ice much to our chagrin, for since the season for getting home is passed we had hoped that we might remain in our position far up this channel which would have enabled our spring parties to go a hundred miles farther North than the English could have reached and moreover if we get out into Lancaster sound we shall have no rest this winter spending it under Summer arrangements.

Off Barlow Inlet

Tuesday Oct. 8th 1850

Wind	force	Weather	Air
NNW	5 to 2	b. bc.	10° 6°

Here we are off Barlows Inlet (and not fetched up yet) as Jack would have it. Capes Hothany, Spencer and Beechey Island all being in sight makes us feel at home again taking away even the pleasure of looking on undiscovered land. The wind has uncovered much of the land and driven the snow in drifts wherever it could find an obstacle costing us many a boot full as it is difficult to calculate where the drift is knee deep on the rugged surface of our floe; which by the way, might rejoice with the author of a certain song at being afloat. Lovell caught a fox in his gum[98] and is trying to tame it.

Strange it should continue warm so long.

Wednesday Oct 9th 1850

Wind	force	Weather	Air
North	3 to 4	om.	17° 8°

Drifted first a few miles in a NE direction and then returned to the southerly drift about the same distance so that we are just abreast of Barlow inlet only two miles distant; but firmly imbedded in the ice and the constant motion of the floes and lanes render it unsafe to send a party off of our floe. The third time that we have been frustrated in the very act of sending a party ashore to make a cache of provisions which would be so useful to the surveyors of this channel in the spring or at least to leave some notice of our having failed in the attempt to reach home where the English think we are gone, but all is for the best. Had no fire to-day and kept part of the hatch open all the forenoon to be comfortable.

Lancaster Sound

Thursday Oct 10th 1850

Wind	force	Weather	Air
North to WNW	2 to 6	om. s.	13° 6°

Well here we are in Lancaster sound again having passed Cape Hothany by 2 P.M. and drifting to S. E. quite finely, have raised Beechey Island and Cape Riley wonderfully; in fact we are one third of the way accross the channel.

Once caught in Lancaster sound and we will not attempt to prepare as is usually done for winter by vessels spending them in this country. But surely if the ice is not going to destroy us it is going to hold us as the quaker did his friend. The acid acetic which was stowed in the after cabin lockers in glass jars of half a gallon each was found frozen or rather commencing to freeze but not injured as one part of the frozen makes strong vineager mixed with seven parts of water.

Read Fernande in the original and was delighted with it being so much more chaste than I expected to find it and rather exposing the abyss into which woman falls when she stoops to folly, than excusing or paliating it as Bulwer often does.[99]

					Friday Oct 11th 1850
Lat *	Long cr	Wind	force	Weather	Air
74°44'N	92°45'W	Southd	3	bcm	6° 2°

The change of wind has driven us first into the middle of the channel and is now sending us up it again nearing the eastern shore; about the same route by which we went up before. This is all pleasant enough except that the constant and easy motion of the ice assures us of its ability to keep underway all winter. I took a cruise on the ice and having got on one of the old floes, found large pools of fresh water ice smooth enough to skate upon but as it was detached from our floe, and I got one leg into the drink in recrossing the crack I did not advise any one to go there.

Definition of Star Shooting

Star shooting or observing is a very cold and troubles[ome] sport, embittering the extremities of Arctic cruisers, especially on cold windy nights, sometimes resorted to by those unfortunate men used to navigate vessels of war for the purpose of finding their position in cases of emergency but more frequently like Arctic meteorogical observations to swell the pages of a narrative or as in our case for the amusement of old asses who sit at home in comfort wondering why we didnt make ten thousand other observations with which they might gull the people in their meteorogical tables and other scientific works on Arctic and other spots rarely visited by men and never without falsifying all their far fetched theories about winds, currents, tides, temperature &c.[100] About equal to our doctors who having by some means obtained twice as much skin clothing as any of us, that they may be enabled to go or stay

below whenever they please, criticize our logs, and dont hesitate to say that
they are useless, not correct because the hourly observations on temperatures, Barometer &c are not taken always at the minute appointed. Although
the person appointed to observe may at the same time be engaged in duty as
much more important to even their comfort and safety as finding Sir John
would be to giving old Miriam a perfect set of observations.

Saturday Oct 12th 1850

Lat Altair[101]	Long c Arcturus[102]	Wind	force	Weather	Air
74°54'N	92°53'W	South	6	om. bc.	12° 2°

No excitement except the escape of Lovell's fox which was almost tame but
being tied out gnawed the rope close to his collar and left.

Commenced a novel called A man made of money and find quantities of
excellent wit in it besides the moral which is good.[103]

Drift Near the West Coast

Sunday October 13th 1850

Wind	force	Weather	Air
South	2	o. os.	19° 14°

Didnt change our position at all. A party failed in an attempt to reach the land
which is about three miles off finding a lead between us and the shore which
would not bear. Lovell's fox was caught in the same trap which first caught
him.

Monday Oct 14th 1850

Wind	force	Weather	Air	Barom. max
S. N.	2.0.1	bcm. os. b.	16° 2°	30.79 in.

Quite a pleasant day. No attempt to reach the shore. Barometer rose so high
that we anticipate a gale judging from the past. Griffin's gum has a fox.

Tuesday Oct 15th 1850

Lat	Long	Wind	force	Weather	Air
74°59'N	92°48'W	North	1 to 3	b	2° 4°

Very fine day, sun though very weak shone pleasantly. Murdaugh got within
musket shot of the land but found an intervening lead. People think they see
a flag on the shore but Murdaugh couldnt find it. It was particularly cold

observing to-night and quite amusing to see the perfect coolness with which some of our scientific drones would remark from the depth of their furs that there and here was another star that we might get in half an hour taking pains not to expose their hand to point them out. All very fine Messrs big bugs Murdaugh & Carter will find you a cord of stars, only you come and get their altitudes after fixing the horizon and glasses in a nice breeze and at blow finger temperature.

Cant Land Commence Winter Arrangements

Wednesday October 16th 1850

Wind	force	Weather	Air
North	3 to 5	b.	3° -3°

Very pretty day. Took a very long walk on a very smooth piece of ice (a lead lately frozen). Shot a fox. The ships are drifting slowly southward. Barlows inlet being a few miles south of us and Cape Riley again in sight.

Thursday Oct 17th 1850

Wind	force	Weather	Air
NNE	4	b	6° -3°

Another bright day but the constant low temperature makes it cool and the fresh breeze penetrated a quantity of woolen clothes. Still drifting slowly southward. The Advance commenced to put her stores on the ice again and we hope with better success than before as no water can be seen anywhere and the crack which opened alongside of her before has ice two feet thick on it now.

Friday Oct 18th 1850

Wind	force	Weather	Air
NE	4. 1 6.	bc. b.c.	9° 2°

Walked as near as I could get to the shore a mile to Northward of Barlow inlet which from the ship seemed to be only two miles off but after walking four, we came to water about half a mile wide which seemed to extend to the land. Griffin's fox seemes untameable and makes unceasing and sagacious efforts to escape. He is a beautiful specimen of the Arctic Fox—pure white, fur very soft, and large black eyes with no stealthy or cunning look, but rather, a tranquil but determined air making him a beautiful animal. A fresh wind this afternoon and night gives us a prospect of another month under summer arrangements.

Much the Same

Saturday October 19th 1850

Wind	force	Weather	Air
Northd	3 to 1	bc. b.	8° 1°

Still drifting a little to the Southward and approaching the Western shore. We are now about four miles ENE of Barlow inlet. A party trying to reach the shore found water intervening. The Advance put up two stoves to-day having cleared the hold to the beams and will be ready for all hands in a week. We have had beautiful nights lately but somehow the big bugs didnt want observations, while Murdaugh and myself have no fancy for the amusement and usually wait till desired or ordered to indulge in it. Read Peer's & Parvenu's by Mrs Gore[104] and was much pleased. Wonder if such society as she describes is always to be found at Naples.

Sunday Oct 20st 1850

Sd. NNE.	4	bc.	6° 0°

Fine day rather fresh. Drifting slowly South. Off Barlow inlet dist 4 miles, water still intervening. Commenced Jame's Anxious Inquirer[105] and find a treasure, making explanations and exciting to study the bible in a way I have never done before. I advise readers of this little book to follow the advice in the introduction while reading it.

Monday Oct 21st 1850

NNE	4 to 0	b. bm. om.	2° -5°

Drifting a few miles to the Southwestward opening the cape beyond Cape Hothany and bringing Barlow inlet to Northward of us. Cant get ashore yet. I wasted my time to-day on a book called the Tartar Chief[106] which professes to give the character of the Tartars but is something of a humbug.

Tuesday October 22nd 1850

Wind	force	Weather	Air
Sd	1	m	4° -3°

A southerly wind bringing thick weather set us a few miles to Northward again. Nothing funny or interesting occurred except perhaps the astonishment of our fleet surgeon, the crack chess player of the expedition, at finding himself schollars mated.[107]

Spent the forenoon quite rationally reading Paleys Nat Theology[108] and Spanish but after dinner got hold of an annual and wasted all the afternoon on it.

Wednesday Oct 23rd 1850

North 2 oms 7° -5°

We have remained stationary to-day and done nothing worthy of note. The parhelia are so common that it is becoming snobbish to notice them, and stars not being in request have declined appearing, so that we cant remark more than the inhabitants of a prison on external things and our thoughts or emotions having been for several days unexpressed, on board the Rescue, had perhaps as well be dismissed without further notice.

Thursday Oct 24th 1850

North 5 to 3 om. s. 3° -4°

We are farther south now than at any time since our capture having drifted several miles in a Southeasterly direction. Every body is seized with a short hair mania and some are chopped as close as a padre. The commo & Murdaugh have cut their beard. I find mine a great comfort in these cold winds and cant spare it.

Time gets along faster now than when we were actively employed and I dont find the confinement irksome yet though I should dread a second winter without a new stock of books.

Leave the West Coast

Friday October 25th 1850

Wind	force	Weather	Air
NNW	2	bc	0° -14°

Drifting slowly to SE are now fairly in Lancaster Sound. An extensive sheet of water about two miles south of [us] stretching nearly accross the mouth of Wellington channel. Nothing new to day except lemon ices and Roman punch which are frozen with much less trouble than at home being simply exposed to the open air a few minutes.

Saturday Oct 26th 1850

North   I   om.   3° -6°
Still going South; are about equally distant from Capes Hothany and Riley. North Somerset is in sight. The water to Southward has closed into a narrow lead extending as far as the eye can reach toward the East & West. We are all longing for a SE wind as a Norwester would perhaps serve us hardly. The sun is getting very lazy, not getting up much before nine and consequently retiring shortly after three.

Sunday 27th 1850

Nd   2   bc   3° -12°
A lovely day and although the temperature is low not cold to the feelings.

A very large pool of water to Southward several miles wide and long as ever. We still go Southward. Can see the land as far as Cape Hurd. Six weeks ago we would have given anything to be in that pool and now we would give anything to be as far from it as we were then fearing that a few unfavourable circumstances may force us to give everything to the ice.

Monday October 28th 1850

Wind	force	Weather	Temp Air
Calm	o	b	-10° max -15° min

Another beautiful day. Still drifting South can see the coast of North Somerset from deck. The men were sent on board the Advance to sleep. No water in sight, the pool to Southward being frozen by last nights calm. Murdaugh & myself walked nearly to the middle of it when we found it breaking under our feet and had to run for it to a double layer we found that we could kick a hole through any part of the pool although it was four inches thick.

Tuesday 29th 1850

Lat ☽	Wind &c	Temp Air
74°36'50"	Calm o b. f.	-10° -17°

A light air from Southward brought a fog concealing the land so that we cant see whether we have drifted. Got a mer alt for Lat and found handling the sextant quite cooling. The sensation when a piece of metal at a very low temperature touches the face is very similar to that caused by a hot piece and the effect the same. Lovell let his fox go as he didnt thrive and was not half as tame as when he was first caught. A journeé manqué [lost day] for me. The Advance's galley was put below but upon starting the fire all hands were smoked out.

Winter Arrangement Move on Board

Wednesday Oct 30th 1850

Wind	force	Weather	Air
Nd	1	b. om.	-3° -14°

We have not altered our position to-day. Walked to the pool to Southward and found only a few seal holes. Saw a great many seal and very tame but had no gun.

All hands took up our quarters on board the Advance which vessel we find prepared for us as follows. The cargo was taken out down to the upper beams fore & aft and down to the lower beams, five feet forward and abaft the main hatch; Boards were then placed on the upper beams from the forecastle aft to the beam forward of m[ain] hatch and from the beam abaft the m. h. to the cabin bulkhead, both bulkheads being removed. The men have the forward and the officers the after part of the vessel; the galley occupies the space under the main hatch and the space abreast of it on each side screened off for kitchen and pantry. The Rescues officers have cots hung in the space between the cabin and galley which is very comfortable except that the space between decks there being less than four feet it is awkward to move about. There are two stoves one in the Fcastle and one in the cabin which together with the galley keep a high temperature below, although the deck is not yet housed over and one hatch is kept partly open. The Rescue is a deserted mansion, her deck filled with the most valuable of the Advance's stores which were on the ice. Our cabin stove was brought on board the Advance and put up in the caboose[109] which is used as a laundry. The galley funnel passes through a patent snow melter fixed in the main hatch which being filled from deck supplies water. So that if the ice remains fixed we are at last in winter quarters.

The Advance

Thursday Oct 31st 1850

Wind	force	Weather	Temp Air
North	1	bc. om.	-9° -19°

Getting gradually into the ways of the new ship and of course don't like it yet. The land not being visible during the day cant tell about drift.

Strange fatality which has kept us from communicating with the English squadron at Assistance harbour when we were so long within reach of them, and also strange that no record of our having failed to get home after leaving them under the impression that we are at home. The trip to Assistance harbour is now given up as unsafe and being a days journey from the land I dare say it will be impracticable to attempt reaching it.

A cloudy night saved Murdaugh and myself from a cold job for the Amusement of others.

Fragment of a dialogue

Com. "Why Capt Sabine[110] made observations all winter."

M. "Yes! and got pay & credit for it besides having assistants and a comfortable place with nothing else to do."

C. "Come Buck we've got to overhaul the sailors clothes & bedding before dinner. (Aside) pity that *at arms* was not added to our titles. I wonder if Parry & his second did nothing but play cards for their share of the credit."

G. "Im sure I should take great pleasure in taking observations but for my eyes."

C. (Aside) "Yes, starlight is killing to the eyes."

Friday November 1st

NNW 4 bcm. om. -8° -13°
Spent this day in our usual serious manner.

Beechey Island Again

Saturday Nov 2nd 1850

Wind	force	Weather	Temp Air
NW South	3. 0. 2	om. s. m.	-5° -16°

Find the ice breaking up very much between us and the Eastern coast which we are approaching rapidly being now only about five miles from Beechey Island. Saw a number of seal in the pools caused by the sluing of the floes as they grind against the land which however are frozen over very soon after they are opened shewing that the water is getting cold.

Sunday 3rd

ESE 5 bm. m* -11° -14°
This easterly wind is very refreshing as it brings relief to our fears of being broken out of our winter quarters which were great yesterday. It brings a fog so that we cant see its effect upon the pack. The last time that we saw the land

we were about three miles from Beechey Island. The vane on the galley funnel not turning when the wind shifted the ship was filled with gas from that
fire and the officer of the watch not being aware of its effect suffered us all to
sleep several hours in it so that we have been a sick party, all day suffering
with violent head aches and nausea. Lovell and myself were the only ones
that could sit up. It would have been amusing to a well person to see us when
called at 7 ½, each one remarking "what a headache." Some rushed into the
cold air and keeled over like stuck pigs until Jack Frost reminded them of their
nakedness. Others encountering a beam would fall before reaching the door.
All were up to dinner but still having aching heads. A few hours more of such
sleep and most of us would have given no more trouble to our friends. The
forecastle being screened off from the galley the men didn't suffer at all.

Hibernating Sunset

Monday November 4th 1850

Wind	Force	Weather	Temperature
SE	5. 2	m. s.	-5° -14°

The land which was visible for a few hours this morning shows us that we
have not drifted at all to the Northward but a little to the Eastward. The sun
has no altitude now but refraction showed him to-day.

Wintering is to me much the most comfortable part of the cruise so far
and to those who are so fortunate as to get into a harbour ought to be glad
when winter comes to release them from the constant labour of the working
season. Even we who drifting about with the pack are in constant apprehension of being left shipless have not had such easy times since we left home. A
party failed to reach the shore, finding water intervening and the floes in constant motion.

Tuesday 5th

South. SE   2. 6   bcm. o. s   -3° -9°

The drift scarcely perceptible. Cut a fire hole[111] in the ice alongside.

Wednesday 6th

SE   8   o. bcm.   -1° -4°

Quite a fresh gale and one that makes hummocks by wholesale and such as
corroborate Backs account of them.[112]

The ice is broken to within fifty yards of the Rescue. The sun was not visible at all to-day though it was clear enough at noon to have seen him.

Winter Quarters Off Beechey I[slan]d

Thursday November 7th 1850

Wind	Force	Weather	Temperature
ESE. NE	5. 2	bcm	0° -9°

The wind ceasing it becomes warmer though the Thermometer falls. Drifted a few miles NW.

Friday 8th

NNE, NW	4. 1	b. bc.	-4° -14°

Drifting Southward & Eastward quite rapidly. The ice about 150 yards to Eastward breaking up with a loud roar similar to the noise made by heavy machinery with occasional shrieks and other singular sounds. We are required to keep regular watch now and somebody of my size is the first sufferer.

Saturday 9th

NNW. ESE	1. 8	bcm	0° -18°

Blowing a gale with heavy snow drift making it very unpleasant on the ice, or as Parry would say "impossible for any one to exist many hours."

Sledges and tents are being made in case of a break up and we are making preparations for a sojourn on the ice in event of losing the little vessels.

The temperature rose to 0° soon after the commencement of the gale. Hoisted the boats up between fore and main rigging to prevent their being injured when the break up comes.

Ice Breaking Up Near Us

Sunday November 10th 1850

Wind	force	Weather	Temperature
ESE	9	om*	+10° +2°

The gale very steady and the temperature rising. Divine service was performed for the first time. A very large fox was caught in a gum.

Monday 11th

ESE   7 to 1   North 2 to 6   os. m.   +14° +4°

When the wind abated leaving the temperature at 14° the weather was oppressive to us while exercising and pleasant while still. The melting of the snow from the housing keeps the deck wet. The ice is broken all around us a crack passing under the Rescue fore and aft and listing her to Starb[oard].

We all keep regular watch now, being unwilling to get such rebukes as it seems a permission to come below during the watches leaves us liable to. A bear came alongside but left precipitately when he found them to be inhabited.

Tuesday 12th

North   8 to 4   bm.   +4° -19°

The commo told me that he did not intend to reprimand me the other day and that he was incapable &c. Sore head cured.

Wednesday 13th

South NNW   4   bcm   -10° -20°

Drifting slowly to Southward & Eastward.

Thursday 14th

Nd West   2   b. bm. s.   -11° -19°

A bear came within gunshot and was fired at on the run but declined stopping.

Beechey Island

Friday November 15th 1850

Wind	force	Weather	Temperature
Ed	2	om. b	-4° -11°

The bear paid us another flying visit. A beautiful night. Exercised the crew drawing the sledges which is a much heavier work than I had any idea of, carrying only about thirty days grub. There are three of them for the men and one being made for us.[113]

Saturday Nov 16th

Eastd   1   bc. om. s   -2° -15°

Commenced baking bread for the crew and buckwheats were introduced into the cabin.

Sunday 17th

Calm   b. bm   -4° -20°
A very fine clear day and night.

Monday 18th

Nd   1   b   -15° -27°
Considerable drift to Southeastward. Leopold Island is in sight. Murdaugh &
myself followed the track of a bear making a circuit of the vessels. Some of
the hummocks to Northward of us are tremendous.

Tuesday 19th

SE   5 to 9   b. bm   -6° -18°
Another specimen of these still quiet Arctic days blowing a young hurricane,
a very heavy snow drift covering every thing. Two faint paraselenae were visible during the morning watch. Forgot to put the lat and Long in yesterdays
remarks. But we are off Beechey Island.

Snow Buildings

Wednesday Nov 20th 1850

Wind	force	Weather	Temperature
Sd & Ed	9 to 3	om	0° -4°

Gale abated leaving lots of snow banks for travelers to fall into.

Thursday 21st

Nd   1   bcm. b   0° -14°
Caught a white fox. Cape Walker was in sight by refraction we think.

Friday 22nd

North   1   bc. o.   -2° -14°
[No entry.]

Saturday 23rd

Nd   2   bc. oms   0° -12°
Building a snow wall and out houses to our establishments. Large blocks of
snow are cut from the snow drifts with spades which are sufficiently strong to
build with, are easily shaped, and become very firm after exposure, needing

no cement, and when the building is made with a little care has a very pretty effect resembling white stone.

Sunday 24th

Nd & Wd   3   bcm   -6° -10°

The Log is marked drifting to the Eastward but as we drift about a great deal without materially changing our position the small changes I dont notice.

Monday 25th

Eastd   1 to 5   om*   -5° -11°
[No entry.]

Ice Breaking Again Aurora Borealis

Tuesday November 26th 1850

Wind	Force	Weather	Temperature
SE Sd	5 to 0	bcm	-6° -17°

[No entry.]

Wednesday 27th

South Wd   1   om   -6° -11°
[No entry.]

Thursday 28th

Nd & Wd   1   bm. om   -6° -16°

A great deal of the fog which indicates water is seen to the Eastward.

Friday 29th

WNW   3   om. s   -1° -5°

The ice is considerably disturbed by even this light breeze from NW being a good deal broken and ground at the edges of the floe. Lovells 21st anniversary.

Saturday 30th

Wd   1 to 4   0. om   -2° -19°

The hour of dim twilight which we have at noon shows us water all around us, and from the port beam around by the stern to the starb[oar]d beam the crack is within 300 yds.

Sunday December 1st

WNW   4   o. bcm. b   -21° -34°

Are quite near the land to-day, but the mist is so thick that we cant distinguish what land it is though all think that we are off Gascoigne inlet. A very pretty Aurora Borealis was visible for a couple of hours of the first watch in the form of a belt extending from one horizon to the other through the zenith in a NW & SE direction.

Gave very little light although very pretty to look at.

Pretty Cold   Anticipate a Crack

Monday December 2nd 1850

Wind	force	Weather	Temperature
WNW	3 to 5	bcm. om	-24° -33°

This temperature is quite exhilarating and I daresay that even an Esquimaux would call it bracing. But nothing checks the Easterly drift which is daily carrying us from the contemplated field of action and to the anticipated scene of danger. All of us are preparing for a run, collecting such articles as would be necessary for a sojourn on the ice.

The commo gave me a very fine skin jumper worth a bale of pea jackets.

Tuesday 3rd

WNW   5 to 2   bcm   -22° -25°

Our floe is breaking more and more each day. And to-day we are thrown into a state of excitement by the ice breaking within thirty yards of our bows and opening into a crack a hundred yards wide and extending an indefinite distance North and South, perhaps accross the sound to the southward as it appears to go to the land North of us.

We have drifted to the enterance of Rigby bay and are still going Eastward.

All the provisions &c were brought aboard from the sledges and the latter made fast to the channels for fear a crack may open between us and the sledge houses.

We take all of our valuables from the Rescue as it is resolved to desert her if she is seperated, the want of stoves rending it useless for any one to attempt to stay by her.

Fitted out one of her boats to take when she goes & all of us are fitting ourselves with knapsacks and bells preparatory to a sojourn on the ice. I however in hopes that we may not have to go until I get well of a lame foot and a very bad cold for which last I have just had my throat swabed out with nitrate of silver in a most suffocating manner.

Wednesday December 4th 1850

Wind	Force	Weather	Temperature
West	2	bcm	-15° -23°

Still drifting Eastward. Leopold Island is in sight and bearing South.

Thursday 5th

Sd & Wd	5	bcm	-10° -18°

Great excitement this morning—the ice all around us breaking up, a crack passing under us fore and aft, the ship righted. The crack passed between us and the Rescue. Made fast to the largest piece and put a quantity of stores upon it. Leopold is a little to the Westward of South and we are nearer to it. Still going. Toward evening the opening of the 3rd inst closing and piling up hummocks making a great variety of unearthly noises.

Friday 6th 1850

Eastd	3	bm	-13° -19°

The crack opened so as to let us float again and rendering our position any thing but pleasing—by midnight it was six feet wide. We are all fixing up in earnest for an icy home. A sleigh was finished for the officers to draw and numerous other preparations are being made to heave out necessaries in case she wont bear the pressure when the crack closes.

Hove Up by the Ice

Saturday December 7th 1850

Wind	Force	Weather	Temperature
E to NE	1 to 6	bm	-12° -17°

The crack in which we are all afloat continued opening until it was thirty feet wide and after remaining so a few hours the floes commenced sluing and approaching each other so as to seperate us from the Rescue and our out houses and at last coming together at 2 P.M. after squeezing us so as to endanger her [the Advance's] existance a point off the starboard floe yielding a little was cracked about twenty yards off and a projecting corner passing under her quarter raised her a few feet and the pressure continuing her stern was raised almost out of water, her bow proportionally buried, and the vessel listed several streaks to starb[oard]. The creaking of timbers, grinding of the ice and uneasy trembling and wavering of the vessel were quite exciting though as we could do nothing for her 'twas no use making a fuss so we just passed our goods and chattels on deck, removed the provisions farther from the edge of the floe, and stand ready for what may come. I wish I was to home now.

Sunday 8th 1850

NE   7 to 4   bm. b   -11° -14°

No very annoying movement in the ice. The floes sluing about break up the young ice formed in the openings with much noise and some soft notes resembling an Aeolian harp.[114] Some of this ice piling up under the bows endangered the head gear and had to be cleared away. The men wore their knapsacks to muster and showed considerable judgment in their selection of necessaries.

Rescue Nipped

Monday December 9th 1850

Wind	Force	Weather	Temperature
Nd Ed	1	b	-11° -20°

The ice remained pretty quiet about us but the poor little Rescue got a very awkward nip and has the ice around her completely broken up so that we have to cross a ridge of hummocks to approach her from any quarter. Still drifting Eastward or rather recommenced our drift for the fresh wind of yesterday had checked it for the time.

Tuesday 10th

Nd   1 to 5   bm   -15° -25°

The ice let us rest to-day. Still going Eastward. Are off Cape Herschell or rather about half way between it and Cape Hurd. What would we not have given to be here the 15th of September.

Wednesday 11th 1850

North to WNW   6   bm   -16° -22°

This wind is sending us Eastward at a big lick. Passed Cape Fellfoot.[115]

The timbers keep up a great cracking owing to so much of the vessel being exposed to the air. We also find it much more difficult to keep up a comfortable temperature below from the same cause.

A faint Aurora was visible for an hour of the morning watch but I have not yet seen as bright an aurora in the Arctics as I have seen at home.

Knapsacks, Tents, Sleighs
Slew a Bear

Thursday December 12th 1850

Wind	Force	Weather	Temperature
WNW	7 to 3	bm	-9° -17°

Off Hobhouse inlet to-day and still going out. Strange how warm it continues. No former cruisers record such high temperatures. Banked up snow about the vessel to keep her warm. A party slept in a tent last night by way of experiment and report having been comfortable all night but I observe that they took long naps to-day. Kept my watch with my knapsack on and hope it may get home unused.

Friday 13th 1850

Variable	2	bcm. om.	-7° -11°

Cant distinguish the headlands today. The officers tried their sleigh. I was a wheel horse[116] and find that the cure billet as half the weight of the sleigh had to be lifted over a bank or hummock every five minutes while the spirited leaders as soon as the strain is taken off their brickholds dart ahead careless of the shins and fingers of the wheel horses; however as the other wheel lost the same quantity of bark that I did I dont growl but in future will vote for having the strongest in that place and of course all will strive to obtain it.

A very large bear made an attack upon our lard kegs in my watch to-night and I let him have the right barrell of my gun which caused him to fall but perhaps only with surprize as he was up and off before I could recap the left one which lost its cap in cocking. Griffin drew a bead on him with his unerring rifle but alas it snapped. Lovell's trap caught a fox. I'm going to see after that bear tomorrow.

Lat 74°20'N   Long 86°26'W

Saturday December 15th [14th] 1850

Wind	Force	Weather	Temperature
WSW	2	bcm	-3° -10°

The ice around is all hard and firm again but as the next spring tide will probably bring more break up it is scarcely worth while to build more houses. Still drifting slowly eastward. Cape supposed to be Crauford in sight.

Followed the track of the bear and found him dead about two hundred yards off quite a large male 8 ft 4 in long. not very fat. The ball entered the loins.

Sunday 15th 1850

NW	5. 2	bc. b	+2° -10°

Departed this life quietly the tame fox. Got a mer alt of Procyon[117] giving lat 74°20'N.

Monday 16th

West	4	b. cm. bm.	-4° -16°

Lat 74°20'N   Long 86°26'W

Had to bail the water from the forecastle, the ship being so much by the head that the water wont run to the well. We have most beautiful moonlight now giving more light than the midday twilight and lasting all day.

Tuesday 17th

Wd Sd	4 to 0	bc, om	-8° -16°

Exercised Officers and crew at the sledges going over some high and rough hummocks. Two paraselenae were visible a short time.

The Middle of This Long Night

Wednesday December 18th 1850

Wind	Force	Weather	Temperature
East	1	bcm	-7° -16°

Off Powells inlet. Westerly winds drive us out and Easterly ones dont stop us. All good, get home sooner.

Thursday 19th 1850

SE W	2	bcm	-10° -18°

Got alts of Procyon and Arcturus giving Lat 74°20'N Long 85°11'W.

Friday 20th

Westd 7 b. cm -9° -18°

A very brilliant parasalena. A man had his ears and wrists frostbitten.

Saturday 21st

Westd 6 to o bm. b -14° -21°

The ice again opening near us. Can read the finest print at noon by turning the book to the Southward. Thanks for our safe arrival to midnight.[118]

Sunday 22nd

SW 3 bcm -5° -20°

A man walking a short distance from the vessel frightened a bear by firing at him, both man and bear being in pursuit of a seal. The bear thinking that he had as much right to the seal as the man wouldnt give up the chase until he was fired at when doubtless being shocked at the impoliteness of his fellow hunter left in disgust.

Christmas

Monday December 23rd 1850

Wind	Force	Weather	Temperature
Calm	o	bcm	-2° -12°

Had to bail the water from under the floor of the forecastle. The mist has obscured the land for several days but when it rises a little we can see a high ridge to the Eastward which we suppose to be Cape Warrender.

Tuesday 24th 1850

Calm bcm -4° -8°

[No entry.]

Christmas day

Ed Wd 1. 2 bm cm -6° -15°

Quite a merry Christmas. Saint Nicholas visited and left us many tokens of remembrance in the shape of toys &c. I received a jackknife from my messmates. During the forenoon prize races between some of the men, then all of them ran together and last by all the officers except myself. A pretty fair dinner at which Grinnell and Miss Grinnell were toasted the former with enthusiasm, the latter with feeling (Parceque, élle etait [Because, she was] the fair donor of the cake). In the afternoon rockets, bluelights, and transparences. And in the evening Theatricals, Patriotic and sentimental songs from the stage ending at 10 P.M. with a dance (the hornpipe) to the Jews harp. Fit commemoration of the birth of a Saviour. It being my watch the forenoon and evening I was fortunate enough to be exempted without censure from participating in the race or having to clap at the exquisite performances on the Stage the quarterdeck in the former and the cabin in the latter instance requiring my attention.

Thursday December 26th 1850

Wind	Force	Weather	Temperature
West	1 to 6	bm	-7° -16°

Several cases of unwell to-day. Most of whom attribute the feeling to the race as of course a Christmas pie washed down with four kinds of wine into a reservoir of brandy and water couldnt hurt any body.

Friday 27th

Wd Sd 4. 1 bcm -7° -20°

Very high land in sight a little to the Eastward supposed to be Cape Warrender.

Lincoln (BM) of the Rescue is very ill and thinks he is about to die. Poor old man. I hope the wisdom of our medical Dept. wont frighten him off.

Saturday 28th

WSW 1 bm -14° -18°

Rather sombre day as most of the days are now for we are getting shockingly weary of our confinement. There were a number of very pretty auroras visible to-day but like all that I have seen up here only pretty giving about as much light as a lunar rainbow but passing near the zenith.[119]

Sunday 29th

WSW 3 cm. om. -9° -15°

I fear that my Sabbaths are more lost to me than they have ever been. I try to read and think with small success in this Bedlam of ours.

Off Cape Warrender

Monday December 30th 1850

Lat obs	Long ch.	Wind	Force	Weather	Temperature
74°18'N	82°15'W	Wd	2	bm	-17° -26°

The ice alongside which was water on the 5th inst is now twenty six inches thick only. We are fast getting into Baffin Bay, the effect of which will be something to interest us from day to day for watching the wane of the tedious winter is dull pastime. Poor old Lincoln is in a most unpleasant state actually frightened to Death's door. Though I must yield to the superior judgment of our sapient M. D., a small share of common sense tells me that the treatment which I have seen in this case is such as to frighten a simple mind to die of a pin scratch.

Tuesday 31st

Westd 2 bm -22° -29°

Last of an eventful year. I hail your birth and hope I may have something good to record at the close of your life. Cape Warrender is to the Westward of us so that now we are in Baffins Bay to all intents and purposes, and having passed that cape feel ourselves quite safe for a least a month, as we can hardly drift to any danger in less time. But alas this ice is more fickle than woman and no trust ought to be put in it. Cape Warrender bore NW by N, Cape Osborne NE½N (TM) at 12 M.

New Years Day in Lancaster Sound

Wednesday January 1st 1851

Westd 1 bm -22° -31°

Happy New Years to all who see this and a sigh for the old one.

Not so grand a festival as the Xmass but quite as pleasant. A sleigh scrub race for a purse of blue flan[nel] shirts, one to each horse of the winning sleigh. A good dinner for all hands. But the grand feature was "a greeting from home" in the shape of a cake presented to the Rescue by Miss Grinnell the prettiest I ever saw. No perceptible drift to-day, but something very like land to the Southward.

Thursday 2nd 1851

Westd 3 b. bm -24° -29°

A cold day. The men building a snow house had to be called in being in danger of frost bites.

Friday 3rd

Calm o bm -21° -30°

A beautiful day quite light and being perfectly calm, very mild. Saw the land to Southward very distinctly although Cunningham hills were nearly obscured. A water blink to the Eastward. Cape Warrender bore NW by W½W Cape Castlereigh (S Coast) South (TM).

Saturday 4th

West 3 bm, om -16° -25°

Drifted very little to the Eastward. Cape Warrender bears WNW, Cape Osborne N by W.

Mouth of Lancaster Sound

Sunday January 5th 1851

Wind	Force	Weather	Temperature
SW. NE. Wd	2. 4. 2	om. s.	+5° -16°

About noon the wind shifted to NE and blew quite a little breeze for eight hours, bringing a thick mist. The thermometer rising from -8° to +4° immediately after the change of wind, indicating water to the Eastward. At 8 P.M. the wind changed to West the thermometer commenced to fall and the mist changed into snow.

Rather a sombre day. Sabbath a la Bedlam.

Monday 6th

West 2 om. s. +4° -5°

Snowy day. A white fox was shot within a few yards of the vessel.

Tuesday 7th

West 3. 4 os. cm. b -7° -20°

Got some snow for specimen to carry home, also some sea water from 144 fms below the surface, found that the line was inclined to NW.

Wednesday 8th

WSW   1   bm   -10° -28°

Anniversary of the battle of N Orleans celebrated. Theatricals in the evening. Cape Warrender bore W by N¼N. Castlereagh SW. Cape Liverpool S by E½E.

Thursday 9th

West   2   bcm. b   -8° -19°

The moon commences to give a fine light and by the time that it disappears we will have quite a fine twilight for four hours about noon.

Rupture in the Ice

Friday January 10th 1850 [*sic*]

Wind	Force	Weather	Temperature
Westd	4	bm. bc	-15° -19°

Drifted Eastward a little.

Saturday 11th

Westd   3 to 6   bm. cm   -4° -17°

The ice commencing to break, a crack commencing no where passes within a few feet of the port quarter between us and the Rescue opened and froze over quietly. In about an hour a motion was perceived in the floes ours apparently drifting to Southwestward and continued for several hours grinding and breaking off the projecting points of each other. By midnight the Rescue had seperated from us about 400 yards. The provisions which were on the ice being on the opposite of the crack went with the Rescue. There was a fresh wind all the afternoon but I think that this rupture is caused by the Southerly current known to flow on the West coast of Baffins Bay.

Sunday 12th

West   4   bcm. cm   -5° -10°

Drifting slowly Southward & Westward. The ice remaining quiet most of the day occasionally closing and crushing up the young ice or opening and slueing so as to warn us of its disposition and power to do us harm.

Repassing the Enterance to Lancaster Sound

Monday January 13th 1851

Wind	Force	Weather	Temperature
West	8 to 6	bm. om	-6° -24°

We were all turned out at two A.M. by crushing, roaring, and screaming of the ice which is broken all around us and all the young ice being broken, the edges of the floes coming together made great hummocks and put our vessel in jeopardy. This disturbance continued at intervals until 5. All hands expecting some grand catastrophe.

Having about three hours of bright twilight at noon we have an opportunity of seeing the extent of the nights work and it passes my power of description. The immense masses of thick heavy ice thrown up ten or fifteen feet high and crushed into every shape. The hill and dale where yesterday was a level plain is very remarkable.

The stores on the ice were many of them lost and all buried in the hummocks so as to be extricated with much labour. The Rescue was again unfortunate; the crack passing across her bow, when the hummocks were formed the ridge rose under her forefoot carrying away the cutwater and bowsprit gammoning raising the bowsprit and opening the old fracture very much. A heavy piece of ice on a hummock carried away a part of her bulwarks forward. E[m]ployed the crew saving as many of the stores as could be found and clearing away the ice from under the Rescues bows.

Five cases of slight frost bite.

Cape Hay bore   SW by W

  "   Walter Bathurst South

Rescue Injured by the Ice

Baffin Bay   Tuesday January 14th 1851

Wind	Force	Weather	Temperature
WNW	6 to 4	bcm b	-24° -26°

The openings are all frozen so as to bear a dozen times a mans weight, but there is still an occasional movement. The crack passing fore and aft the vessel opened about a foot leaving the starboard side resting on, and fast to the ice while the port side seems to be a foot from the ice down to the keel, still she will not right nor settle aft; so that with all the creaking and trembling she is still in the old position making our walk an up and down hill, and sleeping like on the roof of a Dutch house. The damage done to the Rescue is more apparent to-day as the clearing away the ice exposes it to view. The bowsprit is broken entirely off and all the woodwork in to the stem piece is wrenched off leaving us a poor place to step a new bowsprit if we can spare beams enough to make it. This is bitter cold weather the constant fresh wind at this temperature making it imprudent to expose the face to the wind for many minutes together. I saved my nose from a sore by rubbing with snow after walking only a few hundred yards to windwards. I didnt feel the pain until after coming in out of the wind when it was very acute, and not relieved until after several minutes rubbing with snow. The foxes still come around us every night though we must be twenty miles from land. The land shows a SE drift but the mist obscured it so as to prevent taking bearings. Mean temperature -24.83

Ice Still Unquiet
Eclipse of the Moon

Wednesday January 15th 1851

Wind	Force	Weather	Temperature
WNW	4	bcm	-16° -25°

Heard the ice breaking up at a distance to the Westward but felt no shock. The water casks being too large to lumber the decks and being in constant danger on the ice were shaken up,[120] and will give some trouble to be recoopered in the Summer. Can't tell about the drift.

Thursday 16th 1851

WNW. NW   3   bcm. b   -14° -24°

Caught a white fox very fine specimen. The foxes are eaten as a great delicacy but I dont like them. The bear which I shot last is now very fine eating having none of the taste so objectionable in the others.

Friday 17th

West NE   1   b   -25° -29°

A sudden and single start in the vessel was felt by all awake at 3 A.M. and a noise in the ice for a few minutes after when all became quiet, leaving no mark in the ice and not altering the ships position.

All of the night was exceedingly bright, the Southern land being visible. A partial eclipse of the moon, was visible for about four hours about noon. The moon being full and near the South meridian. This being a calm day the men worked out and got a good many more of the stores which were drifted off or buried in the ice on the 13th inst. A crack opened about 500 yds to Southward.

Saturday Jany 18th 1851

Wind	Force	Weather	Temperature Air
Westd	2	b. bcm	-20° -29°

The ice was in motion again forming hummocks in the old crack and giving us some shocks. Saw recent tracks of a small bear about the Rescue. An attempt was made to blast a pile of ice under which a quantity of stores were buried but proved a failure.

Lat obs 73°47'N   Long cr. 75°03'W

Sunday 19th 1851

| WNW NW | 6 | bcm | -20° -21° |

Blowing quite a gale making it very cold. The ice still moving occasionally gave us several shocks.

Monday 20th

| NW W | 5 | bm | -17° -21° |

Another cold day. An opening a hundred yards to Eastward of the Rescue about seventy yards wide and extending very far East and West.

Tuesday 21st

| NNW | 5 | b. bm | -19° -22° |

The wind deserves much credit for this perseverance. A beautiful paraselena in the morning watch the circle about the moon being perfect and having a diameter of about 25°. The days are increasing in length and brilliancy very fast. We have at least Six hours of day bright enough to read by. But the fresh wind makes it almost impossible to walk out for any length of time.

Kites the amusement on the tapis.

All Still Again

Wednesday January 22nd 1850 [*sic*]

Wind	Force	Weather	Temperature
Westward	6	bm	-17° -21°

A moderate gale with heavy snow drift.

Thursday 23rd

West 7 to 2 b. cm -15° -21°

The wind moderated at last. Saw the land to Southward and Westward showing that we have drifted to SE considerably. Latitude by observation 73°11'N
being 36 miles to Southward of the Lat of the 18th inst or seven miles drift
daily.

Friday 24th

Sd & Ed 1. o bcm. m -19° -26°

Quite a pleasant day. Took a long walk and found it not cold at all. The SE
wind brings misty weather.

Saturday 25th

NE 2 bcm. os -6° -29°

Spring weather coming again, the low temperature which the calm left us
being raised by the Easterly wind.

My gun having been left on deck for a month I found it frosted about the
muzzle although enclosed in a cloth case within a leather one. The gun had
been placed near an orifice where the moisture from below came through
but I had no idea that the moisture which rises visibly could penetrate both
cases.

The Sun Rose

Sunday January 26th 1851

Lat *	Long chro	Wind	force	Weather	Temperature
73°09'N	72°02'W	NE. NNW	3	om. bm	-2° -15°

Made three degrees Easting since the 18th inst.

Monday 27th

NW   3 to 6   bcm. b   -9° -15°

The NW wind became quite a gale during the afternoon, drifting snow heavily. About one degree of refraction (a common thing here) would show us the sun if the weather were clear but it is singular that although the nights are clear as possible down to the very horizon, the days are cloudy and misty more so at noon than at any other time of the day. Saw some very pretty auroras to the Southward.

Tuesday 28th

WNW   4   bm. b   -9° -16°

A remarkable aurora near the horizon from South to SW. At Meridian about ⅔ of the Suns disc was visible from the topgallant yard. The sun being actually 70' below the horizon.

Wednesday 29th

72°54'N   71°16'W   WNW   1   bm   -16° -21°

The day commenced to dawn at a quarter fore six. The sun was visible for nearly two hours from the deck, only about ⅔ of its disc at meridian. The bearing of the sun at Noon gave 8¼ points variation.

All hands were assembled and gave three cheers. The sun was actually 54' below the horizon.

Stripped Rescues Bowsprit Saturday

Thursday January 30th 1851

Lat *	Long chro	Wind	Force	Weather	Temperature
72°49'N	70°59'W	NW	1	c. om	-6° -22°

Went with a party of men to strip the Rescues bowsprit, it being quite a difficult job from the stiffness of the ropes.

Had Theatrical performances in the evening from which having the mid watch I was excused.

Friday 31st

NW   3   oms   -1° -10°

Several inches of snow fell to-day. Quite a cooling job sending down the Rescues light yards and housing the topgallant mast.

The sun was not visible through the mist. Thermometer rose remarkably.

Saturday February 1st

NW Westd   3   om bm   -7° -16°

Scrub, scrub, thump, thump, scrape, scrape away. But very little comfort here upon a Saturday.

Sunday 2nd

Westd   3   bm   -16° -33°

A very brilliant aurora in the evening. A most singular ticking sound in the ice, caused perhaps by the fall in the temperature but being so universal and without apparent cause or effect as to appear like witchcraft.

Monday 3rd

Nd & Wd   1 to 4   bm. om   -22° -33°

[No entry.]

Mercury Frozen First Time

Tuesday February 4th 1851

Wind	Force	Weather	Temperature
WNW	3 to 5	bm. o. s	-12° -24°

The Rescues bowsprit was brought alongside or rather a part of it and the carpenters are commencing a new one to be made of spare spars.

Wednesday 5th

NW   2   bm   -13° -35°

Daylight is becoming very appreciable for although there is no warmth in the suns rays it is much more cheerful, so that we spend an hour or two at noon enjoying the light.

Thursday 6th

NW   1   bm   -32° -40°

Quite cold. Mercury froze when the thermometer was at -39°. The thermometers vary very much. Some of them having fallen as low as -45° but we use the one which was at -39° when mercury froze that being about the temperature at which it generally freezes. This the coldest day we have yet had but as it was a calm clear one, felt milder than many of the warmer ones have. However no one took off his coat to play foot ball as we have to do some days. The forge was put up on the ice to make some of the ironwork

for the Rescues bowsprit and the rapidity with which the iron cools off seems
to astonish and annoy the Armourer.

Friday 7th

Calm b. m -35° -40°
The ice formed in a hole cut yesterday was six inches thick formed in 24
hours.

Icebergs

Saturday February 8th 1851

Lat	Long	Wind	Force	Weather	Temperature
72°20'N		Eastd	1	bcm. om	-30° -37°

The ice froze only four and a quarter inches in the hole opened yesterday.

Sunday 9th

72°19'N 68°56'W Nw to SE 3 bm. b. -25° -36°
Saw the West coast quite distinctly and something very much like an iceberg
North of us, but it may have been a high hummock raised by refraction.

Monday 10th

SE 3 bm. om -18° -30°
A bitter cold day owing to the dampness in the atmosphere almost always
produced with a SE wind.

Tuesday 11th

Nd 4 om -17° -22°
[No entry.]

Wednesday 12th

Nd 3 c -17° -31°
Some of the sailors have been breaking open the Rescues hatch to get liquor
regardless of several dozen that have been served out this winter for the
indiscreet use of it.[121]

Thursday 13th

NW 1 bm -31° -37°
Saw some more ice bergs to Nd & Wd very distant appearing only by refraction.

Friday February 14th 1851

Lat obs*	Long chro	Wind	Force	Weather	Temperature
72°15'N	68°40'E	Nd & Wd. Ed	1	bc. m. b	-31° -38°

Tried for soundings with 244 fms, finding no bottom, the line showing an Easterly drift. The horizon was most singularly affected by refraction appearing like a high wall of snow surrounding us. More theatricals this evening, which occurring in my watch I had to attend and did feel for the poor ladies who with bare arms and thin dresses suffered somewhat from the lowness of the temperature.

Saturday 15th

East 1 bm. b -36° -41°

Saw the land to Southward & Westward much elevated by refraction.

Sunday 16th

ESE 1. 2 b. bc -31° -42°

The land again visible. Also three icebergs to Westward and one East of us. We have about eight hours of sun now and although the temperature is low still it feels warm under his rays. The thermometer placed against a dark board turned toward the sun rises ten or twelve degrees, but is very little altered when placed on a stick in the sun.

Monday 17th

ESE to West 1. 2 bcm -23° -35° -29.6°

[No entry.]

Tuesday 18th

WSW 1 b -34° -39° -37°

[No entry.]

Cold Theatre

Wednesday February 19th 1851

Lat *	Long cr	Wind	force	Weather	Temperature
		Westd 1		b. bcm	-25° -38° -33.1°

A parhelion having three mock suns was visible for a part of the forenoon. Carpenters fitting a mast to one of the boats and making alterations in her for a whale boat.

Thursday 20th 1850 [*sic*]

72°10'N 68°37'W Variable 1 b. c. m. -25° -40° -33.2°
[No entry.]

Friday 21st

Westd 2 bcm -36° -40° -37.8°
[No entry.]

Saturday 22nd

WSW 1 bm. b -37° -46° -41°
A fine pleasant day in spite of the low temperature which we enjoyed very much on the ice and in the evening assembled on deck to witness Theatricals quite chilling though the latter was the thermometer standing at 45° below zero during the performance.

Sunday 23rd

Nd & Ed 2 bm. om. s -28° -40°
The change of wind acts marvelously on the temperature.

Monday 24th

Nd 1. Ed 1. 4 bm. b. cm -22° -38°
[No entry.]

Tuesday 25th

East 3 bm. o. s -12° -26°
[No entry.]

Frost Bite High Barometer

Wednesday February 26th 1850 [*sic*]

Lat	Long	Wind	force	Weather	Temperature of air
		SSE	1	b. m.	-30° -37°

[No entry.]

Thursday 27th

Variable 1 b. m. -25° -40°
The sun raises the temperature to several degrees above zero in a place sheltered from the wind and exposed directly to his rays.

Robert Randolph Carter, born in 1825, was aged thirty-two when he sat for this portrait in Buenos Aires, Argentina, where he went in 1858 with the second U.S. La Plata Expedition. *Courtesy of the Colonial Williamsburg Foundation*

Robert Randolph Carter was forty when this photograph was taken in Leamington, England, just after the Civil War. Note the shiny top hat which Carter family oral tradition says Robert put away in a Shirley closet on his return home in 1868. (The present C. Hill Carter Jr. recalls seeing it there.) *Courtesy of the Colonial Williamsburg Foundation*

Lt. Edwin J. DeHaven (1819–65), from Philadelphia, commanded the American Arctic Fleet—the *Advance,* which he captained, and the *Rescue,* under second-in-command Samuel P. Griffin, of which Robert R. Carter was acting master. *From the U.S. Naval Institute* Proceedings, *where it appeared in 1928 courtesy of the late Rear Adm. Albert Gleaves, USN (Ret.)*

William H. Murdaugh, first officer of the *Advance,* was acting master and navigator, as was Carter aboard the *Rescue.* His family lived near Portsmouth, Virginia, and were lifelong friends of the Carters of Shirley Plantation. Nicknamed "Buck," like Carter he had served in the Mexican War, on the Arctic Expedition, on the La Plata Expedition, and during the Civil War with the Confederate Secret Service in Europe. *Courtesy of the Colonial Williamsburg Foundation*

Henry Grinnell, civilian sponsor of the U.S. Grinnell Expedition in 1850–51, was a partner in Grinnell, Minturn and Company, a leading mercantile company in New York City. To support the expedition in search of Sir John Franklin, he bore the entire expense of outfitting its ships and even provided the crews' link to home, forwarding newspapers that arrived in July 1851 to put them in touch with the world again. *Photo by Craig McDougal*

Louise Humphreys Carter (1832–1906), wife of the journal's author, Robert Randolph Carter, was the daughter of Mariette and Hector Humphreys. Dr. Humphreys served as a minister as well as president of St. John's College in Annapolis, Maryland, where Robert and Louise met while he was a student at the U.S. Naval Academy. *Courtesy of the Colonial Williamsburg Foundation*

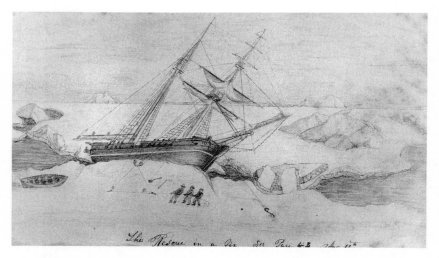

"The *Rescue* in a Fix." On 11 August 1850 Carter noted in his journal: "In the after-noon two floes closing on us, we were nipped and hove down six streaks. A large piece being forced under her bottom lifted her bows three feet." Then he picked up his pen and drew a picture of the scene, including three crewmen trying to warp the ship upright (page 51). *Courtesy of the Colonial Williamsburg Foundation*

"The *Rescue* on a Stiff Breeze." Carter's own caption for the scene describes it well. *Courtesy of the Colonial Williamsburg Foundation*

"The *Rescue* a la Mode Melon Seed." At Barlows Inlet in Wellington Channel on 7 September 1850, Carter's journal recounted: "About this time a large fragment of the floe to which we were fast broke off and both vessels drift rapidly accross the mouth of the harbour toward a berg grounded to leeward of us. The Advance goes clear but the poor little Rescue was caught again. Providentially in the vortex of an angle and was popped out like a melon seed with no damage" (page 70). *Courtesy of the Colonial Williamsburg Foundation*

"Esquimaux Carrying a Canoe to the Water." On 27 June 1850 the expedition was at Greenland and made port at Whalefish Island on which was located an Eskimo village. The next day Carter wrote about the Eskimos: "They have a great many dogs, a half starved wolfish looking set but perfectly inoffensive." His drawing gave a glimpse of them (page 32). *Courtesy of the Colonial Williamsburg Foundation*

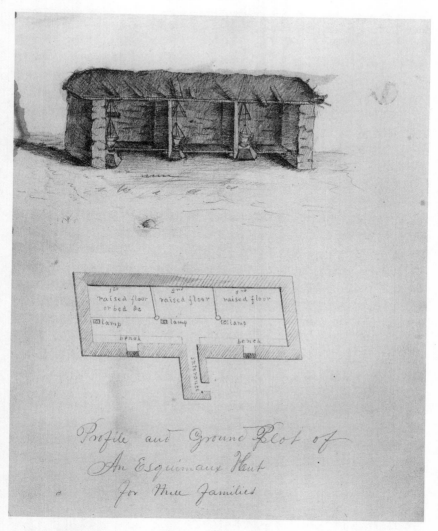

Profile and Ground Plot of
An Esquimaux Hut
for three families

"Profile and Ground Plot of an Esquimaux Hut for Three Families." In late June 1850, while they were in the Greenland Eskimo village on Whalefish Island, Carter was intrigued (and sometimes aghast) at the native Inuit buildings, clothes, and food. He carefully drew this profile of the layout of a typical hut, probably used in cold weather because he reported they slept in tents in the summer (page 32). *Courtesy of the Colonial Williamsburg Foundation*

Shirley Plantation, Virginia. Birthplace of Robert Randolph Carter, who kept this "private journal" on the U.S. Grinnell Expedition to the Arctic, it has been the home of the Hill/Carter family for ten generations. This view, photographed just over the James River on which Shirley is located, shows its original buildings. *Photo copyright by Dave Doody*

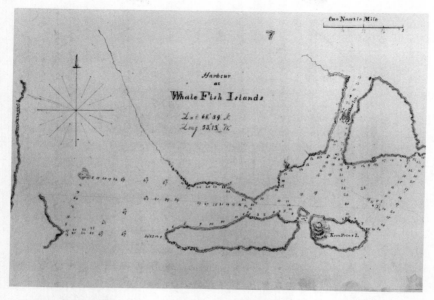

Carter's "Map of Whalefish Island Harbour." As they approached Greenland, acting master Carter discovered they had no map of Disco Bay, or of Whalefish Island harbor, where they should anchor and rendezvous with their flagship, *Advance*. Consequently, he anticipated their return by the same route, and drew this map so he could navigate into port without depending on the same good luck he had on 27 June 1850. Small figures within the harbor indicate the channel depth. *Courtesy of the Colonial Williamsburg Foundation*

Mansion at Shirley Plantation from the land side. The architecture of the mansion with its two-story porticos is almost identical on this land front as on the opposite side, facing the James River. The pine cone on the roof (sometimes called a pineapple) was the colonial symbol of hospitality. A handsome carved walnut staircase runs three stories above the central hall with no visible means of support. Still occupied by the Carter family, as it was when Robert R. Carter lived there, it contains original portraits of their earliest ancestors. *Photo copyright by Dave Doody*

[handwritten journal entry, dated Monday, August 19th 1850, with weather notations and a lengthy log entry in cursive]

A typical page from Carter's "Private Journal" is his entry for 19 August 1850, with its own headline on the first line, and below the date, weather notations which he explained on the journal's last page. His extremely legible handwriting, on pages the size of today's legal pad, was almost artistic, well suited for a naval officer who would keep official logs during his extensive career—first as a member of the U.S. Navy and afterward as an officer in the Confederate navy. *Courtesy of the Colonial Williamsburg Foundation*

Advance ashore. On Sunday, 25 August 1850, Carter reported that the *Advance* had disappeared and that when rounding Beechey Island, "I saw her high and dry on the beech at Cape Riley. Stood down and then off and on until this day ends. It seems that she had stood too far inside of the cape, been becalmed, and drifted ashore with the current near high tide" (page 58). *Courtesy of the Colonial Williamsburg Foundation*

From their original chart, this shows the route of the *Rescue* and *Advance* on their way north along the Greenland coast in late May to mid-August 1850. Sailing first up Davis Strait, the *Advance* preceded the *Rescue*, till on June 24, Carter saw the coast of Greenland and discovered they had no chart of Disco Bay, their first destination. His dead reckoning proved correct, and on the twenty-seventh they arrived at the Whalefish Islands and were reunited with the *Advance*. Here he explored the "Esquimaux" village which he described in detail. (He also made his own chart of Whalefish Island for use when they returned.) *Courtesy of the National Archives and Records Administration*

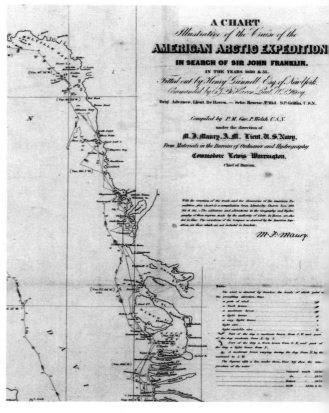

A CHART
Illustrative of the Cruise of the
AMERICAN ARCTIC EXPEDITION
IN SEARCH OF SIR JOHN FRANKLIN.
IN THE YEARS 1850 & 51.
Fitted out by Henry Grinnell, Esq. of New York.
Commanded by E. J. De Haven, Lieut. U. S. Navy.
Brig Advance. Lieut. De Haven. — Schr. Rescue. Æ Mid. S.P. Griffin, U.S.N.

Compiled by P. M. Geo. P. Welch, U.S.N.
under the direction of
M. J. Maury, A.M. Lieut. U. S. Navy.
From Materials in the Bureau of Ordnance and Hydrography
Commodore Lewis Warrington,
Chief of Bureau.

M. F. Maury

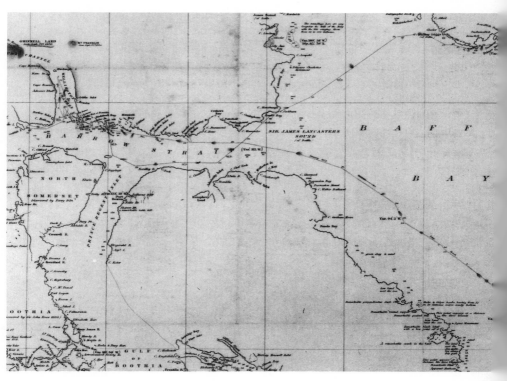

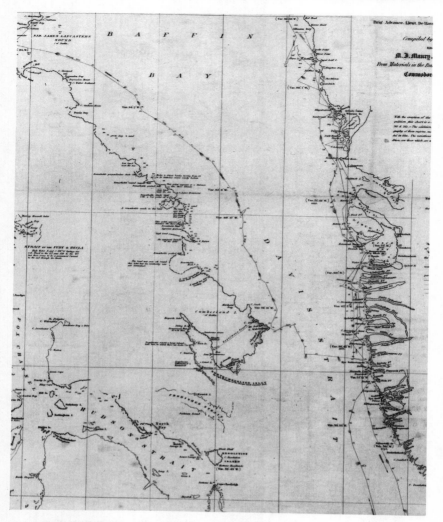

At last in Baffin Bay, they wended their ice-hampered way north and west. They crossed Melville Bay and met some of the British ships and officers also heading for the search in Lancaster Sound, including old Sir John Ross. At tiny Beechey Island, they found the first clues to Sir John Franklin's mysterious disappearance five years earlier, traces of his winter camp, and graves of three crew members. The cairn there told nothing of where he would sail next. *Courtesy of the National Archives and Records Administration*

Floating ice, in which they were beset, propelled the *Rescue* and *Advance* from Lancaster Sound, up and down Wellington Channel, and then east again to Baffin Bay and south from that point. Finding themselves near Greenland's Disco Island, they tried valiantly—in spite of an early winter—to sail up once more to Lancaster Sound in search of Franklin. Their hope futile, on 15 August 1851, Cdr. DeHaven headed south for home. *Courtesy of the National Archives and Records Administration*

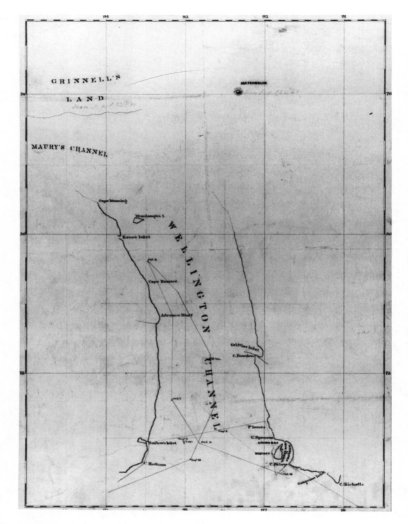

"De Haven Expedition at Wellington Channel, Canada, 1850–52" is this chart's title in the National Archives. It was probably filled in by Carter or Murdaugh, navigators of the *Rescue* or *Advance,* from 13 September to 15 October 1850, while they drifted in Wellington Channel. Their names for its islands or points of land were no doubt changed later by British navigators, as few remain on modern maps. Under a magnifying glass, the faint notation of "Sun., Sept. 22, 1850" can be read below "Grinnell's Land," the date DeHaven named it (it is now called Grinnell Peninsula). Darker dates appear along their route. On the western side of the channel, names read from north to south: Cape Manning, Murdaugh Island, Kanes Inlet, Cape Rescue, Advances Bluff, Barlow's Inlet, and Cape Hotham. On the eastern side of the channel, just above latitude 75 N, are Griffins Inlet and Cape Bowden, and below: Point Innes, Cape Spencer, Union Bay, Beechey Island (with its notation to the east, Winter Har[bor], Franklin) and along the border of Devon Island: Cape Riley and Gasgoigne Inlet. Cape Ricketts is even farther east. Names not associated with the Grinnell Expedition are those previously given to them. *Courtesy of the National Archives and Records Administration*

Friday 27th [28th]

North to NW   2. 5   bm. om   -14° -26°

This has been the coldest day to the feelings for a month. I got my nose frost bitten by being in a fresh gust of wind for five minutes so that I was some time restoring circulation and will have a sore nose for some days. I had been out for an hour exercising and gone below to mark the barometer, all comfortably enough, then going on deck again and finding a gust just commencing I ran out to the slide to take advantage of it but the drifting snow was so unpleasant that I returned immediately, upon reaching the vessel a man told me that my nose was frozen, and sure enough all of one side was as white and senseless as a sperm candle, and required a deal of rubbing with snow to recover its colour. The barometer stood at 31.09 for a short time.

Saturday March 1st 1851

(2☉) 71°55'N   Nd & Wd   2   om. bc. s.   -6° -15°

The mildest and most pleasant day for two months. The ice in the opening of Jany 13th (the last opening about us) was measured, being 3 ft 10 in. thick.

My proboscis being still painful received immediate relief from the application of sweet oil.

Taking our usual exercise found it more pleasant without our coats.

Thick Ice Astern of the Advance

Sunday March 2nd 1851

Lat	Long	Wind	Force	Weather	Temperature
		West	4	om. s	+5° -8°

Commences mildly but the wind freshening makes it less pleasant, a heavy snow fall and drifting fast.

Monday 3rd

SSE   5 to 3   bm. s.   +2° -20°

The wind drifting the snow makes an uncomfortable day and the new snow being so soft makes it almost impossible to walk so all hands were set to work at cutting through the ice astern of us and cutting it from about the Rescues sternpost; found the ice here 8 ft thick that is having cut through eight feet of solid ice the water rushed in and filled the hole but we could feel ice with a boat hook to the depth of eleven feet. The snow was cleaned off the slide but it was not patronized, the work being more novel.

Tuesday 4th

71°54'57"N   66°54'W   Sd   3   bm   -20° -40°

Cutting the ice from around the Rescues stern post to the depth of six feet found that it had been saved from being entirely split by two great pieces placed fore and aft as strengthening pieces a few feet below the upper gudgeon, below which we cant trace the split in the sternpost.

Wednesday 5th

Wd   2   bm   -29° -41°

[No entry.]

Thursday 6th

Sd   2   bm. b   -22° -41°

[No entry.]

Repair of Rescues Sternpost

Friday March 7th 1851

Lat ☉	Long	Wind	Force	Weather	Temperature
71°50'32"		North	1	b	-25° -41°

The sun has great influence on the temperatures now making the hour about noon the warmest and causing a rise in the temperature almost as soon as he appears even in places not exposed to his rays. The Rescues stern post has been fixed so as to appear quite strong and the gudgeon straitened and put on again so that abaft she looks like anything but a wreck.

Saturday 8th

Westd   1   bm. s.   -20° -44°

A bright aurora very near the Southern horizon.

Sunday 9th 1851

71°48'20"N   SE   2   bm. cm.   -24° -36°

[No entry.]

Monday 10th

Nd & Ed   2   bcm   -12° -27°

[No entry.]

Tuesday 11th

North 5 om. s. -7° -18°
[No entry.]

Wednesday 12th

71°41'27" NW 3 bcm. b. -17° -32°
I heard a roaring to the Southward during the mid watch very much like ice breaking up and there was a streak of mist in that direction during the morning but the snow is so soft and deep concealing the fissures in the ice that walking is unpleasant.

First Snow Melting

Thursday March 13th 1851

Lat ☉	Long ch	Wind	force	Weather	Temperature
71°37'20"		NW	3	bcm	-22° -32°

[No entry.]

Friday 14th

NNW 5 bcm -9° -26°
[No entry.]

Saturday 15th 1850 [*sic*]

71°28'N 65°44'W NW 4 bcm. b. -9° -16°
The snow exposed to the sun on a black surface melted at eleven o'clock A.M. This was remarked on the 12th inst but under rather more favourable circumstances the position being entirely sheltered from the sun.

Sunday 16th

71°26'N NW 3 bc. cm. s. -1° -15°
A very mild morning, chilly night.

Monday 17th

71°20'N WNW 4 oms. bcm -9° -14°
Tried for soundings with 310 fms line finding no bottom. This being St. Patrick's day, was celebrated with theatricals, orations, &c by our regular company of actors.

Tuesday 18th

WNW   4   bm   -9° -22°

The snow drifting heavily confines us to the ship for comfort, and the slide being covered there can be no skating so this has been a close day.

Ice Opening Near Us. Dovekies

Wednesday March 19th 1851

Lat ☉   Long chr   Wind   force   Weather   Temperature
71°09'N   Wd 1. SE   1 to 8 b. cm   -5° -26°

The morning commenced beautifully and softly but had March written on its face in its very softness, as the day goes out with what appears to be the beginning of the equinoctial South Easter. Almost every body took long walks and we find that we are almost surrounded by cracks of open water some of them having been open ten days at least. The nearest one about ½ mile South of us has been opening and closing several times (by the formation of its edges) and was undoubtedly the cause of the roaring I heard on the 12th inst.

The largest opening, one about two miles East of us, was several hundred yards wide having also had some hummock action at its edges. Numbers of seal and about a dozen dovekies were seen, which together with the open water make a sight well worth walking miles to see even over this soft snow which at present is most labourious.

Thursday 20th

SE   8   om. cm   +8° -4°

Quite a gale and the snow drifting so as to make objects invisible at fifty yards distant, and covering every thing almost as soon as it is exposed. The particles are so fine that they penetrate the minutest crevice and after being out for five minutes it is impossible to brush the snow from ones clothes.

Friday 21st

71°18'N   NW   4   bcm   +8° -17°

The gale drove us Northward some distance.

Visited the opening south of us and found it about a mile wide and covered with sludge ice. Saw no birds or seals. The snow still drifting heavily.

The Ice Breaking Up

Saturday March 22nd 1851

Lat	Long	Wind	force	Weather	Temperature
71°09'N		NE	4	bcm	-9° -23°

The considerable drift which to-days observed Lat shows makes us think that there is a plenty of open water to Southward of us. The leads near us are constantly shifting. A dovekie was shot in one of them. These birds have an entirely different plumage from the one they have during the summer, being almost white now. The sick of course get the game and the commo being a scurvy patient reports unfavourably upon the dovekie as tough and fishy. A black fox was seen by Dr. Kane.

Sunday 23rd

71°02'N NW 3 bm -9° -18°

The floes are sluing and drifting still, the ships head has altered three points to Northward. the nearest crack was visited at 11 and found to be closed making hummocks on its edges as the floes passed each other. At 1 P.M. it was a mile wide. Narwhals, seals, and dovekies were seen in it. At 4 it was still open and a party visiting it was cut off from the ship by another crack so that a boat had to be hauled over the ice to ferry them across. The last crack is about ¼ mile from us. The frost smoke indicates water almost all around us, but in different directions at different times showing a general commotion in the ice.

Monday 24th

70°55'N 64°04'W NW 4 b. c. m. -18° -20°

Drifting to SE still and the ice loose.

Shot Manufacture

Tuesday March 25th 1850 [*sic*]

Lat	Long	Wind	force	Weather	Temperature
70°46'		WNW	4 to 1	b. bm	-12° -24°

Walked to the opening first seen to Southward and saw several narwhal playing up and down the lead which was about half a mile long and very narrow. Murdaugh fired into one of them but he didnt return to the surface. A party started after dinner with all things prepared to take a narwhal, but not seeing any shot a dovekie and returned.

Wednesday 26th

70°46'N   63°37'W   SW 1. NNE 1   b. bm   -8° -27°
Heard the ticking in the ice similar to that on the 2nd ulto. The ice was much broken up around the cracks but no open water. An attempt to make shot by pouring melted lead through a sieve from the fore yard was a failure.

Thursday 27th

70°42'N   NNE   1   bm   -4° -24°
Much frost smoke on the horizon indicating water almost in every direction. Some of the openings visited were wide and had narwhals in them.

Friday 28th

70°41'N   Calm SSE 1 to 4   bm   -5° -25°
An attempt to make shot from the fore topgallant yard failed.* Sent the bowsprit to the Rescue and fitted the tennon. Most of the provisions put upon the decks in the fall were returned. A party visiting an opening to Southward saw a number of dovekies.
*After this failure, lead was cut up into slugs and rolled in a barrell with no better success.

Thickness of This Winters Ice

Saturday March 29th 1850 [*sic*]

Lat	Long	Wind	Force	Weather	Temperature
70°44'N		SE	4	bcm	-4° -13°

[No entry.]

Sunday 30th

70°47'N   SE   4 to 1   bcm   +3° -9°
[No entry.]

Monday 31st

70°45'N   NE to NW   3   bm. f. s   +6° -12°
[No entry.]

Tuesday April 1st 1851

70°37'N   63°42'W   NW   3   bm. om.   -2° -13°

Measured a floe formed in September and found it seven feet & 2 in thick which we suppose to be the thickness of the winters formation as ice scarcely forms at the surface.

Wednesday 2nd

70°28'N   NW   4   bcm   0° -8°

The clouds appear to indicate a quantity of water to the Northward of us, the mist being thick and scud flying low just as it does over the gulf stream.

Thursday 3rd 1851

70°19'N   NNW   4   cm   +1° -8°

Tracks of a bear going Northward were seen to the West of us a few miles. The cracks are almost all shut up. A narwhal was shot at in a small hole the only one in sight which he seemed loath to leave as he came up in it after being shot at. A party going again in the afternoon found it frozen.

Ice Quarry

Friday April 4th 1851

Lat	Long	Wind	force	Weather	Temperature
70°10'40"N	63°24'W	NW South	4 to 1	bcm. oms	+11° -4°

The barometer commenced to rise rapidly as the NW wind died away but stood still at midnight for several hours.

Saturday 5th 1851

Sd Ed Nd Wd   2   om. s.   +10° -5°

[No entry.]

Sunday 6th

70°03'33"N   Wd Sd SE   1   bm. f.   +6° -16°

The fog was about sunrise, the rest of the day being clear and pleasant.

Monday 7th

East to South   2   cms. om   +11° -7°

A small pool of water to Eastward. Set the crew to digging among the hummocks for provisions supposed to have been buried there the 12th of January.

Tuesday 8th

70°00'49"N   63°18'42"W   Sd & Wd   2   om. bc. b   +11° -2°
[No entry.]

Wednesday 9th

70°02'15"N   SE   3 to 5   oms   +20° +2°
With immense labour for three days we have succeeded in getting out of the
hummocks a barrell of beef, one of salt, and about a quarter of a cord of
wood. Quite a snow storm this afternoon.

Extensive Openings in the Ice

Thursday April 10th 1851

Lat	Long	Wind	force	Weather	Temperature
		ESE	4 to 8	oms. cm	+33° +17°

The snow drifting heavily and melting even in the most exposed places making every thing wet. A large opening in the ice to Northward of us about ½
mile distant.

Friday 11th

SE. S   7 to 3   bcm, oms   +32° +4°
The gale continued until noon by which time the drifts were very deep.

Saturday 12th

Sd SW   4, 2   om. c. oms   +13° -1°
The ice is very much broken up to Northward of us and there are large lanes
of water in every direction except to Westward. The barometer continues rising without bringing N wind.

Sunday 13th

70°12'34"N   63°03'W   SSW   3   om. bc. om   +19° +6°
Max Bar 30.98
Clear pleasant day. Very little water in sight except to the Northward where
there are large pools.

Monday 14th

Sd & Ed. Wd   2. 1   om. oms   +26° +8° 31.03

Broke out and restowed the Rescues hold, or rather the after part of it, leaving out such articles as will be required by the Advance, also taking all the salt from the barrells containing butter kegs to be used to assist the breaking up of the ice.

Water in sight from the mast head just as described on the 12th.

Getting the Rescue Ready to Receive Us

Tuesday April 15th 1851

Lat	Long	Wind	force	Weather	Temperature
70°09'13"N	63°20'W	Calm/ESE	0. 1	om. bcm	+22° 0°

Dug a trench through the snow between the two vessels and put a line of salt upon the surface of the ice which is expected to eat through the ice leaving a crack extending from one vessel to the other so that when the break up takes place we may get together.

Wednesday 16th

70°07'13"N   63°03'W

Broke out and restowed the Rescues fore peak and cleared a space abaft the forecastle for the galley which was struck below to see how the flooring must be placed for it to rest upon.

Thursday 17th

70°04'N   Calm/NNW   2   om/c   +18° +5°

Still working at the Rescue to make her habitable. Laid a flooring for the galley below, and cleared her decks of the remainder of the Advances provisions put there in the fall and scraped out some of the ice from the moisture condensed on the beams, carlines[122] &c so as not to be overflowed when the fires are lighted. The thermometer in the sun rises to 60° about noon.

Friday 18th

69°57'51"N   NW   2/3   om. bc. om   +10° -1°

Working in the Rescues hold and forecastle.

Saturday 19th

69°51'50"N   63°03'W   NW to S   2   om. f. b   +22° -1°

No light was used this night on deck. Lighted the fires in the Rescues cabin and forecastle to melt the ice and dry them out. Found great quantities of it in our lockers and find the clothes &c become damp when warmed. A bear which had been cruising about us all day hove in sight in the afternoon and coming within long range received a carabine ball in his right hind leg which he immediately extracted with his teeth and stood to the Eastward under a heavy press bafling all pursuers. The ball was found where he stopped to extract it.

Sunday 20th

Lat	Long	Wind	force	Weather	Temperature
69°51'43"N		SSE	3	b	+19° -2°

Chilly day, owing to the wind. Two men walking out reported on their return having seen the bear that was wounded yesterday and fired at him four times without killing him. When their ammunition failing they returned.

Monday 21st

The officers moved on board the Rescue to make room for stowing below the Advances cargo. We still mess and keep watch in the Advance. Find the Rescue's cabin still damp but drying rapidly. Brought our chronometers with us. Making stove pipe for the galley which as yet has little effect upon the forecastle. A large opening about a mile and a half to Eastward.

Tuesday

Still working at the Rescue to make her habitable. Carpenter finished putting up forecastle bulkhead and removed all the side lockers making it more roomy. Sent twenty barrells of provisions to the Advance.

Wednesday April 23rd 1851

Lat Long Wind force Weather Temperature
[No weather entries.]

A most disagreeable day. Clearing the Rescues decks and commenced cutting the ice from her sides and under the bows.

Thursday 24th

Open water in every direction but none nearer than half a mile and that due

North of us. I fear that the North winds are done and that our release will be indefinitely postponed. Cutting the ice from about the bows to make room for working at the bowsprit.

Friday 25th

69°46'30"N NW o. 2 oms. o oms +31° 0°

Commenced removing the snow from the ships sides down to the surface of the ice and having cut a hole through that tried a ten foot saw which two men work with great labour; the ice being 5½ feet thick, a formation since the middle of January at which time she floated in a crack about ten feet wider than her beam. The ice on either edge of which is now about eight feet thick. When the hole was cut the water rose four inches above the surface of the ice in the crack.

The armourer who professes to be a cooper by trade having been at work for three days at the staves of the three casks which were knocked up has at last got up one cask which wont hold water and declares that not enough staves remain to make another. A very large flock of geese or brant[123] passed us going Northward.

Saturday April 26th 1851

Lat	Long	Wind	force	Weather	Temperature
69°40'23N		North	2	b	+5° -10°

Rather soon in removing the snow from the sides I fear. Stepped the bowsprit to get it off the deck. Two white birds commonly known among sailors as boatswains[124] were seen.

Sunday 27th

69°35'55"N 63°51'W North 2. 3 c. om. s +9° -6°

The clouds were moving rapidly to Northward almost directly opposite to the direction of the wind. We use one of our chronometers for Longitude differing forty miles from the Advances.

Monday 28th

NW to SW 4 to 1 oms. b +7° -13°

Finished removing the snow from the sides. The clouds were again going to the windward during a part of the day.

Tuesday 29th

69°25'23"N   63°48'30"W   S to N by E 1   b   +16° -17°

There was a great cracking of the timbers during the night owing most probably to the sudden low temperature after the thaw and wet which we had last week.

Wednesday 30th 1850 [*sic*]

69°23'08"N   63°47'15"W   N to E   1   bf. b. bc.   +15° -13°

Commenced the operation of cutting the vessel afloat by digging a trench on the starboard side from the gangway aft. The trench four feet wide and three deep and sawing two lines through the ice in the bottom of it so as to suffer the bottom to rise and be hoisted out.

Thursday May 1st 1851

Lat	Long	Wind	force	Weather	Temperature
69°21'N	63°49'W	Vble	1. 0.1	b	+22° -9°

Broke up and hoisted out the ice sawed yesterday after having to cut the saw dust from the crack with the small saw before we could make the bottom of the trench float by hoisting an ice anchor under it and getting a heavy purchase upon it.

Friday 2nd

Vble   NW   1. 5   f. bcm. s   +23° +5°

Dug a trench from the starb[oard] gangway forward similar to the one aft but deeper so as to lessen the labor of sawing its bottom out. The ice was full of cracks so that while digging the water had to be bailed out constantly. When the bottom was perforated to admit the saw the water rose three inches above the surface of the ice and flowing around the bows ran aft to the port quarter and was four inches deep upon the surface of the ice on that side. Sawed the bottom out of this trench leaving pieces enough unsawed to keep it down until we will have time to hoist it out, as if permitted to rise to the surface it would freeze and require resawing. Saw a few mollemocks.[125]

Saturday 3rd

69°09'47"N   63°46'30"W   Nd   3   bc   +12°

Scrubbing day. A few birds were seen going Northward and an eider duck was killed by an officer of the Advance, it having fallen upon the ice apparently from exhaustion.

Sunday May 4th 1851

Lat	Long	Wind	force	Weather	Temperature
69°04'50"N		North	5	bc. oms	+18° +2°

[No entry.]

Monday 5th

69°00'56"N	63°47'15"W	Sd W. Sd	o. 1	oms. bc. oms	+28° +12°

Cutting the ship afloat. Hoisted out some ice and commenced cutting a trench athwart the stern.

Tuesday 6th

68°58'58"N	South to SE	1 to 4	os. bc. oc	+30° +14°

Long lanes of water to Northward and to Southward of us.

Wednesday 7th

68°58'52"N	SE. West	4 to 8	om. c	+29° +10°

Cut a hole under the port quarter to enter the saw and found the ice 8 ft 9 thick before coming to water, and under that soft ice for several feet more. The water rose six inches above the surface of the old ice.

Thursday 8th

68°47'50"N	63°07'30"W	W	7 to 10	NW 6 to 0	c. +16° +4°

Quite a gale, snow drifting heavily.

Friday 9th

68°42'24"N	62°54'46"W	W to S	3	bc +22° +2°

Employed all hands all day to clear away the snow which has drifted around us.
    A lunar distance makes our chronometer 57 miles too far West.

Saturday May 10th 1851

Latitude	Longitude	Wind	force	Weather	Temperature
68°40'20"N	62°47'30"	Southd	2	b	+30° +7°

Commenced cutting a trench on the port side but the water leaks through the partitions (which on the surface of the old ice are very soft being frozen snow) so fast that we stopped the work as the men had to work standing in sludge ankle deep which indeed has been the case almost all the time since the water was admitted. So Griffin regrets not having completed the trench all around before commencing to saw. A raven flew by going Northward.

A lunar put us 58 miles East of the chronometer again to day which agrees to within a mile of the Advances eight day standard chronometer and I am directed to give the longitude in future by the one of our chronometers (2110 P & F) which varies least from the Lunars using its *old error and rate*, that however is 25 miles too far west by the lunars &c.

Sunday 11th

68°37'51"   62°15' by (2110)   Nd   3   bc. om   +26° +8°
[No entry.]

Monday 12th

68°33'55"N   Nd   5   bc. oms   +13° +10°
Too cold to work at the ice was the order to-day.

Tuesday 13th

68°27'48"N   62°10'W   North   4   om. bc. os   +14° +8°
Working hard all day to get out about three fourths of the ice under the stern which had to be resawed.

Used for first time shears for the saw and found it much easier.

Wednesday May 14th 1851

Latitude	Longitude	Wind	force	Weather	Temperature
No observations		NNW	5	os	+21° +12°

Sawed out some ice from under the starb[oar]d bow cutting it out in triangular pieces because we cant turn the direction of the saw at will but must let it go straight or at least in a very great curve.

Thursday 15th

68°13'47"N   61°51'40"W   NW   6   cms   +20° +12°
Sawing out ice under the starb[oard] bow, wet work and the fresh wind keeping us quite cool. An iceberg which has been in sight since the first of April disappeared to-day to Southward of us.

Friday 16th

68°05'56"N   61°38'50"W   NW   4   b. bc. cm   +22° +12°
Sawing ice. A good deal of water to Northward of us extending to East and west in long lanes. Great numbers of ducks are flying Northward.

Saturday 17th

No observations   NNW   4   0.   +24° +16°

Sawing out ice. Immense numbers of ducks and little auk are flying by to Northward. A bear came alongside the Advance and having received two charges one of which took effect in his port quarter withdrew precipitately and although they thought he made a lame retreat their pursuit was useless as he didnt heave to often even to repair damages until he had placed a long lane of water between his pursuers and himself.

Sunday May 18th 1851

Latitude	Longitude	Wind	force	Weather	Temperature
67°50'N		NW	3 to 7	oms. c. om.	+20° +9°

Read the morning Service in the forecastle for the first time. The little auk were flying by incessantly all day, a few of them were shot as they flew over.

Monday 19th

No observations   NW   4   bc. os.   +20° +8°

The ships head as we say or more properly the floe in which we are frozen has slued four points during the day showing that something has arrested the progress of the Western corner of it. The land appeared in all its glory this afternoon so that we can see the indentations and valleys filled with snow, but cant distinguish any headlands, and the sun not favouring us to day we can only suppose that it is that about Exeter bay.

The birds seem to have stopped going North entirely or we are out of their track. Those killed yesterday were most excellent eating and more appreciated being the first fresh meat we have had since last August, bating[126] the bears and foxes which I never could go knowingly.

Tuesday 20th

NW   3   os   +26° +17°

Fifty three little auk and a duck were brought in by the sportsmen this evening killed as they were flying Northward. We approach and drift by the land very pleasantly, but the snow and mist wont allow us to see its beauties which though not great are very appreciable to us who have not seen any for so long. What we can see is perfectly barren and covered almost entirely with snow.

Wednesday May 21st 1851

Latitude	Longitude	Wind	force	Weather	Temperature
67°12'N	60°53½'W	NW. NE	1	o. cm. os	+35° +22°

The ship floated at last, having cut out the ice about two feet wide on the starb[oard] side, accross the stern and bow and sawed to the port gangway from the stern, upon cutting through the young ice in the opening on the starb[oard] side she came up with a surge disengaging herself from the ice from the port gangway to the bow and rising twenty one inches forward eleven aft. The land still remains obscured by mist.

Thursday 22nd

67°06'N	60°56 ¾'W	Ed, SW	3 / 1	om. com. os	+30° +20°

This constant cloudy weather has affected the eyes of some of the party wonderfully making them blind and causing pain which they concur in saying to be excruciating lasting from 24 to 48 hours and leaving a film over the eyes which remains much longer. The eye is not at all affected in clear weather but there is a glare when the sky is overcast and the lights and shades of the surface of the ice are so indistinct that the eye is constantly strained to see at all and it is impossible to walk without stumbling, no unevenness appearing until it is under the feet.

Friday 23rd

67°01'N	61°01'W	Wd	2	oms. bc 28° 16°

[No entry.]

Saturday 24th

67°03'N	61°08½'W	SE to NE	4	oms 30° 20°

The openings in the ice are becoming very extensive.

Sunday May 25th

NNW	5 to 10 to 8	om	+24° +20°

A heavy gale and snow drifting heavier than I have ever seen it penetrating every crevice. We find it impossible to keep the cabin dry.

Monday 26th

Latitude	Longitude	Wind	force	Weather	Temperature
66°46'N	61°20'W	round comp	8 to 1	oms to b	32° 15°

Got bottom with 243 fms sand and stones.

Tuesday 27th

66°42 ⅓'N   61°20 ⅓'W   SE to NNE   1. 3   bcm   30° 14°

Measured the height and distance of Cape Walsingham measuring base line by sound, found it about seven miles off and one of the highest bluffs near it 1200 feet but it was misty and we were not certain of the cape.

Wednesday 28th

66°34 ¾'N   61°21 ¾'W   Vble   1   bcm   +36° 19°

Very little water visible. Found the spare sails wet and mouldy from the melting of the frost on the beams.

Thursday 29th

66°31 ½'N   61°16'W   Nd   2   bc. om   32° 16°

Saw the high land in the interior covered with snow but cant distinguish Mt Raleigh from the rest from this position. We can perceive by our drift by the land that there is tide here. Very large tracks of a bear were alongside this morning after four A.M. and also about the compass stand. About 12 the bear himself came and having our people in rather better training than the small Doctor we kept quiet until he was within gun shot when he received a volley that rendered escape impossible though he attempted it turning furiously on his persuers when they approached, however a few reserved charges soon stopped him. Very large one; fine skin but badly shot.

Without the Arctic

Wednesday [Friday] May 30th 1851

Latitude	Longitude chro	Wind	force	Weather	Temperature
66°28'N	60°58'W	Nd	1	om. b	28° 18°

We commence to drift off the land rapidly (good sign).

Saturday 31st

66°28½'N   60°41'W   SW to SSE   2 to 4   bc. b. om   32° 19°

Drifting off the coast and the openings becoming much wider.

Sunday June 1st 1851

66°31'N   60°21'W   SE to NE   4   bc. m. om   34° 26°

[No entry.]

Monday 2nd

NE-Sd & Wd   4.0.2   om   44° 28°

The pools of water are getting so wide that we cant see across them from aloft. Can hear the surf on the edge of our floe.

Tuesday 3rd

66°30 ⅓'N   60°04 ¾'W   SEd   3   om. bcm   35° 23°

Great numbers of snow buntings stay about the vessel constantly and so very tame that they will not fly from a man. One of them flew and perched itself upon my hand where it remained a minute but I could not catch its eye and it flew before I got it to my ear.

Wednesday 4th

66°30½'N   59°54'W   Sd & Ed   3   b. bm. om   40° 23°

[No entry.]

Thursday June 5th 1851

Latitude	Longitude (cr)	Wind	force	Weather	Temperature
66°32'	59°40'	S. Ed	3	om. b. bc	38° 31°

We perceived a motion in the ice during the day as if caused by a gentle but long swell and about six o'clock (or nearer at ¼ fore 6) a crack took place between the vessels and very soon after a general break up. The ice breaking into small floes cracking in every direction without noise or violence undulating gently with the swell but not opening wide in any direction.

Friday June 6th

SE. SW. NW   2 to 5   bf   36° 28°

The ice continues breaking up in smaller pieces. And I can hardly express the feeling of pleasure and gratitude at finding ourselves once more capable of motion, however slow it may be at first. A number of Lunar distances put the chronometer about forty miles of Longitude to[o] far West (2 m. 50s) time.

Saturday June 7th

66°21'N   59°12'W   NW 5   Sd 4   b. om.   34° 28°

This afternoon made sail and by boring and warping proceeded about half a mile SW and made fast near the Advance who has also made about half that distance through the ice.

Sunday 8th

S to WNW   2   om. f   39° 28°

The Advance has at last got clear of her friend the ice under her quarter which left during the night, part at 10 and the rest at midnight, carrying with it as a pledge, part of her false keel. She is now even more free than we are for the belt of ice which we left in sawing is not entirely removed and bids defiance to wedges &c. Got underway this evening making some progress to Southward & Eastward through the ice lost sight of the Advance in the fog and at 12 clewed up in close ice.

Monday June 9th 1851

Latitude	Longitude	Wind	force	Weather	Temperature
65°56'N		NWd	2 to 5	f. b. f	35° 27°

Again made sail and progressed slowly to Southeastward saw the Advance about two miles West of us at Noon (for a short time). At 6 P.M. tied up to a large floe—ice and weather being very thick.

Tuesday June 10th

65°22'N   Nd   6. 3. 7   omf. b. om   35° 28°

Made sail and working through the ice to Southeastward, find it getting much looser toward night and by midnight are sailing through streams of heavy floe pieces with edges much washed. Have not seen the Advance all day.

Wednesday 11th

65°23'30"N   NE   7 to 2   om. bc. om   34° 29°

At 2 A.M. passed the last stream of ice and exchanged the thumping and grinding for a heavy cross sea which makes every body very sick. The wind moderated at night.

Thursday 12th

65°34¼'N   53°35'W by the land   NWd   om bc. om   34° 31°

At 8.30 A.M. made the Eastern Shore, the west coast of Greenland very high and at 6 P.M. were within a mile of a small island near Upperment, a small place just North of Sukertopp.[127] An Esquimaux came off to us with no news or articles of trade. Said that the Danish vessel had arrived at Holsteinborg.

Friday 13th

66°25'N   Sd Sd & Wd 3   om. bc.   oms   37° 31°

Sailing up the coast the mist preventing our seeing much of it. Passed over some banks but going too fast to fish.

Saturday June 14th 1851

Latitude	Longitude	Wind	force	Weather	Temperature
67°00'N		NWd, North	1 to 5	bc. om	33° 30°

Working up the coast keeping along the chain of islands which bind it. Passed much heavy floe ice and numerous small bergs. Found a regular tide along the shore.

Sunday 15th

67°22'N   Nd   4 to 0   om. b. f. om   36° 28°

Working up the coast close in shore. On the in shore tacks found banks, 11 fms water about 6 miles off the coast—no fish.

Monday 16th

68°03'   Sd & Wd   0 to 4   oms bf bc   34° 27°

Pass Larger and more ice bergs as we get North but no very large ones yet. At 10.30 P.M. made Whalefish Islands and stood toward them.

Tuesday 17th

68°58'36"N   Ed NE   1 to 5   bc   42° 34°

The wind coming out from Eastd we were until 5 P.M. beating up for the Whalefish Islands. Having anchored the captain went ashore and found a document left by the Advance the day before in the hands of the Dane residing here. So we get underway immediately and stand for Lievely, a Danish settlement about fifteen miles to Northward on Disco Island.

Wednesday 18th 1851

Westd   3   bc   42° 36°

At 1 A.M. anchored in Lievely harbour or Godhaven, found the Advance at anchor arrived ten hours before us did not anchor at Whalefish sailed through and sent a boat ashore. She got out of the ice a day before us but had bad luck coming up the coast becalmed under the land &c. The Danish brig Peru (sent out annually with supplies for the colony) came in this afternoon.

Harbour at Lievely Thursday June 19th 1851

Latitude	Longitude	Wind force	Weather	Temperature
69°14'42"		Eastd 3	b	43° 38°

This is one of the largest and most important of the Danish settlements on the coast but what a poor miserable place. No news, they scarcely know of such a country as the U. States and of course have no idea of such a thing as a search for a lost expedition. The Danish brig just out knows if possible still less, says that the U. S. and Spain are at peace. However here we get plenty of fresh fish, a few birds, and some scurvy grass[128] and the brig gave us a few potatoes, a large quantity of very small beer, a pig, and a quantity of woolens at the low German prices cheaper than we can get them at home.

Got Latitude and some good time sights finding my chronometer (2110) 2m 30s 84 fast by a chart by a Lieutenant G[129] Danish supposed to be right, this error agrees very nearly with the Lunar error of June 5th.

Friday 20th 1851

Vble   1   d   39° 36°

Bad day, went ashore and into one of the Esquimaux huts but was not much amused. The poor creatures live in such filth and what to us appears discomfort but they are or appear contented. Most of the men who come aboard to trade can read and write and are Christianized, consequently they are not so easily satisfied and most of the things we get from them are paid for about seven times the value except skin clothing which we get at perhaps half its real value.

Some willow partridges[130] were obtained from the natives and we find them most excellent eating they are as large as our pheasant. I took a long tramp over the hills and got a fine view of the harbour which is a very fine one, but oh! how desolate. Vegetation is just commencing.

Lievely   Saturday June 21st 1851

No more weather notices; a year in the Arctic being enough. A boat arrived from Whalefish Islands bringing some sea birds eggs, the first we have obtained. They are considered a great delicacy but the season is so backward that they are scarce. All hands went ashore to a fandango and most all danced with the skin clad ladies several of whom (taught by the Danes) waltz and even Polka very well. I could not come to the point and left early sufficiently amused.

Lievely   Sunday 22nd

One of *the* days this, having come off last night at eleven I took the look out until the others should come aboard which they did about two but much to[o] tired to do any thing but go to bed so I had the watch till ten. During the morning we got underway and with much difficulty worked out of the harbour. The Advance having sent us a line to haul herself to windward by, weighed her anchor and dragged us out to the lee side of the bay whence as soon as she had got out, we had to start after warping over to the weather shore we made sail and stood outward but just within the enterance met a light head wind which kept us beating in a narrow passage until eight. At ten Griffin came up and relieved me. By night having got a breeze the Advance was again ahead of us.

Monday 23rd

Beating up the coast against light winds. At noon were off Urag point. Lost sight of the Advance in the Afternoon in a fog.

Lat 70°16'N   Tuesday June 24th

Standing Northward with a fresh fair wind. At 1.30 A.M. made the packed ice too close to penetrate right ahead, hauled up and stood in shore until we came to a narrow passage not a mile wide between the land and ice, this we entered and immediately lost the fine breeze standing along this lead in a dense fog. At 11 it becoming a little clearer we found ourselves inside of Haröe Island[131] and a fair wind freshening took us Northward delightfully. Saw the Advance just disengaging herself from the pack some distance to Westward she probably having entered it near where we turned aside. By midnight were nearly up to Cape Cranstown in a perfect forest of icebergs with much loose ice among them. I counted a hundred and nine from the deck. I suppose there is a large berg factory up this fiord. Passed the krang[132] of a whale.

Wednesday 25th

Came up with packed ice and numerous bergs. Off Storöe I.[133] standing off and on between the land and the pack trying to effect a passage to Northward had quite a gale from SW lasting only a few hours. Toward night finding no opening Northward stood in for a passage among the islands but finding them also joined by ice hove to all night between Storöe and the Islands to Eastward of it in smooth water. The last two days have had thick mist and drizzling rain constantly.

Thursday 26th

Knocking about among the islands all day unable to get out. At 12 midt were jammed in the ice and drifted rapidly to within stones cast of a high rocky bluff before the ice between us and the shore stopped us. I thought she was a gone brig for some minutes, however the check gave us a chance to send a hawser to some grounded ice a hundred yards off shore to which we hung on till morning.

Friday June 27th 1851

Thick Southwest weather with much snow. Managing to work out from among the islands by the passage which we entered. South of Storöe we found a little water to Northward of which we availed ourselves making some eight or ten miles Northward and again found ice across our way.

Saturday June 28th

Finding no passage Northward, tied up to an ice berg about four miles off Proven being unable to get nearer the land. Went to a little island south of us to hunt for eggs but found only numerous old (last years) nests and a burial ground into which some of the party commenced rooting carrying off several old sculls. Saw many eider ducks but they are shy and very hard to kill having such a thick coat of feathers and down. The season being so backward the birds have not commenced to lay their eggs. Many of the nests were protected from the North and some even roofed with stones this is done by the Esquimaux for which they take pay by robbing the nest of all but the last set of eggs with which the ducks are content and return annually.

Sunday 29th

Calm fine day. Ice still close in all directions, our berg drifting a little inshore if anything and the floes drifting off. A party of Esquimaux came off in their kayaks which they carry accross the floes when interrupting their passage. They report a number of whalers having gone North a fortnight ago.

Monday 30th

This afternoon an opening appearing in shore, cast off from the berg and stood in for Proven, a small Danish settlement dependent upon Uppernavik.

Harbour of Proven   Tuesday July 1st 1851

Rainy day. At 3 A.M. came to in the harbour which is a small one formed by islands well protected by the hills from any wind although the ice enters and goes out at will. The governor is a Dane who has become uncivilized as his neighbours, married to a native woman. They share their bed with one married and four unmarried sons, two or three well grown daughters, a maiden aunt and some two or three grand children. The old man prefers keeping his family thus together as his sons (being among the best fishermen or seal hunters) bring in more gain to his coffers, will not permit any more of them to marry as the women rather add to the expense of the household. His salary from the government is a miserable pittance but his sons get a great deal of oil, skins, and other articles which he sends to Denmark in the colony vessels every year. He may like the life but I should not. The school house is the most extensive and comfortable in the settlement. And in it all the officers except myself had what they supposed to be the beauty and aristocracy of the island assembled to a dance until about midnight our men coming off left them a host of the real beauties with whom they had been dancing at the Governors house all the evening however the jaded belles being thus deserted by Jack repaired to the school house and danced with the Gentlemen until the small hours were gone.

Wednesday 2nd

Steady rain all day. The officers were again eclipsed by the sailors all the beauties deserting the school house for the Governors where the Rescues men held forth.

Thursday 3rd

Drizling rain. This afternoon got underway and went out of the harbour to try and get Northward.

Friday July 4th

After knocking about all last night and to day until noon without finding an opening to Northward stood back and anchored in Proven harbour where the Governor arrived soon after us, he having also failed to find a passage Northward to Uppernavik. Got a few eggs and had a nogg.

Proven   Saturday 5th

I took a cruise ashore but was not amused. We shot a good many loons in and about the harbour and find them fine eating.

Sunday 6th

Cleared up with light Northerly wind. Got underway this afternoon and stood out with a rather better prospect ahead.

Latitude 72°30'   Monday 7th

This morning we made two English barques standing down the coast and by noon having met found them to be whalers having given up the attempt to cross the pack to Northward, bound south to try and cross lower down. They were exceeding polite furnishing us with a quantity of fresh provisions and vegetables for which they would not hear of taking pay. They also gave us a number of papers. These old cruisers up here Capts Peterson and Walker think that there will be no getting through the pack until late this season. They left the other whalemen near Cape Shackleton still hoping for an opportunity to get North.

Off Uppernavik   Tuesday 8th

After leaving the whalers last evening we had to work up among floes or rather through a stream of ice between us and the land and during the forenoon followed the Advance into the harbour of Uppernavik, a spacious roadstead partially protected by two islands. We obtained some rein deer meat here and a quantity of loons eggs. The Governors lady and several others wear womens clothes praise enough for the greatest and best in Greenland.

W. Coast of Greenland Lat 73°11'   Wednesday July 9th 1851

Met the American Whaleship McLellan and two English whalers going southward having given up the Northern route as impracticable. Most of us got letters from home (Griffin & myself none from our families) and a quantity of Newspapers (Mr. Grinells kindness). *Bought* of the Yankee captain some potatoes and a small stove at Yankee profit prices. The report of Snow,[134] mate of the Prince Albert, last year speaking so highly of our expedition as to turn every thing into ridicule we hear of with great indignation.

Lat 72°42'   Thursday 10th

During this afternoon we passed through the fleet of English whaleships (eleven) all about to go South. Several of them boarded us and gave us quantities of fresh grub. Sent letters by them to be put on board of fishermen to Southward or carried to England.

Baffin Islands   Friday 11th

Sailing with a fine breeze through a passage between two of the Baffin Islands going five knots the Advance ran her bows as far as the foremast on a rock and of course stuck there. We struck and passed over just in time to haul up clear of the Advances comfortable bed having worked back a short distance we made fast to a small grounded berg and sent our people to assist the Advance but the next high tide left her still high and the following low tide almost dry. However the night tide enabled them to heave her off having lightened her forward and put a shore under the bows at low tide. Took a cruise over the middle island but got no game saw a few old eiders nests. The whalers have scared every thing like game away from the islands though they were formerly abounding in all sorts of it.

Baffin Id   Saturday July 12th 1851

Sailed up to the Northern point of the Easternmost of the islands and being unable to find a passage to Northward made fast to the rocks on shore alongside the Advance. Saw a small vessel to Southward supposed to be the Prince Albert.

Sunday 13th

Thick rainy weather—ice packed closely.

Monday 14th

Foggy and ice close. Made about ¼ mile Nd and tied up to a large iceberg.

Tuesday 15th

Measured the height of the highest peak of this berg and found it 245 feet (inaccessible) but the average height is probably not more than seventy or eighty feet as it is very flat and low except this one peak; it was grounded in 95 fms water. A boat attempted to reach the Prince Albert about 2½ miles to Southward but did not succeed.

Wednesday 16th

One of the Advances boats met one of the Prince Alberts half way and brought the commander Mr. Kenedy[135] aboard. She has letters as late as April for all the Advances officers not one for us. A large floe coming down upon us forced us against the berg and stove in part of the bulwarks and the rail. Shifted our berth to the other side of the berg which became the weather side in an hour after we had sought protection there from a wind in the opposite direction.

Latitude 74°10'   Thursday 17th

Made about 6 miles Northing and again stopped by ice. The Prince Albert also made some Northing and came nearer to us.

Lat 74°11'N   West coast of Greenland   Friday July 18th 1851

Made very little headway with a good deal of warping. The Prince Albert came up and made fast near us. We find the officers very nice people. The chief of the expedition Mr. Kenedey is a Canadian who understands land expedition and from whom they expect much. Mr. Hepburn[136] the man who is mentioned so often in Franklins journey. The ice master an old whaling captain and a French ensign de vaisseau[137] who volunteered for the service and was accepted, knows half the Yankee reefers of 1841 and is a smart and agreeable young fellow. Their appartments are more comfortable than ours but they are not so well supplied with provision or fuel.

Saturday 19th

By an unfortunate circumstance the Advance and Prince Albert got ahead of us last night in Brooks watch and worked through a passage between two floes which closed before we came up to it and they having sailed a mile or two had to tie up while we were warping and heaving for eighteen hours to make a few yards. However we got up to them in the evening just as the ice was opening again so as to have caused no delay but we will return good for evil and help them when they need it.

Lat 74°19'   Sunday 20th

The Advance was the unlucky one to-day and was two miles astern at noon. We sent half our crew and an officer with a boat to assist as also did the P. A. and walked her up to us but by nine P.M. she was again two miles astern sent a boats crew and officer to tow as also did the Prince and towed her up by eleven.

The Englishmen volunteered for both these services and worked with much better will than our men.

Passing a high island we sighted the Devils Thumb.

Off the Devils Thumb   Monday July 21st 1851

Thick rainy weather, Southerly wind. Ice packed tightly warped a short distance to Northeastward. There is a great deal of water to Northward of us if we can pass a few barriers of ice.

Tuesday 22nd 1851

Sailed a little warped and hove a good deal making altogether very little headway on our course. Strong superficial currents making it almost impossible to steer even with a nice breeze. Passed quite near the Thumb and saw the immense glacier on the land commencing about here and running many miles Northward. A very large seal was shot from the vessel but he sunk.

Lat 74°33½'N   Wednesday 23rd

Heaving all the forenoon at a crack between two floes without effect. In the evening cast off and attempting a more westerly passage towed several miles to Westward and making a little Southing withall.

Lat 74°31'30"   Thursday 24th 1851

There appeared to be a good deal of water to Northward of us among the bergs which are very numerous large and new but we were until 4 P.M. heaving through a barrier of ice which closing just as we got clear shut out the Prince Albert so we tied up and sent back to help her through getting clear by seven after which we sailed about two miles to Northward.

Friday 25th

Having again been stopped by a barrier of ice from getting into a large space of water to Northward we entered a crack appearing the most likely to be forced and having hove the heaviest purchase taut remained thus. The wind from SW forcing the floes together gave us a severe nip, listing her four streaks to port. Many bergs around us some to windward and some to leeward of our floes which cause them to squeeze so tightly.

W. Coast of Greenland Off Devils Thumb

Saturday July 26th 1851

Remained all day fast in the ice with SW wind and see no prospect of getting far Northward.

Sunday 27th

Made two or three miles North through loose ice and sailed up a chain of icebergs which holding the field ice together seem to offer us an impenetrable barrier to Northward and with Southerly winds little chance of escape to Southward. Attended Divine Service on board the Prince Albert. Mr. Kenedy officiated and pleased me much. Mr. Kenedy tells me that he has an uncle living in Virginia from Orkney.

Attempting to pass between two floes they closed suddenly upon both the American vessels and having bergs on the opposite sides they come together with tremendous force having by midnight passed about two hundred feet into each other crushing and raising tremendous masses both the vessels have been severely nipped and are in a bed of hummocks. The little Prince just got through in time and lay quietly in a snug little dock and look on with astonishment at our predicament.

I doubt much if she could have stood it like our vessels not being nearly so strong we have rizen over all and have many folds of the ice.

Monday 28th

The SE gale increasing the weather floe comes crushing down and shoves us through the lee one like a plough straining the vessel more than I thought she could bear. Fortunately for us the ice being old is not so hard as the winter ice or we must certainly have been crushed but she creaks and trembles and rolling from side to side rises over the crushed masses beautifully. There are a number of bergs to leeward of us and as we approach them quite rapidly we are preparing for a boat expedition to Uppernavik.

Lat 74°40'N   Long 58°28'W   Baffins Bay   Tuesday July 29th 1851

No appearance of change in the wind which of course leaves no hope of relief from this position. Some narwhals were seen in a pool near us.

Wednesday 30th

Like yesterday no change nor appearance of one.

Thursday 31st

No change in anything.

Lat 74°40'N   Friday August 1st 1851

Well here is the first of August and not released, a week more of this confinement and I shall give up all hope of getting far enough North to do any good this season.

The ice looks equally impenetrable to Southward & Eastward & Westward.

The ice master of the Prince Albert says we wont move an inch till next spring (that is with regard to the ice) but with all due deference to his long yeared judgment I expect to get home sooner than we would if we found a less difficult passage Northward.

Lat 74°40'N   Saturday 2nd

A little wind from Northward gives us a hope of spending tomorrow in our usual laborious manner.

Sunday 3rd

Warping heaving and tracking for sixteen hours to day by the floes but making no Northing as the ice drifts faster than we can warp through it. In constant proximity to old bergs which render our situation very unsafe.

A Southerly wind shuts all up close again by night.

The Prince A. was working all day to get southward but has only put about three miles of ice between us and herself. She has given up the Northern passage and is trying to get South, to attempt to cross lower down the bay.

Monday August 4th 1851

By warping and heaving and with a little NE wind we made about a mile to Northward and got hold of the land floe but there is such a forest of bergs sticking about its edge that the loose pieces cant drift away from it and we cant make any progress either way.

A large bear came near the vessels and the dogs were taken out but no inducement could get them to follow him although they seemed to watch his motions with some interest particularly Griffin's large bear dog (bought for bear hunting at a great price) said to have caught six bears who in order to watch the bear more closely laid down upon the ice. These must be splendid [blank space] dogs since nothing was made in vain and they have been tried at every thing else without success.

Lat 74°41'39"N   Long 58°30'W   Tuesday 5th

After warping about ½ a mile along the edge of the land ice toward the North a South wind came on and we were quickly closed up being unable to get in any direction and having two large bergs ready to pounce upon us. One of them within a cables length of us all the morning ploughing its way through the loose floes.

Wednesday 6th

Remained in the same position as yesterday. In the afternoon I went over to the Prince Albert who is about two miles to Southward of us and in a large pool of water from which she cant escape. They think that they can see an abundance of water to Southward with only one floe intervening and are certain of getting up the West side of the bay if they can only get South now, but if that old ice master once gets them far enough south to insure a safe return I'm thinking they wont get him into the ice again this season East or West sides. Ems only my sentiments maybe I'm mistaken but nous or *somebody* nervous because *we* seem to be safe for another winter in some part of Baffin Bay.

Lat 74°41½'N Long 58°30'W Thursday August 7th 1851

Here we are in status quo we are likely to remain as although the barometer is well up we cant get an opening wind. However its all for the best but shockingly wearisome and the heart begins to grow sick with deferred hope.

Walked over to the Prince Albert again to-day. They talk of going through Hudson Strait and wintering at Repulse bay in event of failing to get up the West Coast.

Friday August 8th 1851

A North wind all day but so light as scarcely to affect the ice only opening the loose pieces about us but not changing a single berg. In fact nothing but a strong Northern wind could, they are so packed about us.

I climbed up on a large berg near us cutting my hands badly and saw some distance to Northward where the land floe appears broken as far in shore as I could see leaving us only a short distance Northward dependent upon it even if we could get through this nest of bergs.

Saturday 9th 1851

A water sky to Southward shows that there is water there not far off. A light SE air squeezes us up tight again.

Sunday 10th

Our day of labour having come we warped about ⅛ of a mile along the edge of the field and tied up again being unable to get farther. Attempts were made to haul out into the loose ice in order to get by the berg which stops us but failed.

A light North wind all day. The Prince Albert has been working all day to get about a mile farther South.

Monday 11th

Northerly wind prevalent. Bergs &c loose ice going to Northwestward. Prince A. still getting to Southward slowly.

Lat 74°41'45"N   Tuesday August 12th 1851

The Advance made all sail and tried to haul out toward the West but it was no go. Prince Albert about ten miles to S of us.

Wednesday 13th 1851

The ice still very close near us but plenty of water to Southward. The P. A. was just in sight from aloft this morning under sail and getting along finely having been ever since the third inst getting out of sight and both expeditions making every effort to go in opposite directions. Many of the bergs have drifted to Northwestward of us making a barrier in that direction but leaving nothing so formidable to Southward & Eastward in which direction I hope we may be able to go by the next labour day as this particular spot has become excessively tedious to me.

Thursday 14th

Completely surrounded by bergs—there is not an opening in any direction. It seems that the more bergs drift past the more there are to come. A raven has been hovering about the ships for two days, lighting upon the bergs to rest.

The water seen occasionally between the bergs is not more than a mile or two off but as it is in the wrong direction is not so interesting.

Friday 15th

This day last year having got clear of ice we passed Cape York and at night landed for water. Now we are just at the commencement of Melville Bay with no water North of us and I have given up all hope of getting that way this season in time to reach Lancaster sound before it will be dangerous to be there.

So good bye Sir John, the Yankees have failed to aid you and can only pray for you. God Almighty aid you to escape from what by this time must be an awful position, if any of your party are still in the hands of Arctic deities.

The little Aauk were going southward in great numbers.

Saturday August 16th 1851

The open water having approached to within about 500 yards of us that is up to the outer edge of the semicircle of bergs by which we are hemmed in we made strenuous efforts to heave throug[h] the sconce[138] pieces by which we are surrounded but made only a few ships lengths.

Sunday 17th

As usual heaving heavily all day and got to within 250 yards of the water. The Advance being in a rather more favourable position got out at 11 P.M. and left us heaving desperately.

Monday 18th

By 9½ A.M. we were clear of that nest of bergs in which we have lain since the 4th inst so unwillingly and stood to Northward & Westward after the Advance coming up with her about noon then running to Northward & Westward through the bergs came to a barrier of them which entirely prevented our going farther (although we could see a good deal of water to Northward beyond it) being then in about [latitude] 74°50' we commenced working to windward against a light SE wind which hauling to Westward brough[t] on a dense fog and the Advance having run into a piece of ice, we both made fast to small pieces and took in sail drifting with loose ice the fog knows whither.

Lat 74°41'30"N   Tuesday 19th 1851

By nine A.M. we were closely beset with floes and fragments and near a number of bergs so holding on to a large floe which was held by two bergs we waited patiently for an opening to occur in the loose ice which was drifting Westward—fog being still thick. At 1 having a light Northerly wind cast off and stood to Southeastward getting clear of the ice very soon but passing numbers of bergs.

Off Wilcox Point   August 20th 1851

Beating to windward to SE all day making slow progress but we find it so delightful to be able to go any where that we dont growl at a head wind even when bound home as we must be now. Made the Pack on the off shore tack. The idea of going home is a very delightful one to me convinced as I now am that our remaining up here longer is useless though I doubt not that we all feel deep regret at leaving even the hope of aiding the unfortunate sufferers and could raise a volunteer party to remain another and a third winter for such a hope but such a hope is not.

Duck Islands   Thursday 21th

Got a fair wind and stood a long way to Westward but losing the Advance in a fog stood more to Southward. At noon we were near the Duck islands.

Buchan Isls   Friday 22nd

Beating to Southward against a light head wind. Joined the Advance.

Saturday 23rd

At 11 P.M. came up with the Advance hove to off Uppernavik with a boat ashore. Hear a report that Sir John Franklin has returned but the vessel which brought it is at Proven.

Sunday 24th

Becalmed all the forenoon off Loon Head. In the evening got a breeze and ran down to Proven heaving to off the harbour at 10 P.M. The vessel here left Denmark before the P. Albert left England so she can only say that the report was left at Omenak (where she got it) by another.

Lat 71°32'   Monday August 25th 1851

Left Uppernavik with a fine Northerly wind and by midnight sighted the Northern end of Disco Island. The Advance in company sparing us all steering sails & foresail. Passed great numbers of bergs and fragments but Providentially came into no danger although it was very dark after ten P.M.

Tuesday 26th

A light fair wind brought us to the Southern end of Disco by midnight. A beautiful mild day.

Wednesday 27th 1851

Light clear and mild weather at 4.30 P.M. anchored in Whalefish harbour found it almost deserted the natives having gone to the main land to Southward after deer. Very little water to be had so eight o'clock found us standing to Southward for Egedesminde, a settlement some twenty miles southward.

Thursday 28th 1851

Anchored at 5 A.M. in Egedesminde harbour and filled with water. This place as large as any that we have visited is the cleanest and most civilized that we have seen. A priest resides here and has a nice house and family, but the poor fellow was made royally drunk at dinner on board the Rescue (Eggnog). No fresh meat to he had. Large codfish are caught near here in great abundance quantities of them being exposed to dry about every hut. I bought a kayak with apparatus complete for a sovereign and engaged a womans dress which I am afraid wont come to hand. The wind shifting this evening blew us alongside the rocks but they were steep and smooth and the little incident only served to break up the dinner party (a hard one) which I escaped by taking a walk over the settlement during the while visiting a very pretty fresh lake a short walk from the town.

Egedesminde Friday August 29th 1851

Left this place early with a fair wind until 12 M standing out through the Southwestern passage which is so long and narrow winding among a group of islands that it appears like a pretty river. Found a heavy SW swell outside and by midnight had its cause to beat against.

Saturday 30th

Fresh head wind, heavy sea, and steady rain.

Lat 67°47'N   Long 54°38'   Sunday 31st

Got a fair wind but heavy head sea. Advance has to run under very short canvass for us. Dark nights but no ice of any sort seen.

Monday September 1st 1851

Arrived off Holsteinsbourg this morning and find a head wind and very heavy swell (shoal water causing it) against which we beat all day trying to weather an island which at eight A.M. was about a mile to windward. The Advance weathers it by ten A.M. and stood in for the port.

Tuesday 2nd

Getting a slaunt during the night stood far enough Southward to bring the port under our lee with the fresh SWester which sprung up this morning and blew us in finely. Find Holsteinsbourg the largest and prettiest place we have been to on the coast, vegetation being much more luxuriant than at any of the others.

Took a guide and went to hunt for Ptarmigan[139] said to be abundant but found them "all gone" as the Esquimaux expressed it. But finding the hills covered with a little black berry something like whortleberry[140] we consoled ourselves with them à le cochon [like a pig]. Found walking in this temperature almost intolerable wonder how it will be at home.

Holsteinsbourg   Wednesday Septr 3rd 1851

Fine day. Governor and suite dined on board the two vessels dividing equally and in evening all adjourned to the Rescue where egg nog, strong punch, and boistrous singing, drawled out the hours till ten.

Governor very gentlemanly and intelligent man (educated) with all his people exceedingly hospitable to us on shore is a bon vivant [one fond of good living].

Thursday 4th 1851

A dance on shore this evening. I staid on board and superintended the fire works, two rockets bursted instead of going up, but fortunately hurt no one.

Friday 5th

The Advance got a large quantity of reindeers meat and six barrells of beer. We of course share. The deer are killed up the fiords by the Esquimaux who go with their families on hunting excursions for a fortnight or more killing great numbers. One of the boats returning to-day came alongside the only man was the father of the family he had with him his wife two lads and two daughters, had been gone ten days and had got fifty-six deer. They bring very little of the meat back killing them principally for the skin. They shoot the deer with rifles.

Saturday 6th

Sailed early this morning with a light Easterly wind which failing outside we had to tow out of danger and at noon got a fine North wind which we again lost by midnight.

Sunday 7th

A light South wind and heavy swell make a poor beginning. Caught ten large codfish in 35 fms.

Lat 66°N   Long   Monday Septr 8th 1851

Light head wind and a heavy NW swell.

This evening from 9 to 10 a magnificent aurora rivaling the brightness of the moon and casting reflections on the water quite as bright dancing and assuming a thousand fantastic shapes with inconceivable rapidity. A wreath of brilliant light was for a few minutes directly over our heads.

Lat 65°17'   Long 53°38'   Tuesday 9th 1851

Got a fine fair wind which but for the heavy sea would be perfection of happiness to homeward bound.

62°40'N   53°50'W   Wednesday 10th

Fine breeze all day, very cheering prospect.

60°50'N   51°W   Thursday 11th

Passed an iceberg, something rare now.

58°30'N   49°46'W   Friday 12th

The wind dying away and hauling ahead.

56°54'N   49°54'W   Saturday 13th

A gale from SE commencing. Advance left us.

N 56°40'   50°21'W   Sunday 14th

A perfect storm from East. Lay to under a small piece of the mainsail, sent down light yards and housed the masts. Sea tremendous.

Lat 55°15'N   Long 50°W   Monday Septr 15th

The gale abating and hauling to Northward & Westward ran her although the sea was high and she was accordingly washed but we are bound home. My Birth day very uncomfortable.

53°47'N   49°24'W   Tuesday 16th

A cross and wet sea, make little progress.

52°21'N   48°04'W   Wednesday 17th

A clear South wester something very strange, a disagreeable sea on drifting us far to Eastward of the dead reckoning.

50°41'   46°16   Thursday 18th

I fell a few feet this morning with my nose across the edge of a half inch board (used to keep the water out of the cabin in heavy weather) and made a pretty figure head of it to go home with. But am very thankful that the edge took my nose instead of the teeth.

50°03'N   47°W   Friday 19th 1851

Had one of those sudden changes of wind common in these regions, but which have proved fatal to so many inexperienced and careless navigators, without any warning the wind shifted from SW to NW coming from the latter quarter in a heavy gust and blowing a storm for about an hour it abated and hauled to SW again leaving a most uncomfortable sea running. Providentially we had just tacked and were heading to Southward & Westward when it struck us (bringing it on the weather quarter) for had it come ten minutes sooner on the lee bow, whar de Rescue?

Lat 49°11'N   Long 48°01'W   Saturday Septr 20th 1851

A most uncomfortable day, heavy sea, head wind and a dull vessel to encounter them. The wind repeated the farce of yesterday but on a much more moderate scale.

48°22'N   48°47'W   Sunday 21st 1851

Head wind and heavy swell.

47°20'N   47°16'W   Monday 22nd

A Continuation of yesterday until 4 P.M. when we got a fair wind and are thankful to see the little boat going toward the looked for end of this horrible passage.

46°01N   49°29'W   Tuesday 23rd

Fair wind continued all this day, moderate and sea not high. Made a sail ahead and actually are overhauling her.

45°24'N   51°45'W   Wednesday 24th

Came up with the sail of yesterday speaking her about six A.M. found it to be the English brig Scotia twenty days from Liverpool bound to Halifax seems to know his position well says he is going North of Sable Island (a dangerous passage) Longitude 25 miles East of ours. The breeze freshening she beat us badly.

44°25'N   54°10'W   Thursday

A glorious breeze from NE with a tremendous sea from NW running out of the gulf of St. Lawrence. Passed the English H. Brig Lima of Liverpool standing to Eastward under short sail, has probably been in heavy weather as there was no officer on deck, the men appearing bewildered at our hail.

Latitude 43°24'N   Longitude 57°36'W   Friday Septr 26th 1851

Another day of fair wind to be thankful for, during which the Rescue has made the greatest run she has yet made—160 miles.

42°46'   59°44'   Saturday 27th

Another day of fair wind with pleasant weather. Saw a large barque working to Northward.

42°34'   62°46'   Sunday 28th

The fair wind gave out this evening and a head wind with heavy sea and damp weather salute an old acquaintance of theirs in the Rescue.

42°26'   63°38'   Monday 29th

Light head wind squally and plenty of rain, wet above and below. Never mind a few more days and we will have houses over our heads.

42°29'   65°03'   Tuesday 30th

Similar to yesterday. A steamer passed us going to Eastward exchanged colors with her and showed a flag at the fore by which we may be known if she will report it in the U. S.

42°50'   66°14'   Wednesday

Head wind until noon when coming fair we kept away to clear the South end of Georges shoal. Boarded Brig Mary of Halifax 19 days from Cuba for Halifax no papers or news from home, told us about Lopez and 30 Americans having been executed at H[avana]. Longitude agrees with ours. Passed 10 small craft standing to Northeastward—probably fishermen.

Thursday Octr 2nd 1851

Latitude 41°34'   Longitude 67°10W

Light fair wind. Find ourselves at noon in some shoal water which corresponds with South end of Georges Shoal although the chronometer is half a degree to eastward of it. Found a strong SW current.

40°33'   68°52'   **Friday 3rd 1851**

A moderate fair wind. Saw numerous vessels.

40°29'   71°11'   **Saturday 4th**

Fine breeze until the afternoon when it hauls so much to Westward as to make us go far to Southward of our course.

39°47'   73°15'   **Sunday 5th**

The wind still shoving us down to Southward so that by sunset we are off Barnegat with the wind at North and have to commence a tedious beat dead to windward. Got a pilot about noon reports the Advances arrival early last week.

Notations for Force of Wind

0 denotes	Calm		
1	Light airs		
2	"	breeze	
3	Gentle	"	
4	Moderate	"	
5	Fresh	"	just carry Topgaltsails
6	Strong	"	single reefs
7	Moderate gale		double reef
8	Fresh	"	treble reef
9	Strong	"	close reef
10	Heavy	"	close r. m. topsl & foresl
11	Storm		Storm staysails
12	Hurricane		No canvass

Notations for Weather

(b,) blue sky or clear weather.   (c,) cloudy, passing clouds
(d,) drizzle   (f,) fog   (g,) dark stormy weather
(h,) hail   (l,) lightning   (m,) misty or hazy
(o,) cloudy completely overcast
(p,) passing showers   (q,) squally   (r,) continuous rain
(s,) snow   (t,) thunder   (u,) ugly threatening

* an asterisk after or under any letter denotes an extraordinary degree[,] thus
f*, means a fog thick enough almost to lean against.

These letters may be combined[,] thus bcm. denotes blue sky, detached
clouds, haze on the horizon. q*pdlt* = very heavy squalls, showers of light
rain with lightening and a very heavy thunder.

Latitude and Longitude are those at meridian. Temperatures marked in
degrees Farenheit[,] no mark or (+) plus or above Zero (-) minus or below
Zero.

Barometer marked in inches and decimals

Lat ☉ = by mer alt sun DA = double alt DR = dead reck
Long c = by chronometer
2☉ means that the artificial horizon was used as it was always when land or
ice were convenient[,] though it is not always marked ☉. ☽ moon ♂ planet
* star

EPILOGUE

Postscript to a Personal Log

WHEN ROBERT RANDOLPH CARTER wrote his own farewell to Sir John Franklin and breathed a fervent prayer for him and his shipmates on 15 August 1851, it was not because he believed the missing explorers were beyond help. The hope he had lost was not for the *Erebus* and *Terror*, but for the *Rescue* and *Advance* and their safe return to Lancaster Sound.

The U.S. Navy's History Division later evaluated the situation on 19 August 1851, when Commodore DeHaven decided to return home. It reported, "The ice was heavier than the previous year, and neither ships nor men could have lasted through another winter. Scurvy had struck, but no one had died. A second winter in northern Baffin Bay would have brought a return of the disease and disaster."[1] For some, the search would continue; for others, their personal role in it had ended.

Back in England that year, seventy-four-year-old Sir John Ross, whom the Americans first met aboard the *Prince Albert* in Lancaster Sound, was promoted to rear admiral in the Royal Navy. Though eager to return to his beloved castle at Stanraer on the Scottish coast, he had to begin raising funds at once when he learned he was deeply in debt for the *Felix*, one of his sponsors having died before he could make the promised contribution for its purchase.[2] Author Robert Goodsir, aboard Captain Penny's brig when it "spoke" the *Rescue* in August 1850, published his book, *An Arctic Voyage to Baffin's Bay and Lancaster Sound*, in London.[3]

Robert Carter, light-hearted as a schoolboy who has heard the recess bell, unloaded his personal belongings from the *Rescue*, which was being returned to the Grinnell, Minturn and Company docks, and sailed for Annapolis, where he paid a long-awaited visit to Louise Humphreys at St. John's College, where her father was president. She had by no means forgotten him, and her family welcomed him cordially.

From there (with heartfelt promises to return) he boarded the Chesapeake Bay steamer to Norfolk, Virginia, and caught another up the James River to Shirley Plantation. No doubt Carter launched his new kayak there, which must have created a sensation with his seven sisters and brothers as well as the neighbors. But his longing for Louise drew him back to Annapolis after a few weeks of reveling in home cooking (a far cry from that of the Eskimos at Disco Bay!) and a family that hung on every word of his adventures as they eagerly turned the pages of his "private journal."

In that well-remembered town where he had first met his dark-haired sweetheart, a whirlwind courtship followed. On 6 January 1852, only three months after the *Rescue* docked in New York, Robert and Louise exchanged wedding vows at St. Anne's Episcopal Church in Annapolis. It was a double ceremony which also united Louise's older sister, Eliza, with Lt. Sam Marcy, one of Carter's former instructors at the Naval Academy. He was the son of William Larned Marcy, former governor of New York and secretary of war under President James Polk, who would be appointed the following year as President Franklin Pierce's secretary of state.[4]

Louise also had an older brother, George, a classmate of George B. McClellan at West Point, who died in 1847 while serving in the Mexican War. (McClellan became a Federal general in the Civil War.) She also had two other older brothers, Fred and Jim, who both died between 1852 and 1854.

After a year's duty aboard the *Preble*, a "practice" ship for the Naval Academy, Carter received an appointment to another of the navy's great exploring expeditions, the Exploration and Survey of the China Seas, the Northern Pacific, and Behring's Strait, the hydrographic counterpart to Commo. Matthew Calbraith Perry's diplomatic mission to open Japan to U.S. trade. St. John's College president, Dr. Hector Humphreys, Louise's father, was quick to write to her from Annapolis, "It is a most responsible, honourable appoint-ment, and Robert owes it to his high character & standing in the Navy, and especially to his Northern Services."[5] Carter served as "acting master" on the flagship *Vincennes,* the same position Edwin DeHaven had held on that ship during the earlier Wilkes Expedition.

In 1855, while in Hong Kong, Carter came down with an acute case of "China fever" (probably a form of malaria) from which he almost died. After the *Vincennes* sailed without him, he was treated by his old friend from the *Rescue,* Dr. Ben Vreeland, before being "invalided" home. Vreeland was serving as fleet surgeon aboard the *Vandalia* in Commo. Matthew Perry's squadron.[6]

From 1858 to 1860 Carter took part in another of the navy's great explor-ing missions to "explore and survey the river La Plata and its tributaries" in Argentina, Brazil, and Paraguay. Commanding the expedition was his distant cousin, Lt. Thomas Jefferson Page, and also serving on it was William H. "Buck" Murdaugh from the *Advance.* Once again, its scientific duties were outlined by Lieutenant Maury at the Naval Observatory and Spencer Baird of the Smithsonian, with Henry Grinnell as an adviser.[7]

Carter resigned from the U.S. Navy in 1861 at the time his father's first cousin, Robert E. Lee, left the federal army.[8] Carter joined the Confederate navy as a lieutenant, and in April 1863, he and Murdaugh sailed from Charles-ton, South Carolina, to England, where they served in the Confederate Secret Service under its European representative, Capt. James D. Bulloch. Carter became a blockade runner, assisted Bulloch in buying the cruiser *Shenandoah* and plotting its future course, and at war's end was in Havana, Cuba, aboard the ironclad ram *Stonewall,* which they surrendered to the Cuban captain general.[9]

As officers of the Secret Service who had served in Europe or at sea were excluded from pardon under the Amnesty Proclamation and threatened with being hung as pirates, Carter booked passage back to Liverpool. He took exams that qualified him for a British sailing master's certificate and then sailed to Brazil to sell several steamers for merchant W. G. Crenshaw. When his father Hill objected strenuously to this and said he would only turn over Shirley Plantation to Robert, Carter negotiated for a pardon.[10] It was issued by President Andrew Johnson in August 1866.[11] Then, reluctantly, Carter left the sea, returned to Virginia, and was master of the plantation until his death in 1888.

After coming back from the Arctic, Sam Griffin headed home to Georgia and later wrote a scholarly treatise on "International Fog Signals," a subject on which the expedition had given him intimate knowledge.[12] Lt. Edwin DeHaven was given leave to recuperate from the effects of scurvy and snow blindness under the tender loving care of his wife in Philadelphia. He then returned to active duty in the office of Coastal Survey. A chart of his geographical work in the Arctic was printed by Lieutenant Maury's staff at the Naval Observatory, as well as several scientific papers dealing with the botanical specimens the expedition had collected. DeHaven's health, however, had been severely affected, and in 1857 he was forced to resign his commission because he had become almost completely blind.[13] He died in 1865 at the age of forty-nine in Philadelphia, and his wife contacted Robert Carter to ask for his testimony to help her in obtaining a Federal pension:

> State of Virginia
> County of Charles City
> Robert R. Carter deposes and says that he was one of the officers of the Arctic Expedition of 1850–51 commanded by Lieutenant Edwin J. DeHaven. That said DeHaven suffered particularly from the effects of the exposure incident to his duties as Commander, and to such an extent that his health may have been permanently shattered so as to finally result in the disease of the lungs of which deponent believes he died. That the hardships which at that time were connected with Arctic Service were such as to affect the strongest constitutions, and though said DeHaven was possessed of a powerful physique, his arduous duties, to which he attended with the utmost fidelity and earnestness, and the necessary exposure attendant thereupon, probably resulted in more permanent ill effects than to any of his brother officers. All men [were] severely tried with the continuous hard work, but, probably because he was an older man, and in addition to the laborious struggle (in which he took the lead) he had the anxious responsibility of directing the expedition, the effects were deeper and more firmly seated in his case than in those of the others.[14]

The "little doc," fleet surgeon Elisha Kent Kane, with the help of his journal, wrote a fascinating account of their experiences, *The U.S. Grinnell Expedition in Search of Sir John Franklin, a Personal Narrative*. It was published in 1853 by Harper and Brothers of New York City and sold sixty-five thousand copies within the first few months.

Although he had returned to his own family in Philadelphia on leave, Kane could not get over the feeling that they had left unfinished business in the Arctic—not only the search for Sir John but also the discovery of Maury's "open polar sea." As he relived those frustrating icebound days while writing his book, he made up his mind that if he could get funding for a second voyage under his own command, he would return.

Henry Grinnell offered to put the *Advance* at his disposal after it was overhauled and repaired from its 1850–51 voyage; and Lieutenant Maury was extremely supportive of his efforts. Maury helped the doctor convince Secretary of the Navy John P. Kennedy and his successor, James C. Dobbin, of the value of another Arctic voyage; but President Franklin Pierce, elected in November 1852, would not recommend it to Congress. The navy did agree to provide Kane and nine volunteers (eight others were civilians) on special duty at "duty-rate" pay and furnish them with medical supplies and some scientific instruments. However, Kane had to raise private contributions from a number of donors (including George Peabody, American-born international financier in London) to finance his expedition, which sailed 30 May 1853. Boatswain Henry Brooks, from the *Rescue*'s crew, the "little doc's" rival in bear hunting, sailed with him.

Considering the evidence found by Captain Penny as well as members of the Grinnell Expedition on Beechey Island, Kane felt positive that after Franklin wintered there, he had proceeded north in Wellington Channel the next spring. Perhaps he had sailed on from there into the "open polar sea" of Maury's hypothesis, which Kane himself longed to explore. When the *Advance* passed Cape York that August he found almost no ice blocking their passage, so they headed north to Smith Sound, which Kane reasoned might also lead to the polar sea. They wintered there in a small inlet.

Although the next spring a party from the *Advance* reached latitude 80°10'N, setting a new "far north" record, they never got into the ocean itself, which does indeed lie beyond Ellesmere Island and Greenland, north of what is now called Kane Basin.[15] (Kane himself wanted to name the basin for Maury, but the modest oceanographer wrote back that he waived the honor and urged Kane to yield to his friends and "let his name go upon the waters.")[16]

The next winter the *Advance* was icebound again, this time at Rensselaer Harbor in northern Greenland; but they accomplished much geographical, meteorological, and geological work, with particularly valuable magnetic data. Kane and his men suffered from scurvy, ran short of provisions, and had trouble with Eskimos stealing from the ship. He finally negotiated a treaty to solve the theft problem, but not until he forced the matter by holding two women he caught wearing outfits stolen from the ship for "ransom"—the return of a sleigh-load of materials discovered missing after an Eskimo visit. The resulting pact promised that "we, the high contracting parties, pledge ourselves now and forever, brothers and friends."[17]

In May 1855, with the *Advance* still frozen in the ice after a year and a half and with two crew members dead, they had to abandon the ship and make an eighty-three-day trek overland to Upernavik, five hundred miles south. There they were met by relief ships sent out by the navy with information which the doctor had left with his father, Judge John Kane, to be used in case a search for him were necessary. (He had learned from Sir John's experience the terrible dilemma faced by searchers with no directions to follow.)

When the navy was organizing the search in March 1855, Robert Carter was so ill in Hong Kong that the *Vincennes'* doctors advised the missionary who was nursing him to prepare him for death, which they thought was imminent. This explains why Carter was the only one of the officers of the first Grinnell Expedition, except DeHaven who was going blind, who did not volunteer for the expedition to find Elisha Kane and his crew. Buck Murdaugh, William Lovell, Sam Griffin, and even Lt. Sherard Osborn, who had commanded the *Pioneer* in Commander Austin's Royal Navy squadron, all offered to join the search when news of it went out. Murdaugh was in Buenos Aires, where the navy thought he should stay on duty, and Griffin was in trouble for some act of insubordination and so was turned down. Lovell, however, sailed as acting master of one of the two rescue ships, *Release* and *Arctic*.

On 11 September they sailed into Godhavn just as the Danish brig *Mariane* was putting out. Aboard her were the "little doc," boatswain Henry Brooks, and twelve other survivors who had arrived at Upernavik only days before. They returned to New York and a tumultuous welcome on 11 October 1855.[18]

Kane named the coast of Smith Sound, separated from Greenland by Kennedy and Robeson Channels, Grinnell Land. Henry Grinnell continued his correspondence with Lady Jane Franklin and contributed liberally to Dr. Isaac Israel Hayes, explorer/surgeon of Kane's expedition, who returned to the Arctic in the schooner *United States* in 1860 and again in 1869, hoping to prove the existence of Maury's open polar sea.[19] Hayes published an account of his exploration of Grinnell Land in May 1854 and his fruitless attempt to reach Upernavik, Greenland, to bring help for the icebound *Advance* in *An*

Arctic Boat Journey. (His futile hike in subzero weather had left him with a maimed foot, and he was in constant pain for years.) He recounted his later voyages in *The Land of Desolation,* published in 1871 and 1872. Unfortunately, the open water he saw and identified as the sea on these cruises later proved to be Kennedy Channel, which separates Greenland from Ellesmere Island.

Undeterred, Grinnell helped finance the 1871 U.S. *Polaris* expedition by Charles Francis Hall, whose work he had supported since 1864. A burly, self-educated, and passionately determined man from Rochester, New Hampshire, he searched for survivors of the *Terror* and *Erebus* or clues to their disappearance for more than a decade (1860–71). Hall felt he had a divine mission to lead any remaining crew members to safety. In his search, he learned many details of the Franklin party's later years and found numerous relics from their travels. At Kodlunar ("White Man's Island") he substantiated the theory that Martin Frobisher had visited there three hundred years earlier while looking for the Northwest Passage. Scientists in his own expedition so resented the influence of this so-called amateur that it was even said they poisoned him by arsenic. (Only a decade ago, scientist Chauncey Loomis exhumed Hall's ice-preserved body and discovered he had indeed been poisoned.)[20]

For his services in attempting to find the lost expedition and its consequent result—exploration and mapping of vast previously unknown areas of the Arctic—Henry Grinnell was honored by the American Geographic and Statistical Society and named its president in 1862. He and his brother Moses had been among its founding members.[21]

From 1850, when Carter's log began, to 1860 thirty-two expeditions by the Royal Navy, the U.S. Navy, and privately funded explorers searched for Franklin, his officers, and his men. It became a quest not unlike that which drove and mystified those attempting to find Sir Walter Raleigh's Lost Colony on North Carolina's Outer Banks, whose settlers disappeared in 1587. How could they simply have vanished from the earth? In both cases, they had not. The clues were simply too subtle or too obvious to be believed, while time, weather, and native scavengers had scattered much of the evidence.

Joseph Réné Bellot, the "agreeable young French ensign de vaisseau" Carter met aboard the *Prince Albert* on 18 July 1851, transferred to HMS *Phoenix* the following year. Detailed in August 1853 to carry dispatches to Sir Edward Belcher in HMS *Assistance,* leading five British ships up Wellington Channel to search for Franklin, Bellot was swept overboard in a freezing storm. His body was never recovered; but a memorial grave site on Beechey Island, next to the Franklin victims, was built to him; and the water separating Somerset Island from Boothia Peninsula was named "Bellot Strait."[22]

In 1854 Dr. John Rae, for ten years resident surgeon at the Hudson's Bay Company's trading post on James Bay (now part of Ontario), and an Arctic explorer who twice previously had searched for the expedition, bought indisputable Franklin relics from Eskimos. They included a silver fork and a spoon scratched with the initials F.R.M.C. (Francis Rawdon Moira Crozier, captain of the *Erebus*); Franklin's medal, a Cross of Hanover, and a circular plate with his name on it; parts of a gold watch which had belonged to James Reid (ice master of the *Erebus*); a knife handle marked "Hickey" on one side and "C.H." on the other, owned by Cornelius Hickey (caulker's mate of the *Terror*); and various other personal items. Dr. Rae was told by one of the Inuit (Eskimos), who years later told the same story to Grinnell's protégé, Hall, that "a party of kabloonans [white men] had died of starvation a long distance to the west of where we then were, and beyond a large river." This event had taken place in 1850, on the mainland at the southern part of Boothia Peninsula, beyond Back's Great Fish River.

At Rae's winter camp on Repulse Bay, other Eskimos came with additional relics to sell and filled in details of that year. On the western shore of King William Island where they were hunting seals, they said, they had met about forty white men heading south dragging a ship's boat and sledges. The men were very thin and short of provisions and were going to where they hoped to find deer to shoot. By gestures they "told" the Inuit that their ship or ships had been crushed by the ice.

That same season, Rae reported, before the summer breakup of the ice, the Inuit found about thirty corpses and some graves on the mainland, and five dead bodies on a nearby island, about a long day's journey to the northwest of a large river (Back River), near Point Ogle and Montreal Island. One other harrowing detail was related—from the mutilated state of several bodies it appeared that some of the starving men, in a futile attempt to stay alive, may have resorted to cannibalism.

When Dr. Rae's report reached England, the Crimean War had started. All the Royal Navy's efforts were diverted to the Black Sea. They did ask the Hudson's Bay Company to send a small overland expedition downriver to

Chantrey Inlet to investigate. Here James Green Stewart and James Anderson in their canoes found several small relics on Montreal Island, but bad weather prevented them from crossing Rasmussen Basin to King William Island and they returned south.[23]

There is another ironic parallel to the Lost Colony here. When Governor John White, in 1587, sailed back from Roanoke Island to England for supplies, the threat of the Spanish Armada forced all British ships to reinforce Sir Francis Drake, and none could be spared to go to the aid of White's New World colony. When at last he returned in 1590 and discovered the clue to its relocated site, a storm off Hatteras blew his little ship out to sea toward the Azores before he could follow its directions, and the ship's captain headed home to England.[24]

Perhaps it would have made no difference in either case. Perhaps the survivors were already dead. And then again, perhaps they were not. Old John White, mourning the loss of his colony, his daughter, and tiny grandchild, Virginia Dare, and Lady Jane Franklin, grieving over Sir John, had heartbreak in common. But Lady Jane could still afford to do something penniless artist White could not—she could, as she heatedly declared, "sacrifice my entire available fortune" if the Royal Navy declined to help.

To public donations she added her own funds in 1857 to buy the 177-ton yacht *Fox*. She hired as its commander a young explorer who had already taken part in three search expeditions, Capt. Leopold McClintock. (The Royal Navy agreed to give him a leave of absence.) Lady Jane told him to search King William Island, south of Lancaster Sound, where Franklin's orders had directed him to sail and where Rae's report said he had indeed gone.

McClintock was forced to winter in the ice off Greenland in 1857, but the following spring sailed as close as possible to King William Island. Peel Sound was only navigable for twenty-five miles, so he and Lt. William Hobson each searched a different area on foot, traveling with man-powered sleighs and dog sleds in subzero weather. In a cairn at Victory Point, on the northwest side of the island, they found a written message, short and to the point, that described the expedition's movements up to 25 April 1848. From it a scenario of events could be written.

Finding southern passages blocked by ice in 1845, Franklin had sailed, as directed, up Wellington Channel (as did the *Rescue* and *Advance*) and became the first to circumnavigate Cornwallis Island. They made their winter quarters in 1845–46 at the site on Beechey Island which Captain Penny discovered in 1850, where three crewmen died, as Robert Carter reported in his personal log. Leaving Beechey Island the following spring, Sir John found Peel Sound, a narrow inlet between Somerset Island and the almost contiguous Boothia Peninsula on the east, and Prince of Wales Island, to westward, unexpectedly clear of ice. (The channel was not navigable again for many years, so none of the 1850 expeditions could explore its shores.) Sir John therefore sailed south to a point near the west coast of King William Island in Victoria Strait, where by September 1846 his ships were beset.

Spring of 1847 brought no breakup, and here on 11 June, Franklin died, according to the message in the cairn. By the following year, nine officers and fifteen men had also perished. On 22 April 1848, Capt. Francis Crozier of the *Terror* and Capt. James Fitzjames of the *Erebus* with 103 other survivors left their ships (or remaining ship) and headed for Back's Fish River, either to hunt deer or to start south for help. No further written message was ever found. Only the testimony of the Eskimos gave clues to the horror of their last days.

McClintock, who was later knighted by Queen Victoria and promoted to admiral, wrote a full report on his findings, which included numerous articles from the ships. He believed these items were hastily abandoned when the 105 men moved south from Victory Point, in his view to try to reach the nearest Hudson's Bay Company post.[25] Later scholars and other explorers who have visited the site presented a more probable case for the supplies having been carefully cached there under canvas for use on their return from a hunting expedition. (It was deer season on the mainland, near Back's Fish River, and many Eskimos hunted there in spring.)

With so much revealed about the expedition's fate, it would seem logical to assume that the long search had ended. But Sir John's grave was not discovered, nor either of his ships or identifiable wreckage from them. In the century and a half since he sailed, not a decade has passed without one or more Arctic expeditions setting out to try to wrest new details from the Arctic ice on that fateful "last cruise" of Sir John Franklin in search of the Northwest Passage. In actuality, some of his party en route to Back's Fish River were within "a stone's cast," as Carter would have said, of completing the last link through Simpson's Strait of the southern passage to the Beaufort Sea above Alaska.

In 1981–82 and again in 1986, a young Canadian anthropologist, Owen

Beattie, examined the well-preserved remains of some of the expedition's members both on King William and Beechey Islands, in hopes that modern forensic methods could determine the cause of death. (Nearly all Eskimo testimony had referred to the death of the majority of the men from sickness, not starvation. Only that small party of survivors seen on the mainland of what is now Canada's Northwest Territory were described as falling in their tracks from hunger.) He took a graphically lifelike photograph on Beechey Island of the frozen, perfectly preserved body of John Torrington, who died in 1846, which *Smithsonian Magazine* had published in 1985 with Bil Gilbert's factual article on the Franklin expedition. In fact, it was so lifelike that a popular tabloid reproduced it later for its supermarket clientele with a blatant headline proclaiming that young, blond, blue-eyed Torrington had returned to life after a century and a half. Beattie determined that scurvy was the principal disease from which they suffered, but he also studied the theory that lead poisoning from solder on meat tins, such as Carter found at Devon Island on 24 August 1850, caused fatalities while their food supply was still plentiful. Beattie found their bones and hair high in lead content and concluded that they did suffer from chronic lead poisoning, which in itself could have killed them or lowered their resistance to other diseases. He reported on this in his book, *Frozen in Time,* on which he collaborated with John Geiger.[26]

Bil Gilbert, historian and naturalist who wrote about the Franklin saga and Owen Beattie's work for *Smithsonian,* personally followed Franklin's footsteps from Great Slave Lake to the Arctic coast, an overland journey Franklin made in 1820–21. The lure of a mystery had never diminished.[27]

In 1991 an officer on the Oceanographic Research Vessel *Endeavour,* David C. Woodman of Victoria, British Columbia, completed ten years of research and analysis on the Inuit (Eskimo) testimonies collected by Franklin searchers and published his extraordinary findings. They dispute assumptions of early explorers that all of Franklin's officers and crew died in 1848 or 1849. He concludes that not until 1851 (when the *Rescue* and *Advance* were forced by ice to return home) did the last survivors leave Starvation Cove on the Adelaide Peninsula at Simpson Strait. The Eskimos visited the *Erebus* and *Terror* before they were abandoned, these testimonies reveal, and some watched as one ship sank. Someday, Woodman feels, their wreckage will be found, possibly near tiny Kirkwall Island, where three stone cairns, never investigated, still stand on top of a ridge, a place one descendant of those who witnessed the disaster, Qaqortingneq, identified to Knud Rasmussen, a Danish anthropologist, in 1923, as "Umiartalik—the place where there are umiaq." ("Umiaq" is the Inuit word for a white man's ship.)[28]

If there were survivors alive in 1851, that knowledge would not have helped the searchers in Lancaster Sound. They already assumed this was true, and worked valiantly, if vainly, against their enemy, the ice, to find them.

In London's venerable old Westminster Abbey today, there is a monument erected after McClintock returned with his report to Lady Jane which brought her tragic news but the comfort of a final answer after years of waiting for one. The monument commemorates Sir John Franklin and his men for "completing the discovery of the Northwest Passage." Its epitaph was composed by Franklin's nephew, Alfred, Lord Tennyson:

> Not here: the white North has thy bones, and thou
> > Heroic Sailor Soul
> Art passing on thy happier voyage now
> > Toward no earthly pole.[29]

By all rights, if monuments were given for devotion, there would be another one alongside it for Lady Jane.

Robert Carter had called Elisha Kane "the little doc" for valid reasons—his slight stature and frail appearance, due in part to his recurring bouts of rheumatic fever which began in his teens. Kane's indomitable spirit often overcame these physical ailments for comparatively long periods of time; but he died 10 February 1857, at the age of thirty-seven. His funeral cortege moved from Havana, where he died, to Philadelphia, where his body lay in state at Independence Hall, through crowds of mourners at every railroad station. Henry Brooks, who never recovered from the effects of scurvy, also died the following year. Gibson Caruthers, a crewman on the *Advance,* died in 1860 while serving with Isaac Hayes on his search for the open polar sea.[30]

In 1903–6, Roald Amundsen of Norway sailed his sloop *Gjoa* through the Northwest Passage, the first explorer to do so. And in 1954 three U.S. Coast Guard cutters followed the route of the *Rescue* and the *Advance* to the Arctic and became the first United States ships to carry out the ambitious orders given the Grinnell Expedition in 1850 to proceed west from Lancaster Sound "if expedient" to the Pacific Ocean.

The navy's aims for the Grinnell Expedition, however, had been threefold: to rescue Sir John Franklin and his men, to complete the discovery of a Northwest Passage, and to obtain scientific data for Lieutenant Maury at the Naval Observatory. It was more than a quarter century later before Maury's theory of the open polar sea was fully tested, and the Arctic Ocean has replaced Polina on modern maps.

Many geographers still believed that Greenland extended across the North Pole to Wrangel Island (Wrangel Land) northwest of Bering Strait above Siberia. Others assumed that in that unexplored polar region numerous islands were separated only by shallow waters. Lieutenant Maury, the pioneer oceanographer who became known as "Pathfinder of the Seas," had studied data of ocean currents from both naval and commercial mariners, and he believed differently, even though his belief in a possible Polina later failed to meet explorers' findings.

The ill-fated voyage of a 142-foot steam bark, *Jeannette,* captained by Cdr. George Washington De Long, in search of the North Pole from Bering Strait in 1879, six years after Maury's death, failed to verify his theory. The *Jeannette,* a former Royal Navy gunboat, was purchased by James Gordon Bennett Jr., owner of the *New York Herald* and an enthusiast of Arctic exploration, in 1878.[31] Like Henry Grinnell in 1850, Bennett offered to outfit the ship for the U.S. Navy's use on De Long's proposed expedition; and the navy provided officers, but the men were members of the merchant marine. They sailed from San Francisco on 8 July 1879. Two months later, the *Jeannette* was imprisoned in the ice east of Wrangel Land at 71°35'N, 175°06'W, as the *Rescue* and *Advance* had been at Lancaster Sound, and in the same manner drifted with the ice pack.

However, De Long's bark did not meet a southerly current, as the Grinnell Expedition did in Baffin Bay, and remained trapped in the ice for twenty-one months before being crushed and sunk at 77°15'N, 154°59'E. Her drift northwestward was a tragic demonstration that Wrangel Land was not contiguous with Greenland.

This historic finding was of no comfort to the *Jeannette's* company, who abandoned ship on 12 June 1881 and watched as she sank the next day. They took refuge in three small ships' boats; and survivors of two of them eventually reached the Russian settlement of Belum six hundred miles away. From there the *Jeannette's* engineer, George Melville, set out on a personal rescue mission. He discovered that after their boats were separated and De Long sent his two strongest crewmen on ahead to Belum, the captain and his companions had died one by one on the Siberian tundra. On 23 March 1882 Melville found their bodies along with the ship's log and De Long's journal with entries up to a few days before his death. He buried the men nearby and constructed a cairn over the graves. A replica of it stands today at the U.S. Naval Academy in Annapolis. De Long's body, along with the bodies of several of his seamen, were later retrieved and buried at Woodlawn in New York.[32]

Three years later Norwegian explorer Fridtjof Nansen learned that recognizable wreckage from the *Jeannette,* along with other items from the Siberian locale, had been found on the southwest coast of Greenland. He determined to allow his strongly reinforced ship, the *Fram,* to be frozen in the ice near where the *Jeannette* had sunk. Nansen theorized that his ship would drift with the currents in the same direction through the Arctic Ocean to Greenland and be set free during spring breakup. In a "voyage" from 1893–96 that was ice-propelled, as the Grinnell Expedition's had been, the *Fram* drifted from the New Siberian Islands to Spitsbergen (Svalbard), northeast of Greenland, over a vast so-called polar sea, now more accurately called the Arctic Ocean, with depths Nansen sounded to thirteen thousand feet.[33] It was not ice free, warmer than its surrounding ice, but it did indeed stretch east to west from Greenland to the Bering Strait.

Through such incredible perseverance in the face of human tragedies, the Arctic was explored. A reading of the names of her sounds and islands, rivers, bays, and straits on a modern map is an heroic roll call of those seafaring scientists.

In 1895 the most northerly of the three administrative sections of Canada's Northwest Territories, which includes Boothia and Melville Peninsulas and all the Canadian Arctic Islands, was appropriately named the Franklin District. Its headquarters are at a trading post on Frobisher Bay, named for the earliest explorer of all to blaze the way to the Northwest Passage, and now the site of a DEW-line (Distant Early Warning) radar and meteorological station.[34]

The Franklin District's entire 549,253 square miles now constitutes a national game preserve. Times have changed; and Sam Griffin's large but lazy Newfoundland "bear dog," who preferred to observe the marauding polar bear threatening *Rescue*'s supplies from a prone position, would find a happy home there today.

NOTES

Introduction

1. Nugent, *Cavaliers and Pioneers*, 93.

2. Rinehart, *Archaeology of Shirley Plantation*, 154ff.

3. Shirley Plantation Collection, John D. Rockefeller Jr. Library, Colonial Williamsburg Foundation (hereafter referred to as SPC-MS91.1.) Four different journals of the *U.S. Peacock*, apparently written by midshipman Hill Carter in 1814–15; Roosevelt, *Naval War of 1812*, 286–88; Heite, "Honors to the Brave," 4–9.

It is possible that President Roosevelt, who had written *The Naval War of 1812* in 1885, also read the *Peacock* logs when he visited Shirley Plantation after speaking at the opening of the Jamestown Exposition of 1907 at Norfolk, Virginia, according to family history (and his signature in the plantation guest book). Robert R. Carter's daughter, Alice, had spent the day cleaning the house in preparation for his visit; but after a thirty-minute tour of the first two stories of the mansion, the historian spent the entire afternoon in the attic, reading the family papers and books that were stored there. Roosevelt's mother, Martha Bulloch Roosevelt, was the half-sister of R. R. Carter's commanding officer, Capt. James D. Bulloch, in the Confederate Secret Service in Europe; although we have no way of knowing if "T. R." was aware of this.

4. Hill Carter, Shirley, to Mary B. Carter, Hickory Hill, Hanover County, Virginia, 7 July 1848, SPC-MS91.1.

5. Beach, *United States Navy*, 178–80, 194.

6. Quinn, *England and the Discovery of America*, 63–64; Morison, *European Discovery of America*, 71–73; Jackson, "Hot on the Cold Trail," 119–30.

7. Ponko, *Ships, Seas, and Scientists*, 181–96.

8. The name of this department was later changed to the Naval Observatory and Hydrographic Office. Williams, *Matthew Fontaine Maury*, 165.

9. Berton, *Arctic Grail*, 24–25; Dodge, *Polar Rosses*, 34–36; Williams, *Matthew Fontaine Maury*, 262.

10. Maury, *Physical Geography of the Sea*, 147–48.

11. Gleaves, "DeHaven Arctic Expedition," 562–68; Snow, *Voyage of the Prince Albert*, 295; Maury, *Physical Geography of the Sea*, 148.

12. Gilbert, "Frozen Sailor," 116–30; Berton, *Arctic Grail*, 144–45; Ponko, *Ships, Seas, and Scientists*, 181; Woodman, *Unraveling the Franklin Mystery*, 13ff.

13. Klutschak, *Overland to Starvation Cove*, ix; Kane, *Grinnell Expedition*, 14. The whaler was the *Prince of Wales*, Captain Dannett (Richardson, *Arctic Searching Expedition*, 17–18).

14. *Dictionary of American Biography*, vol. 4, pt. 2, 2–6.

15. Dodge, *Polar Rosses*, 34–36.

16. Ponko, *Ships, Seas, and Scientists*, 184.

17. Gilbert, "Frozen Sailor," 116–29; Berton, *Arctic Grail*, 121–25; Franklin, *Thirty Years in the Arctic Regions*, passim.

18. Berton, *Arctic Grail*, 38.

19. Woodman, *Unraveling the Franklin Mystery*, 103–4.

20. Dodge, *Polar Rosses*, 24.

21. *Dictionary of American Biography*, 3:401–2; 7:32.

22. Johnson, *Thence Round Cape Horn*, 232–36.

23. "Reefer" was slang for a midshipman, because they were usually the ones sent aloft to reef the sails.

24. Translation:

> Whoever reads this log,
> That which may seem horrid to you
> Is pleasant to me.
>> If you like it, go on.
>> If it bores you, stop.
> Do whichever you please.

The Journal of Robert Randolph Carter

1. The managers of the Astor House offered the hotel as the free headquarters for the officers of the Grinnell Expedition. Kane, *Grinnell Expedition*, 18.

2. This was probably William D. Salter, who was appointed midshipman on 15 November 1809 and became captain on 3 March 1859. He died 4 April 1867. Callahan, *List of Officers*, 480.

3. The forepart of a ship's stem.

4. Fore-and-aft members supporting a deck of a ship or framing a deck opening used to reinforce the smaller beams of a ship. Falconer, *Universal Dictionary*, 78.

5. This was Brooks Brothers store in New York established in 1818. Trager, *People's Chronology*.

6. This was probably Thomas W. Brodhead, who became passed midshipman on 10 August 1847. He died 20 February 1855. Callahan, *List of Officers*, 78.

7. William H. Murdaugh, passed midshipman, was acting master and first officer of the *Advance*. Kane, *Grinnell Expedition*, 22.

8. An aftershave lotion.

9. Lewis Warrington Carter was Robert's older brother.

10. It is not clear what Carter means by "Gr."

11. Sandy Hook.

12. Kane gives this name as Auguste Canot. Kane's roster does not include George Willie but does name H. J. White as a member of the crew of the *Rescue*. Kane's listing of the crew of the *Advance* included: "Officers. Lieutenant Commanding—Edwin J. DeHaven, commanding the expedition. Passed Midshipman—William H. Murdaugh, acting master and first officer. Midshipman—William I. Lovell, second officer. E. K. Kane, passed assistant surgeon. Crew. William Morton, Henry De Roque, John Blinn, Gibson Caruthers, Thomas Dunning, William West, William Benson, Edward C. Delano, James Smith." Kane, *Grinnell Expedition*, 22–23.

13. "Murrain" is an obsolete term for a pestilence or dire disease.

14. Dead lights are wooden covers to replace glass in cabin windows when there is danger of heavy seas breaking the glass. Falconer, *Universal Dictionary*, 96.

15. Watch and watch is the usual arrangement in two watches, alternating in duty. Often noted as W&W. *Naval Encyclopaedia*, 835.

16. The log slate is a slate marked in a manner to represent two pages of the log book. Each day's events are noted on the slate and then copied into the log book. Ibid., 417.

17. It is not known exactly what "R. F. C. W." means, but Carter is probably referring to the weather conditions that Brooks did not write down but tried to remember later.

18. Carter's future wife, Louise Humphreys, daughter of Hector Humphries, president of St. John's College, Annapolis, Maryland.

19. "DR" stands for dead reckoning.

20. William Kurner.

21. Assistant Surgeon Benjamin Vreeland.

22. The expedition was supplied with several chronometers, three made by Bliss and Creighton of New York and the others of English manufacture. Kane, *Grinnell Expedition*, 205. Randall, *Time Museum Catalogue*, 87.

23. Dog watches were the two half-watches of two hours each between the hours of 4:00 P.M. and 8:00 P.M. These watches are known as the "first dog" and "last dog." Kemp, *Oxford Companion to Ships and the Sea*, 256.

24. "Lord have mercy." (A southern expression.)

25. A letter addressed to someone in Annapolis, Maryland.

26. The spar deck is the upper deck extending from stern to stem. *Naval Encyclopaedia,* 766.

27. Sighting for position made at noon. Carter usually used "med" as an abbreviation for "meridian." "Meridian" is used in the archaic sense to mean noon or the highest point in the sky reached by the sun.

28. The bird was probably a northern gannet (*Sula bassana*), related to the booby. Harrison, *Seabirds,* 288.

29. Possibly John Ross, *A Voyage of Discovery made for the Purpose of Exploring Baffin Bay* (London, 1819), but more likely Wilhelm August Graah, *Narrative of an Expedition to the East Coast of Greenland . . . ,* translated by G. Gordon Macdougall with notes by James Clark Ross (London, 1837). Dr. Kane mentions the observations of Graah and Ross, so it must have been part of the expedition's library. Kane, *Grinnell Expedition,* 23.

30. To shake is to disassemble or break down. Bradford, *Glossary of Sea Terms.*

31. Nathaniel Bowditch (1773–1838), mathematician and astronomer, published his *New American Practical Navigator* in 1802. The book went through many editions and was considered the "seaman's Bible." Carter owned the thirty-third edition, published in 1864, which is presently in the Shirley Plantation Collection at the John D. Rockefeller Jr. Library at Colonial Williamsburg.

32. The zigzag route of a vessel forced by contrary winds to sail on different courses.

33. "DA" indicates double altitude and the ☉ indicates the sun was used in the calculation.

34. John Purdy, *The British American Navigator: A Sailing Directory for the Island and Banks of Newfoundland, the Gulf and River of St. Lawrence, Breton Island, Nova Scotia, the Bay of Fundy, and the Coasts thence to the River Penobscot, etc.,* 2d ed. (London, 1847).

35. This comment reflects the experience of many navigators. In a manual published in 1944 the authors observed: "A naval navigator may be the busiest officer on his ship because he is supposed to have so little to do that he comes in for all the odd jobs." Stewart and Pierce, *Marine and Air Navigation,* 345.

36. The taffrail is a rail around the stern of a ship.

37. The Arctic right whale (*Balæna mysticetus*).

38. Sea pies consisted of layers of meat, vegetables, and fish separated by crusts of bread or broken biscuit. Kemp, *Oxford Companion to Ships and the Sea,* 768.

39. Sweeps were long oars used to help propel a vessel.

40. The smallest and most common auk, also called the little auk (*Alle alle*). It breeds on the Arctic coast in the summer. There are twenty-two species of auk, which are the ecological counterparts of penguins of the southern oceans. Harrison, *Seabirds,* 392–93. Bradstreet, "Pelagic Feeding Ecology," 126.

41. A hermaphrodite brig is a two-masted vessel with a square-rigged foremast and a schooner-rigged mainmast.

42. Captain Horatio Thomas Austin and his two sailing vessels and two steam tenders.

43. The store ship was the *Emma Eugenia.* Kane, *Grinnell Expedition,* 37.

44. He is referring to the United States Naval Observatory at Washington, D. C.

45. Kane gives the title as "Royal Inspector of the Northern portions of Davis's Straits." The man's name was Olrik. Kane, *Grinnell Expedition*, 44. Olrik's full name was Christian Soeren Marcus Olrik (1815–70), and his title was "Governor General of the Northern Part of the Danish Settlements in Greenland." He served in that position from 1846 to 1866, when he became director of the Royal Greenland Company. Ostermann, "Bibliografiske oplysninger," 61:724–25. The editors thank Klaus Georg Hansen, head of Groenlandica, National Library of Greenland, Nuuk, Greenland, for providing this information.

46. This is a reference to Commodore Thomas ap Catesby Jones, who mistakenly believed the United States and Mexico were at war, landed a naval force at Monterey, Mexico, and seized the public buildings on 20 October 1842. Morris, *Encyclopedia of American History*, 237–38. Johnson, *Thence Round Cape Horn*, 63–65.

47. The snow bunting (*Plectróphenax nivális*) is circumpolar in Arctic regions and winters as far south as Georgia in the United States. Ornithologists' Union, *Checklist of North American Birds*, 640.

48. Carter used the Beaufort scale for noting the wind force and weather conditions. The scale was developed by Sir Francis Beaufort and came to be internationally used. Kemp, *Oxford Companion to Ships and the Sea*, 71–72.

49. According to Kane this was the first time field ice was encountered. "From this date," he wrote, "really commenced the characteristic voyaging of a Polar cruise." Kane, *Grinnell Expedition*, 49.

50. The seventy-fourth year of the United States.

51. Kane says the boat was an "oomiak, or woman's boat," with four men and three women on board. Kane, *Grinnell Expedition*, 70.

52. This was most likely the black-legged kittiwake (*Larus tridactyla*), which ranges throughout the Arctic regions. Harrison, *Seabirds*, 359. Doctor Vreeland was collecting wildlife specimens for Lieutenant Maury.

53. The Ivory Gull (*Pagophila eburnea*) is the only white gull with black legs. It breeds in the islands of northern Canada and winters from the pack ice to the Gulf of St. Lawrence. It is an Arctic scavenger and aggressive, often called "ice partridge" by Arctic explorers. It is now considered rare. Harrison, *Seabirds*, 363. Snyder, *Arctic Birds of Canada*, 214. Renaud and McLaren, "Ivory Gull (*Pagophila eburnea*) Distribution," 141.

54. Kane said the bear was about nine feet long, "as we afterward found by measuring his tracks." Kane, *Grinnell Expedition*, 89.

55. Also "cavil," "kevil," or "kevel." A sturdy bit or bollard on which the heavier hawsers of a ship are secured.

56. This is a reference to the decoration on the stern of the *Advance*.

57. Symbol for the moon's lower limb.

58. A variation of the spelling of "Squeegee."

59. David Cranz, *The History of Greenland: Including an Account of the Mission Carried on by the United Brethren in That Country . . .* 2 vols. (London, 1820). Carter probably got

the book from the library on the *Advance*. Dr. Kane also mentioned having read it. Kane, *Grinnell Expedition*, 33.

60. Maury, *Physical Geography of the Sea*, 146–49.

61. Kane identified the man as Louis Costa of the *Advance*. Kane, *Grinnell Expedition*, 104–5. See Carter's entry for 13 August.

62. Carter means those people who live near the James River in Virginia, the location of his home.

63. Knightheads are two frames of wood near the foremast and support the windlass. Falconer, *Universal Dictionary*, 324.

64. Streak, or strake, is the breadth of a plank used as a unit of vertical measurement in ship's sides. *Oxford English Dictionary*.

65. Narwhale, usually spelled narwhal, is an Arctic cetacean. The male has a long, twisted tusk extending forward from the upper jaw.

66. Carter probably means 31 July, when he recorded the event.

67. "Filled away" means to trim a sail to catch a wind. The term was first reported in use in 1840.

68. Kane mentions seeing an animal he took to be a "black fox" but does not mention trying to get a shot at it or getting "into a bog." Kane, *Grinnell Expedition*, 146–47.

69. The great auk, a flightless bird, has been considered extinct since 1844, when the last living ones were recorded. If Carter is correct in his identification, the bird was not yet extinct in 1850. Fuller, *Extinct Birds*, 96–100; Ornithologists' Union, *Checklist of North American Birds*, 245.

70. The black-throated diver (*Gavia arctica*) is also called the Arctic loon. Harrison, *Seabirds*, 209.

71. The giant petrel, which ranges in southern oceans, can not be positively identified. Carter might be referring to the northern fulmar (*Fulmarus glacialis*). Harrison, *Seabirds*, 235.

72. The Atlantic puffin (*Fratercula arctica*) grows to about twelve inches long. It is black and white, with a colorful triangular bill, and the color of its legs and feet range from orange to red. It nests in holes in turf and among the rocks of sea islands. Ibid., 404–5.

73. Forenoon watch.

74. This was Dr. Robert Anstruther Goodsir, brother of Dr. H. D. S. Goodsir, who was assistant surgeon on board the lost *Erebus*. Richardson, *Arctic Searching Expedition*, 14; Kane, *Grinnell Expedition*, 158, 172.

75. A small vertical spar under the bowsprit of a sailboat that extends and helps support the martingale.

76. Austin's vessels were the bark *Assistance* and the steam tender *Intrepid*.

77. W&W refers to one watch on and one watch off. See note 15.

78. Dr. Alexander MacDonald. The other surgeon with Franklin was John Peddie. Beattie and Geiger, *Frozen in Time*, 124–25.

79. "Buck" was Murdaugh's nickname.

80. The white whale is also called beluga.

81. These were the graves of William Braine, John Hartnell, and John Torrington, whose bodies were exhumed and examined in 1984 and 1986. Beattie and Geiger, *Frozen in Time*, 23–24.

82. This was Lt. John Bertie Cator (b. 1820), commander of the steam tender *Intrepid*. Kane, *Grinnell Expedition*, 185; Holland, *Arctic Exploration*, 582.

83. Kane does not recount this episode but does discuss the discovery of the graves. *Grinnell Expedition*, 161–62.

84. DeHaven was convinced that Franklin had "gone up Wellington Channel, or to the Westd along the north shore of the straits." He ordered Griffin to search the shore north of Point Innes "as far as practicable, so as to return in 48 hours." Gleaves, "DeHaven Arctic Expedition," 583.

85. DeHaven wrote that "it is not known that any civilized being has ever been up this channel so far. We may be considered its first explorers." Ibid., 584.

86. DeHaven says this event occurred on 30 August. Ibid., 584.

87. DeHaven, Murdaugh, and Kane accompanied Carter on his "cruise" around the inlet. Kane, *Grinnell Expedition*, 176.

88. Probably Sir William Edward Parry, *Journal of a Voyage for the Discovery of the North-West Passage from the Atlantic to the Pacific* (London, 1821).

89. This was William Henry James Browne (d. 1871), who served as third lieutenant on the *Enterprise* in 1848–49 and as second lieutenant on the *Resolute* in 1850–51. Holland, *Arctic Exploration*, 581.

90. Jenny Lind began her American tour at Castle Garden, New York City, on 11 September 1850. Ware and Lockard, *P. T. Barnum*, 19–21.

91. A bower is an anchor carried at the bow of a ship. The "best bower" is the one on the starboard side of the ship. The "small bower" is on the port side and is the same size as the best bower. Smyth, *The Sailor's Word Book: An Alphabetical Digest of Nautical Terms* (1867), quoted in Hough, *Captain James Cook*, 47.

92. Exercise actually accelerates the onslaught of scurvy. Berton, *Arctic Grail*, 146. The *Crow's Nest* was the expedition's newsletter.

93. This was a tract by Justin Edwards, *The Sabbath Manual* (New York: American Tract Society, n.d.).

94. This was probably the American Tract Society, the publishers of *The Sabbath Manual*.

95. A solar lamp, or Argand lamp, was fitted with a cylindrical wick allowing air to pass through both the inner and outer surface of the flame, producing more heat than oil-burning lamps with the usual flat wick. It was named for its inventor, Aimé Argand.

96. Symptoms of scurvy.

97. A bright spot sometimes appearing on either side of the sun, often on a luminous ring or halo.

98. A gum was a trap.

99. "Fernande" has not been identified. "Bulwer" is Edward G. E. Bulwer-Lytton (1803–73), a prolific novelist and playwright.

100. Carter is probably referring to Matthew Fontaine Maury and the staff of the U.S. Navy Office of Charts and Instruments, who helped prepare the expedition's instructions. The instructions required that a variety of scientific investigations be conducted. Williams, *Matthew Fontaine Maury,* 262.

101. Altair is the first magnitude star Alpha Aquilae.

102. Arcturus is a giant fixed star of the first magnitude in Boötes.

103. Douglas William Jerrold, *A Man Made of Money* (London: Punch Office, 1849).

104. Catherine Grace Frances Gore, *Peers and Parvernus: A Novel* (New York, 1846).

105. John Angell James, *Anxious Enquirer after Salvation* (New York: American Tract Society, n.d.).

106. This was probably Aleksandr Marlinskii, *The Tartar Chief: or, A Russian Colonel's Head for Dowry* (New York: William H. Colyer, 1846), or possibly *Temugin; or, The Tartar Chief: An Historical Romance* (London, 1843). The editors thank Professor Steve Jobe of Hanover College, Hanover, Indiana, for providing this information.

107. Also called fool's mate—a checkmate in four moves.

108. William Paley, *Natural Theology, or, Evidences of the Existence and Attributes of the Deity* (Hallowell, Maine, 1819).

109. A ship's galley, usually on deck and resembling a sentry box. Kemp, *Oxford Companion to Ships and the Sea,* 127.

110. Carter is referring to Sir Edward Sabine (1788–1883), British astronomer, who accompanied Sir John Ross (1818) in the search of the Northwest Passage, and three years later accompanied Sir Edward Parry. Ibid., 737.

111. A fire hole is a hole made in the ice to give access to water in case of fire. For a description of a fire hole, see Hayes, *Open Polar Sea,* 183.

112. Sir George Back (1796–1878) had twice accompanied John Franklin to Canada's Northwest Territories, and later conducted two expeditions of his own in search of Sir John Ross, missing in the *Hecla* and *Fury* from 1829 to 1833, when he was found. Back published two books, and Carter was probably referring to the latest of these, *Narrative of an Expedition in H. M. S. Terror* (London, 1838), as his first book recounted his experiences on the overland expedition to the mouth of the Great Fish River, now called the Back River.

113. Even though they were aware that Eskimos used dogs for hauling sleighs, neither the British or Americans were comfortable with them. They used men-in-harness to manhandle sledges until the twentieth century. Berton, *Arctic Grail,* 42–43. For an early-twentieth-century photograph of the procedure, see Scott, *Scott's Last Expedition,* photograph 8b preceding p. 235.

114. A box-shaped musical instrument having stretched strings on which the wind produces varying harmonics over the same fundamental tone.

115. Carter must mean Fellfoot Point at latitude 74°30'N and longitude 88°40'W. *Index-Gazetteer of the World.*

116. A wheel horse is a horse harnessed between the shafts of a vehicle, next to the wheels, as distinguished from the leader (*Oxford Universal Dictionary*). Carter means he was the person closest to the front of the sleigh.

117. A star of magnitude .38 in Canis Minor. Also called the Dog Star.

118. Winter solstice.

119. On this day Kane commented that all the officers were ill except Griffin. *Grinnell Expedition,* 271.

120. Carter probably uses the word "lumber" in the sense that the casks, if put on deck, would clutter it and obstruct the crew. The casks were therefore "shaken up" or disassembled.

121. DeHaven mentioned in his journal that one sailor was flogged for breaking into the hold of the *Rescue,* stealing liquor, and getting "outrageously drunk." Gleaves, "DeHaven Arctic Expedition," 589.

122. "Carline" is an alternate spelling of "carling." *Naval Encyclopaedia,* 114.

123. Brant are dark wild geese of the genus *Branta* that breed in Arctic regions.

124. Carter is probably referring to the Arctic skua, a large predatory sea bird of the genus *Catharacta.* According to the *Oxford Universal Dictionary,* the Arctic skua was called "boatswain" and gives the earliest usage as 1835 in Sir John Ross, *North-West Passage,* iii, 40. The commonly known boatswain bird is a tropical, pelicanlike bird. *Guide to the Gallery of Birds,* 72.

125. A mollymawk is a species of albatross. Because they are mostly confined to the Southern Hemisphere, Carter's reference cannot be positively identified. Harrison, *Seabirds,* 221–22.

126. Excepting.

127. Sukkertoppen.

128. Scurvy grass, or sea kale (*Crambe maritina*), is a European seashore plant of the mustard family used to treat scurvy.

129. Blank in the original.

130. Probably the willow ptarmigan, a small Arctic grouse. Snyder, *Arctic Birds of Canada,* 113.

131. Carter evidently means Hareöen Island, Greenland, at latitude 70°30'N and longitude 55°W. *Index-Gazetteer of the World.*

132. The carcass of a whale from which the blubber has been removed. Also spelled kreng or crang.

133. Storöe, or Storer Island, at latitude 62°58'N and longitude 66°47'W. *Index-Gazetteer of the World.*

134. W. Parker Snow praised the Americans for their expert seamanship and daring. Snow, *Voyage of the Prince Albert,* 293–304.

135. This was William Kennedy (1814–90), leader of the *Prince Albert* expedition in

1851–52. Holland, *Arctic Exploration,* 597. Joseph-René Bellot, Kennedy's second-in-command, noted that the American sailors were fed up and planning to desert and that DeHaven was badly shaken. Berton, *Arctic Grail,* 193, 197.

136. John Hepburn had accompanied Franklin on his 1820 expedition. Berton, *Arctic Grail,* 196. Franklin, *Thirty Years in the Arctic Regions,* 42 and passim.

137. Joseph-René Bellot was a sublieutenant on leave from the French navy who volunteered for the expedition. Berton, *Arctic Grail,* 193.

138. A small fort or defensive works.

139. Ptarmigan is any of various grouses (genus *Lagopus*), with completely feathered feet, of northern regions. Snyder, *Arctic Birds of Canada,* 113.

140. Either of two deciduous shrubs, *Vaccinium myrtillus,* of Eurasia, or *V. corymbosum,* of eastern North America, having edible blackish berries.

Epilogue

1. Department of the Navy, *Dictionary of American Fighting Ships,* 6:16, 81–82.

2. Dodge, *Polar Rosses,* 34–36.

3. Woodman, *Unraveling the Franklin Mystery,* 373.

4. Beach, *United States Navy,* 194ff. In 1845, Sam Marcy's father, William Larned Marcy, then secretary of war, was an enthusiastic supporter of Secretary of the Navy George Bancroft, who was determined to set up a naval academy, but he faced strong opposition in Congress. One of Marcy's sons, either Sam or his brother, both "passed midshipmen," had been assistant to schoolmaster William Chauvenet, a longtime advocate of a real "naval school." Consequently, the story goes, Marcy arranged to be temporarily absent for the day, leaving Bancroft as acting secretary of war to officially sign over Fort Severn at Annapolis to the navy. Here Bancroft quietly set up his academy and moved the various ship's schoolmasters and schools into it without debate. The academy's first class graduated the following year.

5. Dr. Hector Humphreys, St. John's College, Annapolis, Maryland, to Louise Carter, Shirley, 25 March 1853, SPC-MS91.1.

6. Robert Randolph Carter, Hong Kong, to Louise H. Carter, Shirley, 6–13 April 1855, SPC-MS91.1; Robert R. Carter's naval journal, 1853–60, with daily entries from Hong Kong in 1855, SPC-MS91.1.

7. Robert R. Carter's pocket journal for 1858–59, on the La Plata Expedition, and his accounts' ledger on that expedition, SPC-MS91.1.

8. Louise H. Carter's memoirs of the Civil War at Shirley, SPC-MS91.1.

9. Bulloch, *The Secret Service of the Confederate States,* 1:232–37ff.

10. Hill Carter, Shirley, to Louise H. Carter, Annapolis, 7 November 1865, SPC-MS91.1.

11. Pardon of R. R. Carter from President Andrew Johnson, 22 August 1866, SPC-MS91.1.

12. "South's Contributions to History," 115.

13. *Concise Dictionary of American Biography*, 226.

14. Original copy of Robert R. Carter's deposition to Mrs. Edwin H. DeHaven regarding the state of her husband's health on the 1850–51 Arctic cruise in the *Advance* written after DeHaven died in 1865, SPC-MS91.1.

15. Ponko, *Ships, Seas, and Scientists*, 188–98.

16. Lewis, *Matthew Fontaine Maury*, 82.

17. Ponko, *Ships, Seas, and Scientists*, 188–98.

18. Corner, *Dr. Kane of the Arctic Seas*, 220–23. For Kane's description of the expedition, see his *Arctic Exploration*, passim.

19. Information on Isaac Israel Hayes (1832–81) of Chester County, Pennsylvania, *Dictionary of American Biography*, 4:445–46.

20. *Encyclopaedia Britannica*, 4:856. Woodman, *Unraveling the Secrets*, 31–49. Jackson, "Hot on the Cold Trail," 119–30; Stefansson, *Greenland*, 267–69; Hall, *Narrative of the Second Arctic Expedition*, passim.

21. *Dictionary of American Biography*, 4:2–6.

22. Beattie and Geiger, *Frozen in Time*, 99.

23. *Encyclopaedia Britannica*, 8:384; Woodman, *Unraveling the Secrets*, 23–38.

24. Porter, *Adventurers to a New World*, 39–44.

25. McClintock, *Voyage of the Fox*, passim.

26. Beatty and Geiger, *Frozen in Time*, 127–29ff. Also see Woodman, *Unraveling the Secrets*, app. 4, pp. 336–38. Woodman did not concur with Beattie's findings, believing lead poisoning was at most a contributing factor to deaths in the Franklin expedition.

27. Gilbert, "Frozen Sailor," 118.

28. Woodman, *Unraveling the Secrets*. Information on his research ship, McGill-Queen's University Press, Montreal, Canada.

29. Tennyson's epitaph quoted by Beatty and Geiger, *Frozen in Time*, 49.

30. Hayes, *Open Polar Sea*, 35–36.

31. Guttridge, *Icebound*, 4, 26–32; Jackson, "Stout Ship's Heartbreaking Ordeal," 86.

32. Guttridge, *Icebound*, 308–11; Department of the Navy, *Dictionary of American Fighting Ships*, 3:509–11.

33. Department of the Navy, *Dictionary of American Fighting Ships*, 3:509–11; *Encyclopaedia Britannica*, 1:1119.

34. *Encyclopaedia Britannica*, 4:330.

GLOSSARY

abaft	Toward the stern.
azimuth	Horizontal angle of an observer's bearing measured from a celestial body, usually Polaris.
bating	Excepting.
beat	To sail in the direction from which the wind blows.
Beaufort scale	A scale on which successive ranges of wind velocities are assigned code numbers from 0 (calm) to 12 (hurricane) corresponding to wind speeds from less than one mile per hour to more than seventy-four miles per hour. Used by Carter for wind forces in his daily log, according to the weather notations appearing as the last page in his journal.
bight	A bay formed by a curve or bend in a shoreline.
bluelights	A pyrotechnical composition which burns with a blue flame, used at sea as a night signal.
bobstays	Ropes to steady the bowsprit. Part of the ship's rigging.
bowsprit	A spar extending forward from the stem of a ship to which the stays of the foremast are fastened.
brickhold	Referring to a grip that held leaders (in this case, horses) "as tight as a brick."
bulwarks	Part of ship's sides above the upper deck.
caboose	Galley.
capstan	A device used for hoisting weights or for warping the ship

through ice floes. A vertical, spool-shaped cylinder rotated manually around which a cable is wound as it is rotated.

carlings	Short fore-and-aft beams framing a hatchway, mast hole, or other deck opening to support the inner ends of partial deck beams in way of the opening. Sometimes spelled "carline."
cavil	Also spelled "kevil" or "kevel"; a heavy bit or bollard on which the heavier hawsers of a ship are secured.
cutwater	The forepart of a ship's stem, to the rear of the bow.
"cure billet"	Used when Carter was describing pulling the officers' sled on 13 December 1850, it is undecipherable. "Billet" may be a typographical error for "billed," and he obviously meant "cargo" for "cure." Ergo, the "cure billet" as half the weight of the sleigh meant "the cargo billed as half the weight of the sleigh."
deadlights	A strong shutter able to be screwed against the inside of a porthole in bad weather. Often wooden.
dog watches	The two half-watches of two hours each between the hours of 4:00 P.M. and 8:00 P.M., known as the "First Dog" and "Last Dog."
dolphin striker	A strut that projected straight down from the bowsprit to keep taut the series of lines and chains that brace it.
doubling it	Sailing around it.
D.R.	Abbreviation for dead reckoning.
filled away	To trim a sail to catch a wind.
forecastle	That part of upper deck at bow in front of the foremast.
FN	Forenoon (i.e., watch).
forepeak	Section of the hold at the bow of the ship for cargo storage.
gudgeon	Socket for the pintle of a rudder.
gum	A trap to catch an animal.
head guys	Part of the rigging; ropes to the forward part of the vessel.
humplugs	Variation in spelling of "humbugs."
ice master	An expert on Arctic sailing, usually an experienced whaler hired by the navy to advise the officers.
James Riverian	Person who lives on the James River in Virginia.
knees	Braced angles between two framing timbers.
knightshead	One of two large timbers rising obliquely from the keel behind the stem to support the bowsprit.

krang	The carcass of a whale from which all the blubber has been stripped.
lead	An area of open water between ice floes.
lumber	Clutter, or cumbersome articles.
murian	Marrain, a curse.
mouchetach	French for mustache.
paraselene (pl., paraselenae)	A bright spot appearing on either side of the moon or a luminous halo around it.
parhelion (pl., parhelia)	Counterpart to a paraselene or luminous halo around the sun.
pintle	The pin on which a rudder turns.
Polly longlips	A phrase Carter used in describing the shot which killed the bear on 5 September 1850, at which both Kane and Lovell fired. It may have been an affectionate term Henry Lovell used for his long rifle.
proboscis	Nose.
scorbutic	Pertaining to scurvy (as in scorbutic symptoms).
shrouds	Ropes from the mast head (top of a mast) to the sides of a ship, part of the rigging.
slue	To turn sharply, to veer.
sounding	Taking a measurement of the water's depth by use of a weighted hand-held line.
sovereign	Formerly a gold British coin. In 1817, valued at about twenty shillings.
stand off and on	To take a course alternately away from and toward the shore.
stem	The curved upright beam at the fore of a ship.
streak	A degree. When Carter says the ship listed "four streaks to port," he meant four degrees to the port (left) side of the prow.
studdingsail	Pronounced "stunsail." An additional sail set only in fine weather when wind is abaft the beam. They are set outside the square sails of a ship by extending the yards with booms. They are usually set on the topgallant and topmast yards, the topmast studdingsail extends across the depth of the upper and lower topsails.
sweeps	Long oars used to help propel a ship.
taffrail	Rail around the stern of a ship.

tapis	Old-fashioned phrase; "on the tapis" meaning "on the table," that is, under consideration.
to make any weather	To pass to the windward of, in spite of bad weather.
transparency	A picture, print, or inscription on a translucent material, sometimes glass, made visible by a light placed behind it.
veering	Changing the course of a ship by turning the stern windward.
W and W	One watch on and one off duty.
warping	Moving a ship by hauling on a line fastened to or around an anchor or piling, a capstan or windlass. Carter frequently speaks of "heaving" in relation to warping the ship, referring to heaving or pulling on the line being used in the process. Sometimes he says "boring and warping," literally, forcing the ship through ice by warping it.
wheel horse	The horse in a team that follows the leader and is harnessed nearest the front wheel when pulling a wagon or other vehicle.
windlass	A horizontal cylinder turned by a crank so that line attached is wound around it.
windward	The direction from which the wind is blowing.
winter solstice	December 21. Santa Lucia Day in some Scandinavian countries.
Yankee reefers	Midshipmen. So called because they were usually the ones sent to climb up a mast to reef the sails. "Yankee" at this period simply meant an American, without reference to the North or South.

BIBLIOGRAPHY

Manuscripts

Shirley Plantation Collection. John D. Rockefeller Jr. Library. Colonial Williamsburg Foundation, Williamsburg, Virginia.

Periodicals

Bradstreet, Michael S. W. "Pelagic Feeding Ecology of Dovekies, *Alle alle*, in Lancaster Sound and Baffin Bay." *Arctic* 35 (March 1982): 126–40.

Gilbert, Bil. "A Frozen Sailor Summons Up Tale of Heroism." *Smithsonian*, June 1985.

Gleaves, Albert. "The DeHaven Arctic Expedition: A Forgotten Page in American Naval History." United States Naval Institute *Proceedings* 54 (1928): 579–91.

Heite, Edward F. "Honors to the Brave." *Virginia Cavalcade*, Spring 1967.

Jackson, Donald Dale. "Hot on the Cold Trail Left by Sir Martin Forbisher." *Smithsonian*, January 1993, 119–30.

———. "A Stout Ship's Heartbreaking Ordeal by Ice." *Smithsonian*, March 1997.

Renaud, Wayne E., and Peter L. McLaren. "Ivory Gull (*Pagophila eburnea*) Distribution in Late Summer and Autumn in Eastern Lancaster Sound and Western Baffin Bay." *Arctic* 35 (March 1982): 141–48.

"The South's Contributions to History." *William and Mary Quarterly*, 1st ser., vol. 16, p. 115.

Books

PRIMARY SOURCES

Franklin, Sir John. *Thirty Years in the Arctic Regions.* Reprint, with introduction by Bil Gilbert. Lincoln: University of Nebraska Press, 1988.

Hall, Charles F. *Narrative of the Second Arctic Expedition.* Washington, D.C.: Government Printing Office, 1879.

Hayes, Isaac I. *The Open Polar Sea: A Narrative of a Voyage of Discovery Towards the North Pole.* New York: Hurd and Houghton, 1869.

Kane, Elisha Kent. *Arctic Exploration in the Years 1853, '54, '55.* 2 vols. Philadelphia: Childs and Peterson, 1856.

————. *The United States Grinnell Expedition in Search of Sir John Franklin: A Personal Narrative.* Philadelphia: Chiles & Peterson, 1856.

Maury, M. F. *The Physical Geography of the Sea.* New York: Harper & Brothers, 1855.

McClintock, Leopold. *The Voyage of the Fox in the Arctic Seas: A Narrative of the Discovery of the Fate of Sir John Franklin and His Companions.* Philadelphia: J. T. Lloyd, 1860.

Nugent, Nell Marian. *Cavaliers and Pioneers.* Richmond: Dietz Press, 1934.

Richardson, John. *Arctic Searching Expedition.* New York: Harper & Brothers, 1852.

Scott, Robert Falcon. *Scott's Last Expedition: The Journals.* New York: Carroll & Graf Publishers, 1996.

Snow, W. Parker. *Voyage of the Prince Albert in Search of Sir John Franklin.* London: Longman, Brown, Green, & Longmans, 1851.

SECONDARY WORKS

Beach, Edward L. *The United States Navy: A 200-Year History.* New York: Henry Holt, 1986.

Beattie, Owen, and John Geiger. *Frozen in Time: Unlocking the Secrets of the Franklin Expedition.* New York: E. P. Dutton, 1987.

Berton, Pierre. *The Arctic Grail: The Quest for the North West Passage and the North Pole, 1818–1909.* New York: Viking, 1988.

Bradford, Gresham. *A Glossary of Sea Terms.* New York: Yachting, 1928.

Bulloch, James D. *The Secret Service of the Confederate States in Europe, or, How the Confederate Cruisers Were Equipped.* 2 vols. New York: T. Yoseloff, 1959.

Callahan, Edward W., ed. *List of Officers of the Navy of the United States and the Marine Corps from 1775 to 1902.* New York: L. R. Hamersly, 1901.

Checklist of North American Birds. Baltimore: American Ornithologists' Union, 1957.

Concise Dictionary of American Biography. New York: Charles Scribner's Sons, 1964.

Corner, George W. *Doctor Kane of the Arctic Seas*. Philadelphia: Temple University Press, 1972.

Department of the Navy. Naval History Division. *Dictionary of American Fighting Ships*. Vols. 3 and 5. Washington, D.C., 1978.

Dictionary of American Biography. 11 vols. New York: Scribner's, 1946–58.

Dodge, Ernest S. *The Polar Rosses*. New York: Barnes & Noble, 1973.

Encyclopaedia Britannica. 15th ed. 32 vols. Chicago: Encyclopaedia Britannica, 1985.

Falconer, William. *An Universal Dictionary of the Marine*. London: T. Cadell, 1780.

Fuller, Errol. *Extinct Birds*. New York: Facts on File, 1987.

Guide to the Gallery of Birds in the Department of Zoology, British Museum. London: British Museum, 1910.

Guttridge, Leonard F. *Icebound: The Jeannette Expedition's Quest for the North Pole*. Annapolis, Md.: Naval Institute Press, 1986.

Harrison, Peter. *Seabirds: An Identification Guide*. Boston: Houghton Mifflin, 1983.

Holland, Clive. *Arctic Exploration and Development c 500 bc to 1915: An Encyclopedia*. New York: Garland Publishing, 1994.

Hough, Richard. *Captain James Cook*. New York: W. W. Norton, 1997.

Index-Gazetteer of the World. London: Times Publishing, 1965.

Johnson, Robert E. *Thence Round Cape Horn*. Annapolis, Md.: Naval Institute Press, 1963.

Kemp, Peter, ed. *The Oxford Companion to Ships and the Sea*. London: Oxford University Press, 1976.

Klutschak, Hendrick. *Overland to Starvation Cove: With the Inuit in Search of Franklin, 1878–1880*. Toronto: University of Toronto Press, 1987.

Lewis, Charles Lee. *Matthew Fontaine Maury, Pathfinder of the Seas*. Annapolis, Md.: Naval Institute Press, 1927.

Morison, Samuel Eliot. *The European Discovery of America: The Northern Voyages*. New York: Oxford University Press, 1971.

Morris, Richard B., ed. *Encyclopedia of American History*. New York: Harper & Row, 1976.

A Naval Encyclopaedia. Philadelphia: L. R. Hamersly, 1884.

Ornithologists' Union. *Checklist of North American Birds*. Baltimore: American Ornithologists' Union, 1957.

Ostermann, H. "Bibliografiske oplysninger." In *Grøland i Tohundredeåret for Hans Egedes Landing*, pt. 2. *Meddeleser om Grønland*. Vol. 61. Copenhagen: Kommissionen for Ledelsen af de Geologiske og Geografiske Undersøgelser i Grøland, 1921.

Oxford Universal Dictionary. 3d ed. Edited by C. T. Onions. London: Oxford University Press, 1955.

Ponko, Vincent, Jr. *Ships, Seas, and Scientists*. Annapolis, Md.: Naval Institute Press, 1974.

Porter, Charles W., III. *Adventurers to a New World*. Washington, D.C.: Office of Publications, National Park Service, 1972.

Quinn, David Beers. *England and the Discovery of America, 1481–1602*. New York: Alfred A. Knopf, 1974.

Randall, Anthony G. *The Time Museum Catalogue of Chronometers*. Rockford, Ill.: Time Museum, 1992.

Rinehart, Thomas R., ed. *The Archaeology of Shirley Plantation*. Charlottesville: University of Virginia Press, 1984.

Roosevelt, Theodore. *The Naval War of 1812*. Annapolis, Md.: Naval Institute Press, 1987.

Snyder, L. L. *Arctic Birds of Canada*. Toronto: University of Toronto Press, 1957.

Stefansson, Vilhjalmur. *Greenland*. Garden City, N.Y.: Doubleday, Doran, 1942.

Stewart, John Q., and Newton L. Pierce. *Marine and Air Navigation*. Boston: Ginn, 1944.

Trager, James. *The People's Chronology*. New York: Henry Holt, 1994.

Ware, W. Porter, and Thaddeus C. Lockard Jr. *P. T. Barnum Presents Jenny Lind: The American Tour of the Swedish Nightingale*. Baton Rouge: Louisiana State University Press, 1980.

Williams, Frances L. *Matthew Fontaine Maury: Scientist of the Sea*. New Brunswick, N.J.: Rutgers University Press, 1963.

Woodman, David C. *Unraveling the Franklin Mystery*. Montreal: McGill-Queens University Press, 1991.

INDEX

Advance, 7; aground, 146; beached, 58, 68; freed from ice, 139; modified for winter quarters, 95; officers and crew of, listed, 179 n. 12; officers and crew of *Rescue* moved to, 95; sailing qualities, 20

Anderson, James, 171

Annapolis, naval school at, 2–3

Arctic Council of Royal Navy, 6, 9

Argentina, 3

Assistance, 7, 63, 68, 75, 169; beset in Wellington Strait, 76; encountered, 57

Assistance Harbor, 72, 79, 95

Astor House, 10, 17

aurora borealis, 73, 102, 108, 117, 122, 157

Austin, Horatio, 7, 31, 66, 71, 75; arrived at Beechey Island, 63; squadron sighted, 54

Back, George, 9

Baffin Bay, 35, 37–39, 175; ships drifting into, 109; vessels searching for Franklin in, 7

Baffin Islands, 146

Baffin, William, 4

Bagg, Rufus, seaman on *Rescue,* 20

balloons used to distribute news, 66–67

Bancroft, George, secretary of the navy, 3

Barlow's Inlet, 68, 70, 91–92

Barnegat, 160

Barrow, John, 9

Barrow Straits, 11, 73, 79

bear dog, 150

bear, polar, 40, 42–43, 45, 47, 49, 50, 68, 100, 105, 107, 130, 137

Beattie, Owen, 172–73

Beechey, Frederick W., 9

Beechey Island, 9, 60–61, 88, 96, 172; relics of Franklin expedition found at, 57

Bellot, Joseph Réné, 147, 169–70

Bellot Strait, 170

Benjamin, Smith, seaman on *Rescue,* 20

Bennett, James Gordon, Jr., 175

Benson, William, ill with scurvy, 80

Best, George, 4

birds: auk, great, killed, 53, 182 n. 69; auk, little, 50–52, 135, 153; black-throated diver, 53, 56; boatswain, 131, 185 n. 124; booby, 24; brant, 131, 185 n. 123; dovekies, 30, 33, 56, 124, 125; ducks, 25, 35, 134–35; ducks, eider, 36, 132, 143; geese, 131; great petrel, 53; gulls, 28; gulls, ivory, 39; kittewake, 38; loons, 30, 144; mollymawk, 132, 185 n. 125; ptarmigan, 156, 186 n. 139; raven, 133; snow bunting, 33, 138; willow partridge, 141

Boothia Peninsula, 10

Bowdin, Cape, 78; land party sent to, 61

Braine, William, grave of, found, 60–61

Brodhead, Thomas W., 18, 179 n. 6

Brooklyn Navy Yard, 17

Brooks, Henry, boatswain, 2d officer on *Rescue*, 20, 62, 167, 174
Browne, William Henry James, 73, 183 n. 89
Bruce, Robert, armorer on *Rescue*, 20
Buchan Islands, 154
Bulloch, James D., 165
Bureau of Ordnance and Hydrography, 5

Cabot, John, 4
Canot, Auguste, 179 n. 12
Carey Islands, 54
Carter, Charles, 2
Carter, Hill, 1–2, 165
Carter, John, 2
Carter, Lewis Warrington, 19, 179 n. 9
Carter, Mary Randolph, 1
Carter, Robert "King," 2
Carter, Robert Randolph: description of journal, 11–13; first officer of the *Rescue*, 7, 20; joined Confederate navy, 165; later career, 164–65; naval career, 2; pardoned, 165; U.S. expeditions served on, 3; wedding, 164
Cartier, Jacques, 4
Caruthers, Gibson, 174
Castlereigh, Cape, 110, 111
Cator, J. B., 7; suspected of concealing evidence, 61
Christmas celebrated, 107–8
chronometers, 19, 24; Bliss and Creighton, 23
Clay, Henry, 7
Committee on Naval Affairs, U.S. Congress, 7
Constitution, 2
Cook, James, 4
Cornwallis Island, 72, 171; searched, 69
Cranstown, Cape, 34, 142
Crauford, Cape, 55
Crows Nest, expedition's newspaper, 80
Crozier, Francis R. M., 6, 172
Cunningham Hills, 110

Daly, Alexander, seaman on *Rescue*, 20
Danish missionaries, influence on Eskimos, 37
Danish Settlements, Governor General of, 31, 32, 181 n. 45. *See also* Olrik, Christian Soeren Marcus

Davis, David, sailmaker's mate on *Rescue*, 20, 61
Davis Strait, 5
deer, 156
DeHaven, Edwin J.: appointed commander of U.S. Grinnell Expedition, 5, 179 n. 12; early naval career of, 5; instructions to, 10–11; later career of, 166; suffers from scurvy, 125
De Long, George Washington, search for the North Pole by, 175–76
Depot of Charts and Instruments, 5
Devil's Thumb, 38, 40, 147–48
Devon Island, 173
Disco Bay, 31
Disco Island, 23, 31, 140, 154
Dorothea, 8
Duck Islands, 154
Dudley Digges Point, 53–54

Egedesminde, 155
Ellesmere Island, 169
Endeavour, 173
Enterprise, 6
Epervier, 2
Erebus, 6, 169, 172
Erie, 2
Eskimos: clothing of, described, 32, 33; dogs of, 33; food, 32; harpoons of, described, 33; houses of, described, 32, 141; hunting methods of, 33; religion of, 37
Exeter Bay, 135
Exploration and Survey of the China Seas, the Northern Pacific, and Behring Strait, U.S. Expedition, 3
Exploring Expedition, U.S., 3, 5

Falmouth, 2
Felix, 7, 163
Fellfoot Point, 104, 185 n. 115
fire hole, 97
fire works, 156
Fitzjames, James, 172
food, sea pie, 29
Forsythe, Charles C., 7, 58, 61
foxes: Arctic, description of, 91; black, 83, 125; grey, 85–86; trapping, 86–88, 90, 98; white, 110, 113
Fox, 171

Franklin expedition: bodies of members of, found by Inuit, 170; graves of crew members of, found, 60; relics of, found at Cape Riley, 58
Franklin, Lady Jane, 6, 8, 168, 171; encourages search for Sir John, 7
Franklin, Sir John, 8; career of, 6, 8; expedition vanished, 1; monument to, in Westminster Abbey, 174; overland expedition in Canada, 8–9; search for, 6–7
Frobisher, Sir Martin, 4

Gascoigne Inlet, 57, 102
Georges Shoal, 159–60
Gilbert, Bil, 173
Gilbert, Sir Humphrey, 4
glacier, described, 53
Godhaven, 140
Goodsir, Robert Anstruther, 54, 60, 164, 182 n. 74
Great Fish River, 9
Greenland, 29, 139, 147
Griffin, Samuel P., 11, 18; acting master of *Rescue*, 20; later career of, 166
Griffith Island, 72, 74
Grinnell, Cornelius, 10
Grinnell Expedition, U.S., 3, 4, 12, 174–75
Grinnell, Henry, 7, 10, 167, 169
Grinnell, Joseph, 7
Grinnell, Minturn & Co., 7
Grinnell, Moses, 19, 169
Grinnell, Moses Hicks, 10

Hall, Charles Francis, leads expedition in search of Franklin, 169
Hareöen Island, 142
Hartnell, John, grave of, found, 60–61
Hay, Cape, 112
Hayes, Israel, leads expeditions to Arctic, 168–69, 174
Hepburn, John, 147
Herschell, Cape, 104
Hill, Edward, 2
Hill, Elizabeth, 2
Hobson, William, 171
Holsteinborg, 139, 155, 156
Hotel Astor. *See* Astor House
Hothany, Cape, 58, 61, 63, 64, 67–68, 71, 75, 88, 92, 94

Hudson, Henry, 4
Hudson Strait, 151
Hudson's Bay Company, 7, 170, 172
Humphreys, Louise, 21, 179 n. 18; marriage to Robert Randolph Carter, 164
Hurd, Cape, 56, 60, 94, 104

icebergs, first seen, 25
ice mate, absence of, 26
Innes, Cape, searched, 61, 62
instructions to DeHaven, 10–11
Intrepid, 7, 68, 72; encountered, 57
Investigator, 6

Johnson, James, seaman on *Rescue*, 20
Jones Sound, entrance to, closed, 11, 54, 72

Kane, Elisha Kent, 12, 67, 69; death of, 174; described conditions on English vessels, 66; later career of, 166–68
Kator, J. B. *See* Cator, J. B.
kayaks: description of, 31; women's, described, 32
Kennedy Channel, 169
Kennedy, William, commander of the *Prince Albert*, 146, 147, 149
King, Richard, 10
King William Island, 170–71
Knauss, A., cook on *Rescue*, 20
Kurner, William, steward on *Rescue*, 20

Lady Franklin, 7, 54
Lady Jane. *See* Franklin, Lady Jane
Lancaster Sound, 41, 79, 152
La Plata Expedition, Second U.S., 3, 165
Leopold Island, 56, 100, 103
Liefly, 32
Lievely, 140–42
Lima, 159
Lincoln, William, boatswain's mate on *Rescue*, 20, 108–9
Liverpool, Cape, 111
Loon Head, 154
Lovell, William I., 61, 69, 179 n. 12
lunar eclipse, 114

magnetic pole, located, 6
Martyr, Cape, 75
Mary, 7, 159

Maury, Matthew Fontaine, 5; supplies scientific instruments, 10; theory of open polar sea, 5, 175

McClintock, Leopold, leads expeditions in search of Franklin, 171–72, 174

McDonald, Alexander, 59

McLellan, 145

Melville Bay, 45–46, 49, 51, 152

Melville, George, 175–76

Melville Island, 47

Montreal Island, 170–71

Murdaugh, William H., 18, 63, 70; first offfcer of the *Advance*, 179 n. 7; in Confederate Secret Service, 165

Nansen, Fridtjof, expedition of, 176

narwhal, 51, 67, 125–27, 182 n. 65

Naval School, U.S., 2–3

New Year's Day celebrated, 109

North Somerset, 94

North Star, 7, 60

Northwest Passage, search for, 4–5

Ogle, Point, 170

Olrik, Christian Soeren Marcus, 181 n. 45

Ommanney, Erasmus, 7, 57, 69; suspected of concealing evidence, 61

Osborn, Sherard, 7

Osborne, Cape, 109–10

Page, Thomas Jefferson, 3, 165

paraselene, 100, 107, 114

parhelion, 84, 87, 93, 119

Parry Islands, 9

Parry, William Edward, 4, 8, 9, 59

Peacock, 2

Peel Sound, 171

Penny, William, 7, 54–61, 71, 76, 172; description of, 60; squadron sighted, 54

Perry, Matthew C., 3, 165

Peru, 140

Phoenix, 169

Pioneer, 7

Polaris, 169

Polina, 175; open polar sea theory, 5

Ponds Bay, 59, 64

Port Leopold, 56, 59

Powells Inlet, 106

Power, Lt., Admiralty Agent, 33

Preston, William B., secretary of the navy, 14

Prince Albert, 5, 7, 54, 146–49, 151–52, 163, 169

Prince Regents Inlet, 56

Proven, 143, 144, 154

Radstock Bay, 56, 60

Rae, John, 170–71

Raleigh, Mount, 137

Rasmussen Basin, 171

Rasmussen, Knud, 174

recreation: dances, 141, 156; foot races, 41; football, 39, 117; running, 87; skating, 83; theatricals, 111, 116, 119, 120; whist, 39

Repulse Bay, 151, 170

Rescue, 3, 7; damaged by ice, 55, 112, 113; description, 17–18; officers and crew of, listed, 20; officers and crew of, moved to *Advance*, 95; poor workmanship, 21; refloated, 136; repaired, 116, 122, 129, 130; sailing qualities, 20

Resolute, 7; described, 64

Richardson, John, 9

Richardson Point, 9

Rigby Bay, 102

Riley, Cape, 56–58, 60, 61, 88, 91, 94; relics of Franklin expedition found at, 58

Ross, James Clark, 4; career of, 6

Ross, Sir John, 4, 6–8; later career, 163–64; sighted with Horatio Austin, 54

Sable Island, 159

Salter, William D., 17, 178 n. 2

Sandy Hook, 19, 20

Savannah, 2

Scoresby, William, 5

Scotia, 159

scurvy: DeHaven suffers from, 125; first case of, discovered, 44; symptoms of, among crew, 83

seals, 43, 82, 96, 107, 124, 125

Shackleton, Cape, 145

Shenandoah, 165

ships: clipper, description, 3; drifting into Baffin Bay, 109; English, described, 55, 64, 66; English whale, 345; life on board, 48, 77; preparations made to abandon, 98; sheathing of, with iron, 47. *See also* specific names of ships

Shirley Plantation, 1, 164; manor at, description of, 2
shot, attempts to make, 126
Smith Sound, 11, 72
Snow, W. Parker, 5, 7, 145
Sophia, 7, 54
Spencer, Cape, 88; relics of Franklin expedition found at, 59–62
Stewart, James, seaman on *Rescue*, 20
Stewart, James Green, 171
Stonewall, 165
Store Island, 35
Storöe Island, 142, 143
St. Patrick's Day celebrated, 123
Sukkertoppen, 139

Tasmania, 6
Taylor, Zachary, 7, 13
Terror, 6, 169, 172
Torrington, John, grave of, found, 60–61, 173
Trent, 8

Ubekfent Island, 34
Upperment, 139
Uppernavik, 35–36, 143–46, 149, 154; harbor of, described, 145
Urag Point, 142

Vandalia, 165
Van Diemen's Land, 6
Verrazano, Giovanni da, 4
Victory, 6
Victory Point, 171–72

Vincennes, 3, 5, 165
Vreeland, Benjamin, 165; surgeon on *Rescue*, 20

Walker, Cape, 11, 56, 100
walrus, 53
Walsingham, Cape, 58, 137
Walstenholme Island, sighted, 54
Walter Bathurst, Cape, 112
warping, description of lines used for, 38
Warrender, Cape, 107–11
Washington No. 4, pilot boat, 20
weather notations, 160
Wellington Channel, 11, 56, 59, 61, 72, 169, 171; closed by ice, 59
Wellington Strait, expedition beset in, 76
Whalefish Harbor, 154
Whalefish Islands, 30–33, 140
whales: Arctic right, 180 n. 37; beluga, 183 n. 80; Greenland, 28; white, 60
White, H. J., seaman on *Rescue*, 179 n. 12
Wilcox Point, 153
Wilkes, Charles, 3, 5
Williams, John, quartermaster on *Rescue*, 20
Willie, George, carpenter's mate on *Rescue*, 20
wind force notations, 160
Woodman, David C., 173–74
Wrangel Island, 175
Wrangel Land, 175

York, Cape, 152; crimson cliffs at, 52–53; purple snow at, 52–53